Black Bourgeois

Black Bourgeois

CLASS AND SEX IN THE FLESH

Candice M. Jenkins

Excerpts from *Citizen: An American Lyric,* copyright 2014 by Claudia Rankine, are reprinted with the permission of The Permissions Company, Inc., on behalf of Graywolf Press, www.graywolfpress.org. Reproduced by permission of Penguin Books Ltd.

Chapter 1 was previously published as "New Bourgeoisie, Old Bodies: Performing Post–Civil Rights Black Privilege in *Tar Baby* and *School Daze,*" *Criticism* 58, no. 4; copyright 2016 Wayne State University Press; reprinted with permission of Wayne State University Press. Portions of chapter 3 were previously published in a different form in "'A Kind of End to Blackness': Reginald McKnight's *He Sleeps* and the Body Politics of Race and Class," in *From Bourgeois to Boojie: Black Middle Class Performances*, ed. Vershawn Ashanti Young and Bridget Tsemo; copyright 2011 Wayne State University Press; reprinted with permission of Wayne State University Press.

Published by the University of Minnesota Press
111 Third Avenue South, Suite 290
Minneapolis, MN 55401-2520
http://www.upress.umn.edu

Printed in the United States of America on acid-free paper

The University of Minnesota is an equal-opportunity educator and employer.

Library of Congress Cataloging-in-Publication Data
Names: Jenkins, Candice Marie, author.
Title: Black bourgeois : class and sex in the flesh / Candice M. Jenkins.
Description: Minneapolis : University of Minnesota Press, [2019] | Includes bibliographical references and index.
Identifiers: LCCN 2018055521| ISBN 978-1-5179-0579-8 (hc) | ISBN 978-1-5179-0580-4 (pb)
Subjects: LCSH: American literature—20th century—History and criticism. | American literature—African American authors—History and criticism. | American literature—21st century—History and criticism. | African Americans in literature. | Class consciousness in literature. | Social classes in literature. | Human body in literature.
Classification: LCC PS228.S63 J46 2019 | DDC 810.9/896073—dc23
LC record available at https://lccn.loc.gov/2018055521

UMP BmB 2019

Race is the modality in which class is lived.

—Stuart Hall, Chas Critcher, Tony Jefferson, John Clarke, and Brian Roberts, *Policing the Crisis: Mugging, the State, and Law and Order*

Contents

Preface

This anxiety about propriety and place, race and class, marks me as hopelessly bourgeois, I suppose.

—Patricia J. Williams, *Open House*

Class is a weird, weird thing for black Americans. Maybe I should only speak for myself, though recently published essays about what might be summed up as class ambivalence, one in as storied a venue as the *New York Times,* suggest black people's strange feelings about class, and especially class privilege, run wide and deep.[1] Among those of us—especially those of us grown folks—who can presently be counted as middle class, very few have lived inside that location in an uncomplicated, comfortable way since birth, and even fewer can point to a long legacy of ancestors so positioned. Instead, in each generation some of us, via education, aspiration, hard work (our own, and our parents') and luck, find ourselves much more comfortable than our parents were—and some of those who started out in relative stability fall out of their family's class position, at rates much higher than for white Americans.[2] For many of us, middle-class status is neither a given nor a permanent status, and it is only rarely bolstered by the kind of generational wealth that would make it unnecessary to, say, borrow significant money for one's education, accumulate consumer debt, or even live paycheck to paycheck.

But this describes only black folks' complex relationship to the *economic* matter of class. We also tend to have a thorny relationship to other kinds of class markers, markers that are hardly acknowledged, at least not openly, to be about class at all, even as they have the potential to shape how we are perceived and treated and to affect the resources to which we gain access under this nation's system of white supremacy. An anecdote might illustrate this better than any list of statistics. For much of graduate school I wore my hair cut very short, nearly bald—about two millimeters away from Danai Gurira's General Okoye. When I let my hair begin to grow back in my final year there, a black woman administrator I liked said, upon seeing me with hair for the first time, "Candice! I didn't know you had *naturally curly hair!*" I talked with friends about this later, trying to understand her pleased, incredulous tone. As they pointed out, she'd said it as if my hair texture were a talent or skill I'd been keeping hidden, like a secret ability to play the cello, or perhaps practice telekinesis. And while her comment was made in passing, and likely nothing she would even remember saying later, it was clear in that moment that my status had somehow improved, in her eyes, simply because my hair (for the record, generally a 4A on Andre Walker's scale, with a few 3B/C sections mixed in) was less kinky than she must have expected, based on my coloring and features.[3]

This scenario captures one piece of what this book is about—the way class status can be, for black people, *in the body* in particular, phenotypical ways. But that tells only part of the book's story. I make a larger argument, in these pages, that narrative representations of black class privilege in the late twentieth century, even those that pay little attention to skin color, hair texture, and the like, are particularly interested in the body—and not simply because "class," for black people, is always closely related to, and often ambivalently projected *through,* the embodied identity categories of race and gender. This narrative preoccupation with the physical, or corporeal, also reflects the way that these fictional stories of class privilege are disrupted by a visceral sense of racialized *vulnerability,* such that even the most privileged black subjects are never quite insulated from racism. Class privilege is, in these texts, a complicated and even paradoxical matter: never as simple, or as safe, as it might first appear.

Class has never been a simple matter for me, either. Maybe for that reason, it has since childhood been a source of fascination and no small confusion. After my parents separated when I was nine, my mother—an alumna of Tuskegee and the first in her family to go to college—raised me on her own in the Midwest, moving us from the East Coast back to the Ohio city where my parents had met, years before, because she was able to return to an old job there. We were nowhere near our sprawling working-class family in Houston, though we had stopped there for a while on the way to our new life away from my volatile father; my Texas cousins told me with no particular malice that I "talked proper." I am an only child, and I was lucky enough never to want for any genuine necessity, never to be hungry or homeless—my mother, whose degree was in biochemistry, was always able to work, in various kinds of modestly salaried, middle-class jobs (medical writer; drafter of abstracts for scientific publications; SSI claims adjuster) that kept the bills paid. But I remember different sorts of what I only now, when comparing my childhood to that of my own children, recognize to be deprivations—wearing mostly thrift store clothing; not having cable, or even color, television; and living in a rental apartment, not a house.[4] Thinking back, it would be overstating the case to say that I consciously felt myself on the outside of any sort of class barrier, looking in, but I do remember noticing the differences between how we lived and how some of my mother's (also black) friends from graduate school or the office did, in comfortable, suburban houses, where you could take your dirty towels down to the basement instead of, as we did, carting them to a nearby laundromat.

Yet I also remember, clearly, that the apartments we rented were decidedly not in "the 'hood"—like many other middle-class black people, my mother used what financial and cultural capital she had to keep us in spaces she perceived as safe, which in Columbus, Ohio, in the 1980s, typically meant moderately integrated but majority-white areas on the north side of town. We never made our home in truly wealthy enclaves—those areas were outside of the city proper and not accessible by public transportation, and we didn't always have a car, yet another example of the precariousness of our middle-class status. Instead, we lived in townhouse apartment complexes set on the fringes of quiet neighborhoods not far from the bus route, where folks who had worked for the telephone company or the post office for twenty years tended patches of lawn in front of modest colonial or ranch-style homes. This is all to say: I didn't exactly grow up poor, but I didn't have many of the things that I associated then or now with being truly middle class, either. No single "class" category has ever felt like my home, an experience that is certainly not unique, especially for black folks, but for me has become an angle of vision on the world that I can't quite shake. This sense of liminality traveled with me to Spelman College—a place where I finally saw the scale, and variety, of what both "blackness" and "the black middle class" could mean—and has continued to shape my thinking about the very notion of *class,* which has always seemed, to me, to be about much more than the money one has in the bank.

I once, in my mother's hearing, talked about growing up "not exactly middle class," and she later asked me, concern in her voice, whether I really felt that way—didn't I think she had raised me to be middle class, at least in terms of values? The answer to this question is yes, but the question itself gets at the other part of what I am trying to do in *Black Bourgeois*—that is, to think through class as performance, and black class privilege in particular, as informed by *culture.* It seems to me that the ways that we signal class positioning—via behavior, consumption, or style—and the stories we tell ourselves about what that positioning means matter at least as much as the numbers on our balance sheets. Not because numbers are irrelevant—they clearly are not—but because those numbers tell only some of our specific class stories. And they are always already skewed against us by structural factors that we cannot control. News outlets reported in 2018, for instance, that women of color in academia make sixty-seven cents for every dollar that white men make—just the most recent in an avalanche of data that point to the persistence of both income and wealth inequality in the United States.[5] Given such factors, it makes sense that "class privilege" might mean something more than simply money for black people.

My project in this book has been, then, to unpack some of the complexities of class privilege for black Americans by considering how texts from the post–Civil Rights era through the turn of the twenty-first century represent the embodied dilemma of being both black and middle class. This dilemma is one I know I will continue to ponder even as I send the manuscript off to press, because I am continually reminded—by a specious arrest at Starbucks or a microaggression in the office—of the ways that "privilege" is often paradoxically fragmented and incomplete for black people, and not just because of financial pressures. I wonder if, as Patricia Williams suggests in the epigraph, my persistent "anxiety about propriety and place, race and class" operates as its own kind of class credential.[6] Like her, I am "hopelessly bourgeois" because I continue to be intrigued, or haunted, by where I come from and the place to which I've tenuously arrived. Like so many other members of the "black middle class," the complicated distance between those points stays with me, its own kind of hidden talent—an ever present reminder that seems to reside in my very flesh.

Introduction

The Black and Bourgeois Dilemma

> We both know that we can't dress ourselves out of the perception of who [we] are in the dominant society. She and I, dressed in the kind of professional attire anyone would expect a college administrator to be wearing in the middle of a work day, are still targets for hate.
>
> —Dr. Bob Hughes, Seattle University

(Black) Class as Culture

This book has at its center a kind of oxymoron, the precarious and seemingly impossible cultural position of the black and bourgeois subject, and the centrality of *embodiment* to that impossibility. The quotation above, drawn from a June 2016 blog-post-turned-op-ed written by longtime educator Bob Hughes, illustrates the nature of this oxymoronic position. As Hughes recounts, he and his black female colleague, dressed professionally, gainfully employed, legitimate participants in the capitalist, consumer marketplace, as Starbucks patrons—in other words, evidently *privileged* subjects—are spit upon and accosted with racial slurs by a "clean cut, well dressed," and "visibly angry" young white man.[1] Their privilege does not protect them from racial violence, as in this moment their black flesh, and in particular his colleague's *black and female* flesh—Hughes notes that the young man "seemed only to see a woman of color," a fact highlighted by the specific insult he hurls in their direction, "fucking nigger bitch"—supersedes any "access and status" that he and his colleague had attained.

In the epigraph above, Hughes says he and his colleague are well aware that their privilege cannot protect them from such racist violence. Yet the fact that he makes repeated, fetishistic recourse to the evidence of this privilege—education and employment, exhibited in the embodied, performative marker of "professional attire"—suggests subtle expectations that persist, a continued assumption that material privilege can, or should, insulate certain bodies from the violences to which black flesh is routinely subjected. Indeed, Hughes's telling use of the word "still" in the final sentence of the epigraph—clothed in their professional attire, he and his colleague "are *still* targets for hate"—not only subtly reinforces the notion that the assault should not be happening to such mundanely middle-class figures as "college administrators," but also overlooks the ways that, particularly in this highly charged historical moment, the visible collision of blackness and privilege may itself serve as provocation for the attack. Does the young man's rage arise from the fact that Hughes and his colleague are not only black but black *and* privileged, acting in ways that he perceives as out of place (read: *uppity*) by publicly enjoying a professional meet-up over coffee? Or is the attack simply a racialized refusal to recognize the "socio-economic status, educational accomplishments or . . . age" that Hughes would expect to lead to "respect or deference"?[2] While we ultimately cannot know the young man's motives, Hughes's own language, his insistence that "the young man didn't see educated college administrators sitting at the table. He saw two Black people," suggests that the very fact of blackness (as Fanon might put it) in this instance renders the protective qualities of privilege illegible.[3]

It seems fitting that Hughes's first awareness of the young man, and his hostility, begins with a fleshly sensation—with Hughes "realizing that my right hand was wet," only later to understand that "the liquid I felt on my hand was [the man's] spit." In Hughes's retelling of the incident, competing versions of black embodiment struggle for dominance, as the contained and respectable body of the "college administrator," buffered and armored by its "professional attire," is contrasted to and disrupted by the black flesh violated, wet with saliva, vulnerable to assault, violently reduced to the non-human by an epithet, *fucking nigger bitch,* which, like the man's spit, is hurled at Hughes and his companion twice. And while the violence of this encounter is most certainly "about" race and gender, the story is framed as a professional rendezvous, replete with "the kind of innocuous catch-up talk that two college administrators do," a meeting that takes place on the occasion of Hughes's colleague securing a new position in his area, prompting him to "welcome her to the neighborhood and her new job." These details signal something other than race, or rather, something co-constituted with race, shaping Hughes's experience perhaps as much as race does, in simultaneous if competing ways—that is, *class,* and specifically class privilege. Part of what Hughes struggles to reconcile in his essay is the same contradiction in terms that animates this book—the ontological conundrum, if you will, presented by a subject who is black and materially privileged, vulnerable and presumably protected, a subject that is simultaneously (black) flesh and (bourgeois) body.

This book began as a project solely about "identity" in contemporary African American fiction, evolving very slowly into a project about the way that such fiction narrates black class privilege. As the project shifted in this direction, however, it quickly became clear that to talk straightforwardly about black class privilege was far more difficult than it first would seem, not only because the very meaning of "class" for African Americans has always been a complex affair but also because the way that class *privilege,* in particular, applies to "black" subjects tends to be inextricable from those subjects' bodies, and particularly from bodily performances that are more readily understood as racialized and gendered. In Lisa B. Thompson's words, "class performance is bound up with the performance of racial and gender identity."[4] Under these circumstances, class becomes a cipher or hieroglyph to be, first, detected—is *class* even operating here?—and then interpreted, teased from the braid of identity threads that form the (black middle-class) subject.

A small number of scholars in sociology and anthropology have argued for an approach to the study of class that considers the category not merely in the Marxist sense, as "the social positions generated by the organization and logic of capitalism," but also as a form of *identity,* one that "comes to be known equally by markers that exist outside of discovering one's position in paid labor . . . lived out in private life and personal relations—in short, class culture."[5] But despite critical precedent for understanding class in this way, such scholars have also readily acknowledged class as a "hidden" discursive category:

> Class exists in America but cannot be talked about; . . . there is no language for it, but . . . it is "displaced" or "spoken through" other languages of social difference—race, ethnicity, and gender.[6]

This displacement is crucial to my project in this book. The way that class is a sort of invisible or submerged identity category for which we have minimal language, and the way that it gets subsumed by race, gender, and ethnicity, means that black people often understand the *cultural* implications of their class position largely, though not entirely, through their (racialized) bodies. Class as culture is thus about what and how those bodies signify and perform, how they are styled, how they are read as successful or striving or respectable or "ratchet"—which has to do with everything from physical phenotype to styles of dress, hair, and speech, none of which are neutral, all of which speak to a kind of social performance, or perhaps *performativity,* that is never entirely conscious.[7]

The notion that class is lived *through* race thus has special emphasis in this project. Stuart Hall, Chas Critcher, Tony Jefferson, John Clarke, and Brian Roberts wrote the words of the book's epigraph in 1978, arguing that working-class black Brits "comprehend, handle, and then begin to resist the exploitation which is an objective feature of their class situation" via the prism of race, which "structures, from the inside, the whole range of their social experience."[8] And while it seems no particular stretch to apply this insight from Hall and his coauthors to working-class black Americans, in *Black Bourgeois* I want to think through how and why it also might be true of the black middle-class subjects at the center of the post–Civil Rights era texts that ground this study. This last is a trickier proposition, in part because Hall and his coauthors, via their interest in how working-class blacks "comprehend, handle, and then begin to resist" *exploitation,* clearly signal their Marxist investment in "class" as hierarchical economic structure and their privileging of labor and proletarian class consciousness as precursor to structural resistance. My interest in this project is less in this macro version of class consciousness per se, one that presumably "unfolds automatically from the relations of production," and more in the "micro level of identity formation, where the circulation of cultural meanings produces the material that makes various subjectivities possible."[9]

Of course, my focus on class as culture and embodied performance is in no way meant to dismiss or even diminish the structuring role of capitalism "as a set of discourses, practices, and institutions in the world."[10] Indeed, the material realities of capitalism vis-à-vis class structure are particularly relevant to any examination of the black middle class, in part because black Americans tend to be disproportionally affected by structural shifts that contribute to, for instance, the general precarity of the category "middle class" within contemporary global capitalism, the dramatically increasing economic disparities and inequality that concentrate wealth among the group that has come to be described as the 1 percent, and so on.[11] Yet these material realities must be thought simultaneously with class as *culture,* with the ways that people understand themselves and others as not simply economic actors but as subjects in discourse. As Lisa Henderson writes, "Even though class is traditionally an economic category, a lot of variation occurs within those stations of the cross of class historically defined through labor-capital analysis (in the Marxist tradition) or empirically defined by occupation, income, and formal education (in the liberal one)."[12] Or in Rita Felski's words, while "work continues to play a major role in the shaping of social status and life chances, . . . class distinctions are also shaped by consumption practices and lifestyle patterns that do not bear any simple relation to the basic division between capital and labor."[13] Class, in other words, is not *merely* objective and structured by labor; it is also a cultural site and what Sherry Ortner calls "an identity term," albeit one that is informed by—indeed, visible largely *through*—other identity terms.[14] As Ortner goes on to write, "there is no class in America that is not always already racialized."[15] Because of both the intersectional way that identity works and the manner in which class is discursively hidden, to write about class for black people is always already to write simultaneously about those sites onto which class *as identity* is "displaced"—race and gender.[16]

Questions about these sites—and about race in particular—seem especially urgent in the moment in which I write, as the rallying cry of a new civil rights movement, Black Lives Matter (BLM), gains traction in the wake of increasingly visible police killings of unarmed black people. The BLM movement places emphasis on the black body's absolute vulnerability to racism and state violence, not only in the form of police killings but also in the everyday reminders that black bodies in white spaces can be policed and disciplined for simply existing while black. A mass movement that works to turn our collective attention to the precarity of black life, to the ways that black lives are apparently *not* understood to "matter" under white supremacy, BLM seems a stark corrective to expansive narratives of black progress that dominated social discourse until very recently, arguably well into Barack Obama's first term as president. But this seemingly abrupt discursive shift, in the second decade of the twenty-first century, from the post–Civil Rights moment to the BLM moment, from a cultural emphasis on privilege and progress to an emphasis on precarity, actually can be understood as a discursive pendulum swing between two interrelated positions that remain, in fact, in tension.

This epistemic tension is related to and a reflection of the ontological tension I outline in this book—one that lies at the heart of the "black middle-class" subject, between the symbolic and literal *vulnerability* of the black body and the covering, and sometimes confining, protection, again both symbolic and literal, of material privilege. The texts I study in this volume transform this ontological dilemma into a representational one in which narrative depictions of black fleshliness repeatedly intrude upon and challenge narrative treatments of material privilege. These works depict protagonists who struggle continually with and repeatedly return to the corporeal as they navigate raced and classed subjectivity, highlighting the ways that black class privilege operates as lived conundrum and rhetorical contradiction. This conundrum, what I call the "black and bourgeois dilemma," encompasses both the intimate way that privilege can be, oxymoronically, written in and on the very black body that interrupts its seamless operation, as well as a larger, fraught interaction between externalized performances of middle-classness and of blackness, always embodied, precarious, and mutually disruptive—even, sometimes, deliberately and proudly so. Attending to these representational disruptions, as I do in this project, productively complicates—and conjoins—

our disparate understandings of both "blackness" and "privilege" in the United States, particularly in the present moment. These concepts are, of course, far from totally discrete entities, despite how they are popularly perceived; thus in the following sections I endeavor to clarify how our *theoretical* senses of blackness and of class privilege are already historically and discursively imbricated with and defined against each other.

Body and Flesh

When we consider what I am calling the black and bourgeois dilemma, a tension or contradiction between the precarity of the black body and the supposed protection of privilege, an obvious and fair question arises: Does material privilege offer any *real* protection from the operation of black vulnerability? In light of the magnitude of that vulnerability, it would surely be easier to dismiss any possible relevance of class privilege to conversations about black racial identity and to focus instead on the risk all black people share. Indeed, we need only to look at the numerous examples of wealthy blacks' experiences of workaday racism—from Harvard professor Henry Louis Gates being arrested for "breaking into" his own home in Cambridge to Oprah Winfrey being denied buzzer entry to the Hermès boutique in Paris—to understand that even extraordinary privilege does not actually "cover" the "black" body fully, nor with any reliability or coherence.[17] And yet the (often unvoiced) expectation that it *should,* that indeed such protection is part of the point of laboring to achieve in those ways that would produce material gain, creates the ontological tension I speak of. In the Gates and Winfrey examples, a part of the outrage at the racism is the particular mis-recognition at its heart—"Don't you know who I am?" being the words that we imagine in the mouths of such figures—a mis-recognition that is both ironic and inevitable, attaching as it does to black subjects who are not only highly visible (is there any black person on the planet more recognizable than Oprah?—perhaps Beyoncé?) but also visibly black.

This last is crucial, for the effectiveness of class "protection," indeed, the question of whether the cover provided by privilege is real at all, hinges upon the body—by which I mean it depends upon any given body's corporeal nuances, how it is read in specific moments of (typically cross-racial) encounter, but also on the ways that the black body in general disrupts the expected operation of privilege. Harvey Young calls this generalized black body "the imagined and, yet, highly (mis)recognizable figure who shadows the actual, unseen body," both an "externally applied projection blanketed across black bodies and an internalization of the projected image by black folk."[18] *This* black body, this projection that comes to live within as well as without, creates the conditions of possibility for black vulnerability, a vulnerability that shapes our present historical moment and frequently makes intraracial distinctions of class, as well as, for some critics, demarcations of history, seem particularly irrelevant.

Indeed, in response to Hortense Spillers's description of the "originating metaphors of captivity and mutilation" perpetuated within the "dominant symbolic activity" surrounding the black subject, Jared Sexton has written, "this claim, if taken seriously, chastens our *desire* to discover in political and popular culture something new about contemporary representations of racial blackness, whether we designate this moment post–civil rights, post–Cold War, post-9/11, and so on."[19] Sexton's caution seems particularly important in this moment of renewed attention to the precarity of black life, in which "Black Lives Matter" coheres as a phrase in part because of repeated, violent, and visceral reminders of what Sexton calls the "absurdity" of a world in which such a statement *needs* making.[20]

And yet Spillers, in the same essay that Sexton references, advances several ideas that I find generative for thinking blackness alongside figurations of class, ideas that may be more compatible with Sexton's skepticism of the new than they first appear, precisely because they suggest that the fraught relation of the black subject to privilege is not at all a recent phenomenon. Spillers in "Mama's Baby, Papa's Maybe" famously addresses what she calls "patriarchalized gender" and the way that captive bodies (as well as their "liberated" counterparts) are necessarily excluded from the gender relation as it is conceptualized in the West. This seems a particularly applicable, and evocative, way of thinking about what material privilege might mean for black bodies in the United States. If patriarchalized gender is the only gender there is (Spillers 73), could the same be said of class? Or at least of class privilege, which relies upon an engagement with the property relation that is very different than *being* property—that instead suggests being *propertied*? The connection comes to mind first at a moment from "Mama's Baby" that has been crucial to earlier work of mine on black intimacy, in which Spillers discusses "Family" as a vertical relation:

> It seems clear, however, that "Family," as we practice and understand it "in the West"—the *vertical* transfer of a bloodline, of a patronymic, of titles and entitlements, of real estate and the prerogatives of "cold cash," from *fathers* to *sons* and in the supposedly free exchange of affectional ties between a male and a female of *his* choice—becomes the mythically revered privilege of a free and freed community. (74)

Those "titles and entitlements," that "real estate," not to mention the "cold cash," are all markers of wealth, particular signifiers that raise the specter of material privilege even as the passage's focus is on a social, intimate relation. Thus, the racial "vestibularity" Spillers outlines, which removes black bodies from the Western "Family" relation, and from gender, might *symbolically* remove those bodies from class (status/privilege) as well.

Spillers writes, for instance, that "the captive body . . . brings into focus a gathering of social realities as well as a metaphor for *value* so thoroughly interwoven in their literal and figurative emphases that distinctions between them are virtually useless" (68). And further: "The captive female body locates precisely a moment of converging political and social vectors that mark the flesh as a prime commodity of exchange" (75). Captive black bodies, commodified at the level of the flesh, cannot be understood as active participants—agents—in market exchange unless their corporeal *embodiment* of capital—in other words, their status as chattel property—constitutes "participation." Instead, black flesh figures always and already as fungible object to be owned, exchanged, and exploited.

This book's full title, *Black Bourgeois: Class and Sex in the Flesh,* is meant to suggest precisely the contradiction in terms presented by black flesh that also qualifies as "bourgeois." Spillers's foundational differentiation between body and flesh ("But I would make a distinction . . . between 'body' and 'flesh' and impose that distinction as the central one between captive and liberated subject-positions" [67]) is crucial to my thinking on this point, particularly her assertion that "The flesh is the concentration of 'ethnicity' that contemporary critical discourses neither acknowledge nor discourse away" (67). While Spillers articulates this body/flesh distinction in order to make a point about gender—captive black and female flesh, vulnerable to violation both interior and external, is "female flesh 'ungendered'"—I am interested, here, in how we might draw upon Spillers's distinction to outline more clearly the way that captive *blackness* is implicitly, and perpetually, not just declassed but symbolically expelled from class logics entirely. And while a number of scholars have made explicit the notion that post-Emancipation, black labor and black bodies generally became (or became more visible as) an "excessive and residual Otherness" within the American body politic, the question of what the implications of Spillers's figuration might mean for the so-called liberated black body and that body's positioning in relation to class hierarchy remains undertheorized.[21]

Following Spillers, I would argue that blackness has been discursively and conceptually marked as Other to privilege—and that this obtains despite the documented existence of the propertied black exception.[22] The continuing operation of those "originating metaphors of captivity and mutilation" that circulate within "dominant symbolic activity" in the United States means we might figure black flesh, even "liberated" black flesh, as *ontologically* tied to property, a consequence not only of what Cedric Robinson called "racial capitalism" but also of what Stephen Best has described as slavery's "unique scandal of value," in which "the slave has become a money form."[23] This is precisely why Frank Wilderson and other Afro-pessimist thinkers define the position of blackness in civil society in terms of *antagonism,* although, as I explore in more depth in this volume's fifth chapter, Afro-pessimism rarely considers the question of how the black and the bourgeois might nonetheless, and paradoxically, coexist.[24] Addressing this uneasy coexistence is my project throughout this book.

Alexander Weheliye draws upon Spillers's framework in order to suggest that "flesh" is what exceeds and precedes the (Western) body, a genre of humanity that is not recognized as such; in other words, for Weheliye, "the flesh . . . operates as a vestibular gash in the armor of Man, simultaneously a tool of dehumanization and a relationship vestibule to alternate ways of being."[25] Weheliye's notion of black "flesh" as a tool of dehumanization is certainly critical to my thinking in this book, insofar as that dehumanization—on the basis of black flesh as "fungible accumulation"—collides, always contradictorily and often violently, with the material conditions and cultural performances of black privilege.[26] But that very collision raises, again, his other reading of the flesh, as fugitive surplus and site of possibility, and this reading, too, is relevant to my project here. The texts I read throughout this book force us to ask whether the social strictures of class privilege—especially as those strictures are tied to a particular kind of obeisance to Western logics of humanity and value—constitute not only protection but a cage. How does the insistent presence of the flesh—Greg Thomas's metaphoric use of "proud flesh" as a rejection of "the 'normal' logic of the society that injures [and] . . . imprisons us" seems relevant here—thereby make room within that cage, or point out a means of escape from it?[27] Narrative subjects who navigate the paradox or dilemma of the black and bourgeois also, sometimes, willfully negotiate within and against the *class* restrictions of this dilemma, and not just its racial ones. And, as I discuss below, these restrictions have their own (racialized) discursive implications.

Bourgeois(ing) While Black

Two concepts from French sociologist Pierre Bourdieu seem relevant to understanding how "social class" works more generally and how its application to putatively "black" bodies might operate in specific ways. Young explains Bourdieu's notion of *habitus* as "the generative principle of regulated improvisation," elaborating as follows: "A person from a certain social category is taught how to perform successfully her role as a member of that category. Eventually she inhabits this performance, and her performance of her class becomes the model upon which other members of that same category—and those who fall outside of it—are judged."[28] The performative nature of *habitus* is, of course, hidden from our conscious view as subjects—"we forget that we are performing."[29] While Young draws upon the notion of *habitus,* reconfigured as *black habitus,* to "read the black body as socially constructed and continually constructing its own self," I want here to return *habitus,* at least in part, to its origins in the study of social class.[30] This return might seem easy enough, but it is complicated by the fact that black habitus and middle-class habitus intersect with and work in opposition to one another. Bourdieu writes:

> The individuals grouped in a class that is constructed in a particular respect . . . always bring with them, in addition to the pertinent properties by which they are classified, secondary properties which are thus smuggled into the explanatory model. This means that a class . . . is defined not only by its position in the relations of production, as identified through indices such as occupation, income or even educational level, but also by a certain sex-ratio, a certain distribution in geographical space (which is never socially neutral) and by a whole set of subsidiary characteristics which may function, in the form of tacit requirements, as real principles of selection or exclusion without ever being formally stated (this is the case with ethnic origin and sex). A number of official criteria in fact serve as a mask for hidden criteria: for example, the requiring of a given diploma can be a way of demanding a particular social origin.[31]

What is both fascinating and frustrating about this explanatory passage is that while it gives us tools for understanding the *implicit* aspects of class positioning—criteria that go beyond "occupation, income, or even educational level," the typical measures by which sociologists determine who is "middle class"—we are left to discern for ourselves how these "tacit requirements" operate vis-à-vis race, or vice versa. For Bourdieu, writing in the context of twentieth-century France, "ethnic origin" is one category that functions as a "real principle of selection or exclusion without ever being formally stated." This suggests, for our purposes here in the twenty-first-century United States, not only that *naming* race as a principle of class exclusion would be a taboo, and must be accomplished by other means, but also that those who seek to select or exclude on the basis of race may not even realize they are doing so. After all, as Bourdieu goes on to note, "the schemes of the habitus . . . owe their specific efficacy to the fact that they function below the level of consciousness and language, beyond the reach of introspective scrutiny or control by the will."[32] When it comes to a breach in habitus, a moment of someone's (or, as I will return to shortly, of one's own) failure to conform to class or caste expectations, we as observers may simply have to intuit, to know it when we see it.

The black women's book group ejected from a California "wine train" in 2014 for laughing too loudly provides a fitting example. The incident became a trending topic on Twitter under the hashtag #LaughingWhileBlack. Especially striking about this incident for our purposes is the fact that these middle-class black women, who had, like everyone else, paid their money to participate in the bourgeois activity of wine tasting (in a "luxury rail car," no less), were nonetheless *racially* targeted, expelled for engaging in the same behaviors as whites on the train—talking, laughing, and drinking wine. The practice of wine tasting is a classed one, operating precisely in the arena of "taste," defined as "an acquired disposition to 'differentiate' and 'appreciate.'"[33] The fact that middle-class whites on the train perceived this particular group's laughter as too raucous and complained to management—as well as the fact that the group's lowering of their voices, their attempt to comply bodily with the implicit demand for their restraint, proved insufficient—indicates the black women's incompatibility with the classed scene of the wine train, a failure at the level of (perceived) habitus, which after all "embed[s] what some would mistakenly call *values* in the most automatic gestures or the apparently most insignificant techniques of the body—ways of walking or blowing one's nose, ways of eating or talking"—or, evidently, ways of laughing.[34] #LaughingWhileBlack becomes, then, *laughing blackly,* interacting in a way that, seemingly inexplicably, triggered an unbearable level of discomfort in some of the white passengers.

The whites who complained likely would not have admitted openly to the racial component of their complaint even if race was their conscious and deliberate motive, but what the operation of race as a "subsidiary characteristic" or "hidden criterion" for exclusion from certain middle-class habiti suggests is that these whites may not even have been *consciously* aware that race was the(ir) issue. They simply looked at the book group and perceived it—alone among other, similar groups that were raced differently—as overly "loud" or "disruptive," as a site of *excess,* a response that nonetheless was absolutely legible to the women targeted as a *racially* motivated exclusion.[35] Indeed, the fact that the train company initially justified their ejection of the book group and the supposed necessity of involving police (who met the women as they left the train) with exaggerated claims of "verbal and physical abuse toward other guests and staff" signals the larger meaning of black presence in white (middle-class) space—*danger,* both figurative and literal.[36]

This, then, is precisely the sort of "spectacular event" in which "conceptions of blackness are projected across individual bodies," erasing those bodies' humanity and reducing them, instead, to blackness as *symbolic* pollutant, disruption, and threat—"a valueless form of life."[37] But what of the set of practices that constitute, in Young's words, "black habitus"? Zandria Robinson suggests that "because of the complexity of individual identity intersections and social tastes, most African Americans must work diligently to stay put or to jump into native blackness."[38] Blackness, too, has its *performative* rules for inclusion and exclusion, as the popular metaphor of the revocable "black card" makes clear. We might ask, then, what are the "subsidiary characteristics" that could serve, tacitly, to exclude a putatively black subject from racial belonging? Ironically, middle-class origins or behaviors can function in this way; as Patricia Williams has written of "that utterly paradoxical category of social projection: the 'new black middle class,'" it includes "anyone—from security guards to Oprah Winfrey—deemed not a member of the 'real' black underclass," suggesting that authentic blackness is figuratively associated with black poverty.[39] Black habitus, then, is at its most precarious when it is accompanied by (or, perhaps, disrupted by) performances of class privilege.

Actor, comedian, writer, and producer Issa Rae, now well known for her HBO series *Insecure,* itself a major touchstone of black middle-class cultural production, wryly highlighted this issue in her preceding web series, *The Misadventures of Awkward Black Girl.* The conflict arises during an episode of the series' second season titled "The Friends," in which central character J, played by Rae, meets her new, white boyfriend's (fair-skinned, straight-haired) friend Ty.[40] Ty, who says that he is from South

Africa, tells J that during his childhood his family sent him to the States so he could "grow up in the projects," and proclaims relief at his return to Los Angeles "so I can be with my people." While J can't quite understand Ty's performance of black racial solidarity ("Why does he keep saying 'we'?"), she complies easily enough with his attempt to exclude her from black authenticity based on her class origins. When she reveals to him that she grew up in Baldwin Hills, a wealthy, majority-black area in Los Angeles, Ty pulls away from her physically and responds with the retort, "Oh, where the rich black folk live," concluding, condescendingly, "not all of us African Americans have to struggle."

Not surprisingly, J's initial response to Ty's characterization of Baldwin Hills as "rich" ("Oh—more 'middle class'") fails to mitigate this rejection, and her subsequent attempts to save face and recuperate her blackness escalate, hilariously, to claims that before she was "found" and adopted by a Baldwin Hills family, she had been homeless and lived "in these streets," as well as in "trash homes" (after supposedly being abandoned in a trash can by her birth mother). J generates these extreme fabrications seemingly despite her own best judgment and against her own will—she begins to construct a black habitus that includes this "street" history even *after* she has wondered incredulously to herself, "Is this faux-nigga competing with my black card?" Of course, "faux-nigga" here only emphasizes the irony in their interaction. Ty—who is not only white-skinned but an actual South African who claims to be an African American on a seeming technicality—can nonetheless easily trump J's "black card" by emphasizing his own connections to black poverty ("the projects") and invoking the specter of J's black middle-class *in*authenticity.[41] J's own participation in this process—her seeming complicity with Ty's attempts to cast her as a privileged "pretender to victimhood," in Patricia Williams's words—suggests the tenuous coherence of black habitus as it interacts with bourgeois origins or status.[42]

One irony of the scene in *Awkward Black Girl* is the way the brown-skinned Rae uses a white-skinned South African to question J's class-based authenticity, thereby disrupting the implicit equation of "post-black," "light-skinned," and "new black middle class" that is evident in

Patricia Williams's words and in many broader discussions of the black middle class and its racial loyalties:

> A postblack, on the other hand, is that light-skinned, ubiquitous pretender to victimhood who malaprops his way through the one professional job that should have been divided among ten better-qualified whites and who is known less for the content than the contentiousness of his character.[43]

While it may seem only fitting that Williams's humorous, stereotypical version of the "postblack" middle-class subject be described as "light-skinned," the better to understand his or her status as "pretender to victimhood," the question of skin color is in fact quite a tricky one to address in analyses of black class privilege. Light skin is no guarantee of a particular class standing, and dark skin no guarantee of its absence, yet the complex history of race and class in the United States means that, "for generations of black people, color and class have been inexorably tied together."[44]

This "inexorable" link between color and class has its roots in enslavement and in the sexual exploitation of black women by white men that has led to an array of skin colors among those whom we now understand as "black." And although much scholarly and creative attention has been given to the idea of intraracial colorism, understanding the roots of colorism in *whites'* preference for and prejudice toward whiteness is key to understanding why skin color remains tied to material advantage for blacks (and other non-whites).[45] In a 2015 op-ed for the *Guardian,* Linda Chavers describes the way her status as a "light-skinned black woman with dark, thick, long hair" leads police officers (and other whites) to "profile [her] body" as "pretty," "harmless," "accessible," "approachable and nice," as "one of the good ones."[46] Whatever one thinks about Chavers's final statement in the essay—a sardonic reminder to racist police officers that "you are shooting the wrong ones"—the point she makes about whites' assumptions regarding skin color is supported by research, particularly Lance Hannon's recent study "White Colorism," which uses existing survey data to demonstrate that whites see lighter-skinned blacks and Latinos as more intelligent, as well as an earlier study that showed that whites remember the faces of professional blacks as lighter skinned.[47]

One of the first concerns of this project, then, is how post–Civil Rights narratives speak to the "light-skinned" black body and the privileges that attach to it, particularly as those privileges are also gendered. This returns us to Bourdieu and his concept of "cultural capital," or nonfinancial assets that contribute to social mobility—a concept that, along with *habitus,* might help us better understand the operation of (black) class performance. Throughout this project, I read skin color and hair texture as forms of cultural capital, a kind of capital that in this case accrues *within* (and is revealed upon) the body. This is both a function of what Bourdieu calls "seniority"—"the embodied cultural capital of . . . previous generations," a point to which I will return momentarily—and a side effect of white supremacy, which continues to value whiteness not just legally or politically but across realms of the social, including conceptions of beauty, which means that proximity to whiteness continues in many instances to determine what is understood as the bodily "ideal."[48]

The consequences of this structural devaluing of blackness are repeatedly observable in black cultural production, going back at least a century: we might think, for instance, of the repeated mistreatment, and related self-loathing, of dark-skinned character Emma Lou Morgan in Wallace Thurman's *The Blacker the Berry* (1929), or the stark class and color hierarchy between light-skinned free blacks and the formerly enslaved character 'Liza Jane in Charles Chesnutt's short story "The Wife of His Youth" (1899).[49] These and numerous other textual examples point us to the ways that, both historically and in the present, differing shades of skin color are differently valued in Western culture, with lighter skin privileged and darker skin disadvantaged based on each one's relative positioning vis-à-vis whiteness. This form of cultural capital is particularly applicable to black women, who are especially subject to gender norms that tie value to embodiment. And while, as sociologist Tressie McMillan Cottom has recently pointed out, "Black women have worked hard to write a counternarrative of our worth in a global system where beauty is the only legitimate capital allowed women without legal, political, and economic challenge," counternarratives of beauty that deliberately embrace *black* embodiment do not on their own change the fact that, in Cottom's words, "beauty's ultimate function is to exclude blackness."[50] As such, the antiblack logic of colorism values, and often materially rewards, lighter skin colors (along with smoother hair textures, narrower facial features, and so on) that appear to reveal a closer proximity to whiteness.

This embodied sense of white proximity returns us to the question of "seniority," a kind of "embodied cultural capital" that is inherited. Bourdieu links "aristocracy," "the form par excellence of precocity," to the notion of seniority, through the operation of time:

> Legitimate manners owe their value to the fact that they manifest the rarest conditions of acquisition, that is, a social power over time which is tacitly recognized as the supreme excellence: to possess things from the past, i.e., accumulated, crystallized history, aristocratic names and titles, chateaux or "stately homes," paintings and collections, vintage wines and antique furniture, is to master time, that is, by inheritance or through dispositions which, like the taste for old things, are likewise only acquired with time and applied by those who can take their time.[51]

The question of "seniority" for black American elites, those from the highly privileged black social world that Margo Jefferson calls "Negroland"—a group who are not the entirety of my focus on "the black middle class," here but who do comprise a significant substratum of it—is thus a complex one.[52] These subjects, from "old families," are indeed endowed with an excess of cultural capital, but this is only partly in the straightforward sense that in having some generational wealth they have had longer and more sustained access to the kind of cultural skills and material possessions Bourdieu describes. Black elites' cultural capital operates also in the more subtle and complicated sense that such figures' frequent light-skin privilege is read by both blacks and whites as a *symbol* of the same kind of aristocracy, precisely because it signals a prior association with whiteness. Of course, *association* is the sort of word that masks any number of potentially painful, scandalous, or unsavory connections, including enslaved ancestors who lived in proximity to the white "owner," as house servants; a family history of being raped and otherwise sexually exploited by whites; or the relative freedom, even during slavery, to learn a trade or acquire some literacy when such things were legally forbidden, perhaps because of a benevolent owner (who might also be one's biological father). In other words, skin color operates not only as a "subsidiary characteristic" of black middle-class habitus but also as a form of cultural capital that signals a potential white ancestor yet conceals the "relations between . . . subjugation and sexuality" that make such ancestry possible.[53]

This "signal," importantly, speaks as loudly to whites as it does to other blacks, if not more so. And as Chavers points out, skin color and other such embodied, ambivalent signals of black privilege (via an assumed or imagined link to whiteness) inform blacks' experiences even in our present moment—even, not infrequently, shaping how black precarity applies to specific bodies.[54] It is perhaps not surprising, then, that contemporary fiction's narration of black middle-class subjectivity—especially during the 1980s, when these issues were a strong undercurrent in conversations about the "new," post–Civil Rights black middle class—sometimes explicitly figures skin color and hair texture as classed signs, and explores their meaning as such. Still, such figurations are only part of the way post–Civil Rights cultural production speaks to and represents black class privilege—and even texts that elide, ignore, or subvert the operation of color as embodied cultural capital reflect the larger conundrum that animates *Black Bourgeois,* the tension between black habitus and bourgeois habitus that marks "black middle-class" subjects as a sort of contradiction in terms.

The Post-soul, the Contemporary, and the Present: Notes on Method

This book is, ultimately, concerned with what we might call "contemporary" African American narrative, though as I will argue, the moniker is a contested and problematic one. Arguably, what has become known as "contemporary" African American writing begins in the mid-1970s, at the temporal end of the Civil Rights and Black Power movements.[55] One possible problem with this "contemporary" designation, however, is that 1975 was over forty years ago. That 1975—or 1987, or even 1999—was a very different historical moment from "the present" in which I write, 2018, seems so obvious that it hardly bears mentioning, but if so, the persistence of this improbably broad understanding of the contemporary as a more or less coherent period in African American *literary* history remains puzzling. Especially since the contemporary persists, but not without implicit and explicit contestation. Writing from this period has been described by scholars studying the work as, among other things, "post–civil rights," "post-identity," "post-integration," "post-black," "new black," "post-soul," and most recently "post-racial." This litany of terms, breaks, and critical approaches signals a wide and productive diversity of opinions about and approaches to conceptualizing so-called contemporary black writing beyond the designation 1975–present. Yet these terms' reliance upon the "post-" signals, as well, a certain inability to pinpoint the specifics of the *now* beyond its relationship to what has come before.

Indeed, although there is a longer conversation to be had about periodization in black literary study, particularly in light of Kenneth Warren's infamous claim, in 2011, that "African American literature" ended with the demise of Jim Crow in the United States, what intrigues me most about the very idea of the "contemporary" designation is less the relative fixity of the era's beginnings and more the peculiar, and false, stability in accompanying ideas of the "present."[56] Seemingly based in optimistic, class-driven notions of progress and the perpetual expansion of racial possibility (a particularly ironic point of view to emerge under neoliberalism), this stable present has of late been abruptly unsettled by the rallying cry of a new civil rights movement, "Black Lives Matter." To put it bluntly, Black Lives Matter—as a movement and as an idea—has begun to shift our present from one that emphasizes black privilege to one that emphasizes black precarity and the vulnerability of black flesh. Prompted by the ideological crises precipitated by this shift, in this project I take a more historical view of the present and consider how a specific subset of narratives from the recent past, which often continue to be grouped under the rubric of "contemporary" black fiction, can be understood as operating within and speaking from a discrete moment that is both contiguous with and distinct from the present in which I am writing.

My focus in this book is on late-twentieth- and early twenty-first century, post–Civil Rights, and, crucially, pre–Barack Obama African American fiction. Frequently, I use the somewhat outmoded term *post-*

soul—coined by Nelson George in 1992—to describe this body of work, because I continue to find it useful shorthand for what we might call the aftermath of the Soul (read, Civil Rights and Black Power) era.[57] *Post-soul* refers, in critic Mark Anthony Neal's words, to "those folks, artists and critical thinkers, who live in the fissures of two radically different social paradigms . . . *children of soul,* if you will, who came to maturity in the age of Reaganomics and experienced the change from urban industrialism to deindustrialism, from segregation to desegregation, from essential notions of blackness to metanarratives on blackness, without any nostalgic allegiance to the past . . . , but firmly in grasp of the existential concerns of this brave new world."[58] The term *post-soul,* then, periodizes a collection of writers and artists with strikingly similar experiences and topical concerns.

Post-soul is thus in part useful as a loosely *generational* term—with Toni Morrison as notable exception, the novelists and filmmaker whose work I examine throughout *Black Bourgeois* are black late-stage baby boomers (born in the final decade of the nearly twenty-year span that constituted the post–World War II "baby boom") or black members of so-called Generation X, post–baby boomers born between the early 1960s and the early 1980s.[59] They all—again, with the exception of Morrison, whose 1981 novel *Tar Baby* is included here because it anticipates the concerns of so many post-soul efforts—meet scholar Bertram D. Ashe's criterion for "post-soul," as African Americans who "have no lived, adult experience with [the Civil Rights] movement."[60] For both Ashe and Neal, this generational distance from the Civil Rights movement creates a corresponding distance from "the nostalgia associated with those [Civil Rights] successes," leaving post-soul artists and writers uniquely "positioned to critically engage the movement's legacy from a state of objectivity that the traditional civil rights leadership is both unwilling and incapable of doing."[61]

Crucially, as noted above, the work I examine in this volume should be understood as emerging from not only a post–Civil Rights moment but also a "pre-Obama" moment; these are texts produced in a period of relative political stability and rapid economic expansion spanning the mid-1980s to the mid-2000s—not coincidentally, the period often described as the neoliberal era. These works are written in a paradoxically optimistic moment, a moment of perceived racial newness and possibility, especially culturally—Trey Ellis's 1989 essay "The New Black Aesthetic" captures the exuberance of this era's early years, while writer Touré's *Who's Afraid of Post-Blackness? What It Means to Be Black Now* (2011), with its belated pronouncements against traditional notions of racial authenticity, offers perhaps the moment's last gasp of relevance. I use the phrase "paradoxically optimistic" above because this era's sense of cultural possibility was always tempered by visceral, spectacular reminders of black political and material precarity—for instance, the Rodney King case and subsequent riots in Los Angeles; Hurricane Katrina and its consequences for New Orleans and the entire Gulf region—but many of these reminders at the time seemed to bifurcate and stratify the black community in stark class terms.

We might say that Barack Obama himself, then, constitutes both the apotheosis of and a symbolic break from the post-soul era: his iconic performance of blackness is predicated on a familiar kind of black bourgeois respectability and *cultural* savvy, marking him as a product of the post-soul moment, yet his unprecedented win of the White House diverged sharply from what many, even of the post-soul generation, had believed was *politically* possible for the United States. Obama also arrived in the office of president just as the widespread neoliberal illusion of perpetual, market-driven American prosperity was shattered by the Great Recession, shifting the national zeitgeist and contributing to a resurgence of precisely the open resentment of blackness (and of black privilege) evident in this book's opening anecdote. I also use *post-soul,* then, as a *temporal* term—shorthand for the far more unwieldy "pre-Obama era/era of neoliberal ascendancy." My sense of the post-soul as a period of the very recent past, situated within and overlapping with the broader "contemporary," creates the discursive space to unpack how representations of black class privilege from the 1980s, 1990s, and early 2000s both anticipate and diverge from those emerging in our immediate—BLM, post-Obama, end-of-neoliberalism—present moment.

In my previous book I wrote of my "rather traditionalist" methodological position, that "works of fiction are both products of and responses to a given sociohistorical and political moment, and that it is possible to learn something useful about our 'reality' through rigorous examination of the stories that are told about it," indeed, that "close reading of African American narrative . . . might offer us insight into the ideological complexities of black subjectivity."[62] While I maintain this position here, my thinking on methodology is amplified, in this project, by what may seem to be competing interests in both theorizing the present and historicizing the recent past, and in the somewhat fraught relation between the two—particularly regarding the changeable nature of contemporary understandings of race given that we are "not fixed quantities but ever-shifting qualities."[63]

My analysis of post-soul cultural production throughout this book, while centered on close readings of literary texts, is thus informed by, for instance, Raymond Williams's much-discussed concept of "structures of feeling," or the notion of "social experiences *in solution,* as distinct from other social semantic formations which have been *precipitated* [i.e., sedimented] and are more evidently and more immediately available."[64] In other words, a structure of feeling is a somewhat murky, not-quite-tangible cultural shift—the concept constitutes an "incitement to think about the present as a process of emergence."[65] Throughout this book, I understand the black contemporary to be bound by emergent, constantly shifting affective structures that are only partially visible to us as we live through them but that become clearer in the texts I analyze—as Williams suggests, "semantic figures . . . in art and literature . . . are often among the very first indications that such a new structure is forming.[66]

In my understanding of how to work with the material of (recent) history in this project, I am also moved by Darieck Scott's formulation of "the tools of *theorizing* and *imagining*—inventing by use of the stage set by history without attending too scrupulously to the particulars of historical incident."[67] This formulation, the notion of "work[ing] imaginatively *with*" history, is useful to me here, in part, because of the way that the texts I consider here, while indeed products of their individual historical moments—the Reagan-era 1980s, the uneven economic growth years of the 1990s and early 2000s, and the crisis years just prior to the Obama era—can all, also, be understood as part of a general post–Civil Rights era near present, a recent past that seems not yet fully to have ended.[68] Maintaining a commitment to an imaginative reading of history may allow us to better see what Margo Crawford calls the "productive tension between the residual and the emergent"—and to recognize both the relationship and the differences between discrete historical moments of late capitalism that have passed and a (post)neoliberal "present" that continues to unfold.[69] The impulse to "discover in political and popular culture something new about contemporary representations of racial blackness" is perhaps a function of this emergent present, one that signals less an actual *newness* than an ongoing and fragmentary shift in our collective attention.[70]

Rolland Murray has written of contemporary black fiction, "One cannot read these novels as merely universalizing the condition of the middle class or capital, for they take the class divisions of the present as an opportunity to anatomize both the middle class's solipsism and its contradictory pursuit of hegemony over the black poor."[71] Speaking back to Lukács's ideas about the bourgeois limitations of the novel as form, Murray here argues that black fiction in the late twentieth century—writing in 2010, his paradigmatically expansive notion of the "contemporary" encompasses works from both 1984 and 1998—narrates black class *conflict* rather than simply centering the middle-class experience, "transform[ing] the divides of the present into the animating formal and ideological features of their texts."[72] In other words, this "present," broadly defined, which may be better or at least equally understood as the very recent past, is a moment of heightened attention to the fissures of intraracial difference, "especially differences of class."[73] *Black Bourgeois* marks that attention as it manifests in contemporary narrative, but largely as such narrative rehearses the individual, *intrasubjective* conflict of competing raced and classed performances. I am interested, in this project, in how this intrapersonal conflict both stands in for and, in its uncovering and its (ir)resolution, offers a key to negotiating larger scenes of intraracial conflict.

Put differently, it is my sense that the recent past, the twenty to thirty years just prior to our immediate present moment—we might postulate that this *immediate present* begins in 2012, with Obama's second term as president and, more important, black teenager Trayvon Martin's death and vigilante George Zimmerman's eventual acquittal for it, which inspired Alicia Garza to speak/write the words "Black Lives Matter" into existence—has something urgent to teach us about race and class identity, something that might allow us better to understand that which structures the "now" we currently inhabit. This is, in part, because the exploration, in these post-soul texts, of the ways material privilege fails to "cover" the black body, and of that body's perpetual reemergence, signals something noteworthy about the reciprocal meaning(s) of both privilege and blackness, and, perhaps more important, something crucial about how to *navigate* their interrelation. I am interested, here, in what it might mean to undertake, in Jessica Marie Johnson's words, "a deep and virulent acceptance of our own flesh"—to take seriously the fleshly *integrity* of the black subject, even or especially when that subject is riven, bodily, by competing notions of racial and class performance.[74] These texts push us toward understanding class as embodied and performative, just as we understand race, and gender, and sexuality as embodied and performative. Undertaking this conceptual shift in our understanding of class, I argue, might well take us closer to conceptualizing black subjectivity as a collection of contingent and sometimes opposing needs, positions, desires—and, analogously, to understanding black *community* as, in Reginald McKnight's formulation, a "civilization" whose various constituencies not only intersect, not only occasionally work in opposition to, but also often feed and mutually constitute one another.[75]

This project also highlights the value in (re)reading African American literary and cultural production with the tension between material privilege and corporeal precarity as our starting point. The "contemporary" black and bourgeois dilemma reflects and recasts Du Boisian double consciousness and other narratives of black duality, highlighting the necessity of considering such duality as a *recurrent* preoccupation of black cultural production—and black critical analysis. Indeed, drawing upon Du Bois, C. Riley Snorton has recently argued that double consciousness "simultaneously articulates the feelings that emerge for blacks in America and throughout the diaspora and provides a way to perceive how race and gender are inextricably linked yet irreconcilable and irreducible projects," such that "to feel black in the diaspora . . . might be a trans experience."[76] The irreconcilable simultaneity Snorton articulates across "race" and "gender" here is one we might read across other sorts of racial intersections, including that of blackness with class privilege. Rather than dismissing post–Civil Rights, pre–Black Lives Matter black literature as merely a site of bourgeois irrelevancy, or reinscribing familiar tropes that emphasize the authenticity of black poverty, how might we understand the continued relevance of African American literature in a new century by looking again at how, in these turn-of-the-twenty-first-century narratives, the black and the bourgeois operate in tandem and speak to, with, and against one another? I argue, ultimately, that to better understand the *irresolvability* of this corporeal tension—between black flesh and bourgeois body—is to better understand not only our (immediate) present moment but also all those that have come before it.

Perilous Darkness

Here, then, I want to turn to an early post-soul text that presciently illustrates "contemporary" African American narratives' preoccupation with the black and bourgeois dilemma. Andrea Lee's 1984 novel, *Sarah Phillips,* is set in the "hermetic world of the old-fashioned black bourgeoisie—a group largely unknown to other Americans, which has carried on with cautious pomp for years in eastern cities and suburbs, using its considerable funds to attempt poignant imitations of high society, acting with genuine gallantry in the struggle for civil rights, and finally producing a generation of children educated in newly integrated schools and impatient to escape the outworn rituals of their parents."[77] Like the book's author, its title character was born in 1953 and is ten years old at the time of the March on Washington, an event that, in the novel, Sarah watches on television with both admiration and ambivalence—as she notes, "I wasn't sure what I really thought" (51). The character Sarah Phillips can thus certainly be understood as a post-soul figure, and Lee a post-soul author.

I am most interested in *Sarah Phillips,* however, for the ways that it narrates its heroine's desire to *flee* blackness, to escape "the outworn rituals of [her] parents" into a privileged individualism, a desire that is continually thwarted by the intrusion of Sarah's black habitus—as well as, specifically, her black *body*—into the privileged scene. In one sense, then, *Sarah Phillips* deviates from a number of other post-soul texts under examination later in this project, in that most post-soul characters are less nakedly ambitious about escaping race, and indeed, demonstrate a dogged commitment to—a love for—blackness despite the ways that their class status constrains or disrupts a seamless performance of black identity. In another sense, however, Sarah's character, and Lee's text, constitute particularly nuanced examples of the black and bourgeois dilemma, in that Sarah's body—her body's appearance, but also her embodied experiences and reactions to the world around her—is repeatedly cast as the locus of both her class performances *and* her re-racialization, often against her conscious will. In *Sarah Phillips,* as in the other texts I consider in this study, the "complicated possibilities of [Sarah's] flesh" (85) continually reassert themselves, and make simply disappearing into privilege a poignant impossibility.

We are introduced to Sarah in a chapter titled "In France," the temporal end of the novel, when Sarah is oldest. After "In France," the chapters first move more than a decade back in time, to Sarah's early childhood, before gradually progressing forward again through her adolescence and her college years, culminating with her father's death just before her graduation and a final scene of her "in motion," traveling back to Harvard after his funeral and making vague plans to flee family, home, and country. As Adrienne McCormick notes, we thus end where we begin, and "the fact that the novel does not allow Sarah either to completely escape nor to physically return situates Sarah firmly within a complex postmodernity that looks backwards and forwards at once."[78] The crux of "In France" is a cruel insult that Sarah's French boyfriend Henri, a "big blond" with the "veiled, mean gaze of one for whom life has been a continual grievance" (5), hurls at Sarah one afternoon after she mistakenly raises the sore spot of his own illegitimacy:

> "Don't go anywhere, darling," [Henri] said. "I want to tell Roger all about your elegant pedigree."

> "Tell him about yours!" I said rashly, forgetting that Henri was illegitimate.
>
> Roger gave a thin squawk of laughter, and Henri's face darkened. . . . "Did you ever wonder, Roger, old boy," he said in a casual, intimate tone, "why our beautiful Sarah is such a mixture of races, why she has pale skin but hair that's as kinky as that of a Haitian? Well, I'll tell you. Her mother was an Irishwoman, and her father was a monkey."
>
> Roger raised his hand to his mouth and made an indeterminate noise in his throat.
>
> A small, wry smile hovered on Henri's lips. "Actually, it's a longer story. It's a very American tale. This *Irlandaise* was part redskin, and not only that but part Jew as well—some Americans are part Jew, aren't they? And one day this *Irlandaise* was walking through the jungle near New Orleans, when she was raped by a jazz musician as big and black as King Kong, with sexual equipment to match. And from this agreeable encounter was born our little Sarah, *notre Négresse pasteurisée.*" He reached over and pinched my chin. "It's a true story, isn't it, Sarah?" He pinched harder. "Isn't it?" (11)

As Valerie Smith notes in her foreword to the text, readers of the novel who are familiar with work by earlier black women authors like Ann Petry, Paule Marshall, and Zora Neale Hurston and their characters' struggles for voice (iv) "might wish Sarah to articulate the rage that such an insult is bound to call forth" (xiv), particularly given its violent racial stereotypes as well as vicious misogyny. Sarah's reaction, however, is peculiarly passive and interior.

Retreating to the ladies room, she closes and sits down on the toilet lid, "bending double so that [her] cheek rested on [her] knees. It was a position to feel small in" (12). In an inner monologue, Sarah reassures herself that she was not upset by Henri's racism, given that "nasty remarks about race and class were part of our special brand of humor" (12); instead, she ruminates:

> His silly tall tale had done something far more dramatic than wound me: it had somehow—perhaps in its unexpected extravagance—

> illuminated for me with blinding clarity the hopeless presumption of trying to discard my portion of America. The story of the mongrel Irishwoman and the gorilla jazzman had summed me up with weird accuracy, as an absurd political joke can sum up a regime, and I felt furious and betrayed by the intensity of nameless emotion it had called forth in me. (12)

While the question of what this "nameless emotion" might be (rage? shame?) haunts the passage, I am most interested in both Sarah's peculiar claim that Henri's insult "summed her up with weird accuracy" and the way she occupies her body as she grapples with the consequences of his words. McCormick rightly points out the absurdity of Sarah's suggestion that the insult "summed her up"—"recognizing her 'portion of America' as derived from a history involving miscegenation . . . is one thing, but calling a bestial stereotype of race accurate is quite another"—but the *reversal* Henri enacts is indeed "a very American tale," precisely because it mirrors the operation of racial rhetoric in the United States.[79] The prevailing black-male-rapist-of-white-woman stereotype about miscegenation, evident across history in American cultural narratives from *Birth of a Nation* to Willie Horton, perversely serves to mask and erase the historical truth of enslaved women brutally and repeatedly raped and sexually exploited by white men.

In fact, then, Henri does "sum up a regime" with his caricature—the distorting and totalizing regime of white supremacy. Thus the character Sarah Phillips is, in this moment, perhaps more perceptive than she knows in taking Henri's words as proof of "the hopelessness of trying to discard [her] portion of America." As a black bourgeois subject, hers is precisely *this* inheritance—a slave past that, though she "found it hard to picture the slaves as being any ancestors of [hers]" (26), remains legible in her very body, even as its truths, distorted into stereotype by the reach of white supremacy, are rendered invisible to history, a "silence in the archive."[80]

This is perhaps what drives Sarah into the fetal position—a return to origins, to the (relative) safety of her childhood—and what pushes her to the self-infliction of pain: "'Oh, dear,' I said aloud in English, and, still bent double, I turned my head and gently bit myself on the knee" (12). In the act of "gently" causing herself pain, she brings her body back into focus—pulling herself out of what Bourdieu calls the "objectified body," "trapped in the destiny proposed by collective perception" and into a semblance of *self*-control.[81] It is no coincidence that in this moment she also reverts to speaking English—her natal language provides another means of returning to an earlier, presumably safer or less precarious instantiation of herself. Of course, in Sarah's case, this fantasy of safety is just that, a fantasy, as the novel goes on to reveal that Sarah's existence, and that of the black bourgeoisie that she is so eager to escape, is defined by its certain but also masked relation to precarity and risk.

This relation is the lesson of the chapter "An Old Woman," in which a sixteen-year-old Sarah and her mother go to visit a former parishioner of her father's church, Mrs. Jeller, in a nursing home, and come face-to-face with the intimate horrors of black women's history in the United States. Mrs. Jeller tells them a story about her life in "the back of nowhere in Kentucky" (84), a story that includes her rape at twelve years old, her subsequent pregnancy and forced marriage, and the death of her child in infancy. Before even hearing Mrs. Jeller's story, Sarah is shocked "in a curiously intimate way" by the old woman's "bare legs" and "shamelessly tossing breasts," and compares the feeling to "learning a terrifying secret about myself" (83). And the question of what this secret might be—while found most explicitly in Mrs. Jeller's tragic story—is prefigured much earlier in the text, in the chapter called "Mother."

In that chapter, the narrator—an older Sarah who nonetheless seems to remain identified with the younger Sarah's naive pretensions and ambiguities—describes Sarah's mother, Grace Renfrew Phillips, who "had been brought up with all the fussy little airs and graces of middle-class colored girls born around the time of World War I" (32) but remains a woman of some fascination for her daughter. Central to this fascination is her mother's association with "caves, with anything in the world, in fact, that was dimly lit and fantastic" (32). The narrator recalls a particular story from Grace's childhood that served to "rivet" her and her brother:

> At nine years old, walking home through the cobblestone streets of Philadelphia with a package of ice cream from the drugstore, she had

> slipped and fallen down a storm drain accidentally left uncovered by workmen. No one was around to help her; she dropped the ice cream she was carrying (something that made a deep impression on my brother and me) and managed to cling to the edge and hoist herself out of the hole. The image of the little girl—who was to become my mother—hanging in perilous darkness was one that haunted me; sometimes it showed up in my dreams. (32)

This scene, particularly when read in concert with the later narrative of Mrs. Jeller, can be understood as a richly generative symbol of the position of Andrea Lee's black characters in the wider world—a symbol that resonates with all of the texts under scrutiny in this book. A precocious black bourgeois child walks the surface of the earth, in the "real world," freely participating in market exchange as a consumer (having purchased ice cream from the drugstore, just as, at the start of "An Old Woman," Sarah hopes to purchase "a nifty pair of French jeans" at Saks Fifth Avenue [81]), while all along a subterranean darkness waits to (re)claim her.

The untended storm drain, a product of racially informed structural neglect and carelessness, constitutes a violent breach beyond her control, not entirely unlike the narrow-eyed boy with the gun in Ta-Nehisi Coates's narrative of his childhood in Baltimore—a breach that reinforces her absolute vulnerability, given that, at any moment, she might stumble into that cavern below the surface, a stumble that should rightfully lead to her death.[82] And her liminal position *between* life and death, clinging to the edge of the drain, actually figures most accurately the position of the black bourgeois subject, the precarity of black middle-class identity but also its potential—not only that chance, in moments of extreme luck and fortitude, of surviving the fall into the cavern, but the possibility of returning to the untroubled surface of the "real" world, *changed.* Indeed, what she finds in the world below seems forever after to alter her with its power. Sarah speculates, "perhaps her near-fatal tumble underground was responsible for my mother's lasting *attraction to the bizarre side of life*" (32, my emphasis). In other words, the cavern, and her liminal relation to it, seems to remain ever-present in some part of Grace's consciousness, with her subsequent attraction to the "bizarre" marking her awareness of the unreal and fantastic qualities of darkness.

This is the "terrifying secret" Sarah learns about herself when she encounters Mrs. Jeller—not even, at first, the specifics of Mrs. Jeller's story, but the fact of Mrs. Jeller's unruly and uncontrolled body, her "large, limp breasts," her bare legs and "wild, frizzy mass" of hair (82)—the ever-present black and female corporeal vulnerability that Sarah's class position seeks, in vain, to delimit and control through comportment. The cultivated and restrained body of the middle-class black woman (in the chapter called "Gypsies," Sarah similarly compares the swaying, "long breasts" of the gypsy woman to "our mothers' well-contained bosoms" [43]) masks what Sarah recognizes, after hearing Mrs. Jeller's story, as the "complicated possibilities of my own flesh—possibilities of corruption, confused pleasure, even death" (85). Thus, while, as McCormick writes, "the particular constellation of class privileges that situate Sarah and her mother . . . insulates them from knowledge of black women's systematic rape under slavery, as well as the continuing presence of rape as a gendered crime of power," Sarah's hyperawareness of her body ("I felt very aware of my body under my clothes" [85]) seems to suggest a crucial fissure in this "insulation," a break in the covering protection of privilege that relates, explicitly, to Sarah's raced and gendered "flesh."[83] In a sense, Sarah's black and female body writes her *into* Mrs. Jeller's story, or at least reduces and disrupts her safe distance from it.

That Sarah ultimately cannot escape this story, a fact revealed both in the narration ("It was clear, much as I did not want to know it . . . that for me the bright, frank, endlessly beckoning horizon of the runaway had been, at some point, transformed into a complicated return" [15]) and in the recursive, circular structure of the novel, suggests, as do the remainder of the texts under examination in this volume, that grappling with the complexities and disruptions of black and bourgeois subjectivity is less a matter of avoidance or escape (Sarah ultimately fails as "runaway") than it is a matter of negotiation—or of navigation, of moving *through*.

In the following chapters, then, I close read post-soul African American texts to uncover these negotiations and methods of navigation, methods that tend to shift and metamorphose across the thirty-plus-year period that constitutes the contemporary even as they remain legible within larger theoretical and historical frameworks for understanding racial, gender, and class performance. In chapter 1, my discussion of Toni Morrison's novel *Tar Baby* (1981) and Spike Lee's feature film *School Daze* (1988) explores the ways that post–Civil Rights black and bourgeois subjects use the specular power of the "natural" black body to counter the conscripting effects of privilege. Unpacking the classed metaphor of a black body penetrated by whiteness, this first chapter attends to the 1980s specifically as a period in which representations of the black bourgeoisie both relied upon and sought to transcend outdated notions of skin color hierarchy with roots in American slavery, even as they strained to signify (and contain) a new kind of intraracial class politics.

The remainder of the book considers the structuring role of bodily anxiety in later narratives of black privilege, from the 1990s through the first decade of the twenty-first century. Chapter 2, via readings of Danzy Senna's *Caucasia* (1998) and Rebecca Walker's *Black, White, and Jewish* (2001), explores class-driven tensions between the metaphor of the "cultural mulatto" and that of the "real" mulatto—highlighting the still permeable boundaries between figurative and literal notions of a privileged black body with, in Walker's words, "white inside." I argue that while Walker's uncritical reliance upon the "truth" of the mulatto body serves to elide her memoir's investment in class and association of whiteness with material privilege, Senna's contemporary passing narrative highlights the costs of an embodied notion of racial subjectivity for a "black" subject whose body cannot be read as such. Her protagonist eschews the property of whiteness throughout the novel precisely because of its privileged investments.

Chapter 3 addresses a recurrent theme in turn-of-the-twenty-first-century post-soul narratives: that of the black creative abroad. The chapter considers how two novels from this period, Reginald McKnight's *He Sleeps* (2001) and Shay Youngblood's *Black Girl in Paris* (2000), represent the black creative/intellectual—a figure whose class status is both liminal and contingent upon *place*—in contrasting geographical and gendered contexts. McKnight's narrative ultimately turns on the embodied (d)evolution of a middle-class black scholar at war with his own geographically informed privilege and blind to its implications for a vulnerable, if toxic, black American masculinity. Youngblood's novel, by contrast, emphasizes the ways that geography simultaneously empowers and impoverishes a tenuously middle-class black woman artist, ultimately revealing black women's labor as the hidden cost of the life of the mind.

Using the tropes of futurity and black interiority, the fourth chapter considers Percival Everett's *Erasure* (2001) as a unique exploration of this book's fundamental question: Is it possible to resolve the tension between how class privilege "whitens" and conceals the body and blackness specularizes it? Everett's narrative takes this dichotomy to its most monstrous and threatening extreme, entertaining two equally problematic figurative possibilities: a privileged body that completely escapes sociopolitical constraint, thereby becoming invisible, and a superficially black body that, when severed from its creator's interiority, devolves into a kind of grotesque hyperembodiment. In separating the privileged body's "inside" from its black surface, Everett's text forces us to question the very logic upon which the opposition rests, and it challenges the notion of a raceless future.

The final chapter of *Black Bourgeois* turns to black social death and a related black and bourgeois fatalism. It begins with an analysis of how we might think theories of Afro-pessimism in concert with black class privilege, before turning to Colson Whitehead's *John Henry Days* (2001) and Michael Thomas's *Man Gone Down* (2007). Both novels, which I understand as transitional, (post-)post-soul texts, speak to the precarious position of the black bourgeois subject in the early twenty-first century, a period of resurgent social inequality in which technology has begun to transform both labor and capital. While Whitehead's central character faces the loss of his livelihood as print journalism succumbs to the ascendance of the internet, Thomas's unnamed narrator—an adjunct English professor—pursues a series of temporary, low-wage jobs, as well as a final financial gamble, in order to maintain his family's elite Brooklyn lifestyle. I consider the multiple, embodied vulnerabilities that define Whitehead's and Thomas's protagonists as black and middle class and argue that such vulnerabilities underlie, and belie, the contemporary notion of the post-racial, instead centering the open question of black agency and empty promises of so-called progress.

The book's Conclusion returns to the immediate present and the looming matter of black life. I draw upon key, painful collisions of class privilege with racial precarity in Claudia Rankine's *Citizen: An American Lyric* (2014) to ground my discussion of how both Issa Rae's HBO comedy, *Insecure* (2016–), and Ava DuVernay's OWN drama, *Queen Sugar* (2016–), use moments of social and sexual intimacy to represent black bourgeois vulnerability on the small screen. In my analysis of these Black Lives Matter–era literary and visual texts, I ask, finally, whether and how the embodied negotiation of black privilege and precarity might offer a way to conceptualize solidarity beyond social (class) conformity.

Black Bourgeois is, ultimately, a project in favor of blackness and black community, "pro-black" in a way that might be understood as conventional, or even nostalgic, but that is also forward-looking and curious about the ways that people try to belong to one another, even across accumulated layers of difference, social and material difference that resides with us intimately, in and on our bodies. The texts I examine here portray black characters whose bodies are privileged—and thereby alienated—to varying degrees and yet are always subject, and often deliberately or willingly so, to an enduring vulnerability, hanging always on a precipice between the shiny surface of the world and its inner depths. To navigate, to work with, and through, the perils and contradictions of that position is, at its best, to envision new ways of being in the world. For that precarity is most certainly what makes us not only black but human—as Ta-Nehisi Coates has written, "[our] very vulnerability brings [us] closer to the meaning of life."[84] But the knowledge of "perilous darkness" that comes with such vulnerability may also make it possible to inhabit privilege differently, to bring the *powers* of that darkness, and its capacity to leave what it touches forever changed, with us on our travels to the surface.

1 New Bourgeoisie, Old Bodies

Performing Post–Civil Rights Black Privilege in *Tar Baby* and *School Daze*

> "Your first yalla?" [Gideon] asked. "Look out. It's hard for them not to be white people. Hard, I'm telling you. Most never make it. Some try, but most don't make it."
>
> "She's not a yalla," said Son. "Just a little light." He didn't want any discussion about shades of black folk.
>
> "Don't fool yourself. You should have seen her two months ago. What you see is tanning from the sun. Yallas don't come to being black natural-like. They have to choose it and most don't choose it. Be careful of the stuff they put down."
>
> —Toni Morrison, *Tar Baby*

> This script takes place at a fictitious, predominantly Black college in the South. The student body is divided into two factions: the Haves and the Have-Nots. This division is based upon class and color. The Haves, the affluent students at Mission, are all with light skin, "good hair," blue or green eyes, and so forth. While across the tracks are the Have-Nots. They are dark, have kinky nappy hair, and many of them are the first members of their families to ever get a college education; in other words, the black underclass.
>
> —Spike Lee, "A Note" prefacing the script of *School Daze*

When African American narratives from the 1980s take up the matter of class privilege, they frequently make recourse to the trope of a black body infiltrated by whiteness. Consider Lawrence Otis Graham's revelatory book about the African American elite, *Our Kind of People,* in which

Graham describes his experience of a college party by outlining the hierarchy of skin color and hair texture that structured the campus's black social scene:

> With long, streaked, straight—or straightened—hair flying behind them, the Sisters of Ethos were running in and around the tall French doors, inspecting college IDs as they approved or turned away male partygoers who either passed or failed the ubiquitous "brown paper bag and ruler test." . . . . As I circled the room, I saw reminders of my childhood. The "dark outer circle" was very much apparent. . . . [It was] where one found the geri-curled [*sic*] guys and the dark-skinned women with "bad hair" and bad weaves.[1]

Graham differentiates baldly between the bodies of the light-skinned, straight-haired women at the "creamy center" of this culture of privilege, also literally the gatekeepers at its doors, and those of the group on the periphery.[2] This corporeal distinction is one of aesthetics but also one of social class. Those bodies that most visibly display marks of white ancestry seem, by this logic, to have a special claim upon intraracial class privilege. Or, in Graham's words, "it was a color thing and a class thing. And for generations of black people, color and class have been inexorably tied together."[3]

Graham attends to a particular history of black American affluence, one tied to intraracial distinctions rooted in slavery and to the rule of hypodescent that has governed definitions of blackness in the United States since the seventeenth century.[4] Significantly, most of Graham's examples have to do with the female body, highlighting that what Harryette Mullen calls the "color capital" of the miscegenated body has particular consequences for women and, indeed, that gender structures the way that such capital is evaluated.[5] In the elite black world that Graham describes, the *materiality* of the body has always been central; its shades and textures matter, in specific and historically predictable ways. Indeed, the corporeality of class status, for Graham, has to do with not simply aesthetic manipulations of the body, such as hair styling and straightening, but the raw text, so to speak, of the body itself: skin and eye color, the hair's "natural" kink or wave.[6] Of course, these two concepts are related; the perceived success of aesthetic manipulation often depends on how accurately it mimics the "natural" appearance of miscegenation. Graham emphasizes this even in his description of the Sisters of Ethos, with use of the word "straightened"—this term implies heating or chemically processing curly hair to achieve a flat texture that some possess by birth. Even the mention of "bad weaves" implicates the Sisters. Presumably, some of them sport "good" weaves, undetectable precisely because they approximate the "long, streaked, straight" hair of the most privileged.

But while the figure of the privileged black subject as a corporeally *whitened* one draws upon historical realities with contemporary consequences, it also reflects a problematic assumption about which bodies are classed and, indeed, about what material privilege signifies for African Americans. It should go without saying that bodily marks of miscegenation are not reliable indicators of black class privilege, even as they have taken on figurative meaning as classed signs. While a "mulatto elite" with roots in the U.S. domestic slave system may be the foundation for the black elite that Graham describes, Karyn Lacy reminds us that this elite saw their standing, which was based on "ancestry," diminish significantly in the early twentieth century as they were supplanted by "black professionals and small business owners, the parvenu."[7] Lacy goes on to note that "educational attainment" set this "emerging black middle class apart from the mulatto elite," an effect that became even more pronounced in the years between the world wars, when far greater numbers of blacks began to attend historically black colleges and universities.[8] Rather than completely erase the "mulatto elite," however, these demographic shifts had the effect of merging the two groups, as educated and successful "monoracial black men" married "women from the mulatto elite," solidifying their middle-class status.[9]

Thus the representation of the black bourgeois body as a "whitened" body has had, at least since the early twentieth century, a complex relationship to the actual, lived experience of the African American middle class, with many individuals who identify as such conforming imperfectly, if at all, to the miscegenated bodily model. This explains, perhaps, why some of the Sisters of Ethos in Graham's anecdote wear "straightened" rather than "straight" hair—and why their application of the "ubiquitous" brown paper bag and ruler tests of skin color and hair texture involves, rather counter-intuitively, "inspecting college IDs." Indeed, this attention to *university* pedigree as a form of elite inclusion, signaled by the "ID" as a physical and documentary totem of membership, actually points to higher education's role as a site of class formation in the United States, something social scientists have long acknowledged.[10] Historically, education has functioned as both a "vehicle for upward mobility," enabling a "transition from working class to upper middle class status," and, for those who are already materially privileged before attending college, as "a means of further distinguishing [oneself] from the [lower] classes based on the quality and reputation of the institution attended."[11] As Tressie McMillan Cottom points out, "At heart, higher education is a means both of redressing socioeconomic inequality and of perpetuating socioeconomic inequalities in new guises."[12] For the Sisters of Ethos, then, the inspection of college IDs likely serves as a far clearer and more predictable means of policing class-based boundaries than any examination of ambiguous, and as I have noted, frequently manipulated, bodily markers would.

Graham, however, seems to take the evidently murky link between "color and class" as fairly literal, assuming a correlative relationship between "darker, less affluent, less popular, and less attractive."[13] His uncritical reliance on the penetrated-by-whiteness metaphor for black privilege highlights the unreliability of his narrative and indeed points to the larger unreliability of autobiographical writing; as Sidonie Smith and Julia Watson have noted, autobiography, rather than offering verifiable history, "incorporate[s] usable facts into subjective 'truth.'"[14] So I open with Graham's narrative because it offers readers a parallel insight—parallel, that is, to those of avowedly fictional black narratives—into how class has been *imagined* in post-soul African American expressive culture.

As a kind of constructed storytelling about race, gender, and class, Graham's narrative becomes even more intriguing when we consider, as I noted early on, that his anecdote takes place in the early 1980s, a moment when the contours of the black middle and upper classes were changing yet again—when, indeed, these classes were expanding dramatically in the wake of Civil Rights advances.[15] Because the gains of the previous two decades granted ever larger numbers of blacks access to education and white-collar employment, the 1980s emerge as an unprecedented period of transformation for the black bourgeoisie. The historical association of bourgeois status with a particular kind of miscegenated black body thus becomes, in these years, an even more unlikely indicator of class privilege.[16] Yet fictional representations of the black middle classes in the 1980s continued a long tradition of associating class privilege with a "whitened" black body, even as that connection was frequently drawn in much more ambivalent ways than in years past. These representations challenged the notion that an increasingly complex and nuanced *social* body, the expanding black bourgeoisie, might be reduced to simplistic, and literally corporeal, narratives of light-skinned privilege and dark-skinned exclusion; they continued, however, to tie class privilege to the trope of a black body penetrated by whiteness, even if only symbolically.

Symbolic penetration: here we arrive at the larger stakes of this class metaphor.[17] If it is hardly remarkable that black class privilege historically has been associated with a particular kind of body—after all, Peter Stallybrass and Allon White, following Bakhtin, have pointed out that both the (white) bourgeois body and its working-class complement have specific roles to occupy in the social order—neither is it trivial, particularly given the contradiction that such a (black, and bourgeois) body raises.[18] This perpetual state of contradiction is what I call the black and bourgeois dilemma, an inherent tension between the visibility and vulnerability of the black body and the covering protection of privilege. After all, the "black" body is typically understood to exceed and be excluded from the bourgeois—indeed, in its *excess* of embodiment, what Nicole Fleetwood has called "excess flesh," to personify the subordinated and abject Other.[19] By contrast, the (white) bourgeois body—Stallybrass and White's "classical body"—is *in*vulnerable, constructed as "high, inside and central by virtue of its very exclusions."[20] This presents a problem for the representation of the black bourgeois, a category of identity that, given its internal contradictions, seems constantly in danger of erasing itself. This may explain the ubiquity of the penetrated-by-whiteness trope in early post-soul representations of black class privilege; the fantasy of white corporeal incursion allows putatively "black" bodies to visually approximate the classical standard. Yet if taken to its logical conclusion, this trope also raises the problematic question of just where such "penetrated" bodies' loyalties lie—with an Othered blackness, or with the material privilege that would erase that Other's traces?

In this chapter I juxtapose two very different cultural texts from the 1980s—Toni Morrison's 1981 novel, *Tar Baby,* and Spike Lee's 1988 feature film, *School Daze*—in order to theorize the shifting relationship between class and embodiment for black subjects in the post–Civil Rights era, and ultimately to illumine how both novel and film explore the sometimes contradictory relationships between race, gender, and class for black bourgeois subjects. As I noted in the introduction to this volume, my use of the terms "middle class," "class privilege," "black bourgeois," and the like, while informed by sociological understandings of class as primarily economic, also relies on the notion of class as culture—the sense that for African Americans, social class historically has been shaped by less "objective" markers, such as aspiration and, in William Muraskin's words, "social perception."[21] Further, my interest in reading class as *bodily* performance shapes my analysis of these texts. As andré carrington has recently noted, "the presentation and reception of distinguishing features makes the body meaningful in racial terms," such that "qualities typically described in terms of 'ethnicity' might be reconsidered as performance."[22] Diana Taylor's suggestion that performance is a kind of epistemology, that indeed "embodied practice, along with and bound up with other cultural practices, offers a way of knowing," also informs my assertions here, as does the black feminist concept of intersectionality, deliberately attentive to what Valerie Smith has described as "the contingencies, differences, and discontinuities upon which identities and consensus depend."[23]

Throughout this chapter I am interested in how *Tar Baby* and *School Daze* unpack such contingencies, differences, and discontinuities, particularly as they surface in the arenas of class, race, and gender. In distinct but often overlapping ways, Morrison's and Lee's works appear to delimit the sprawling problematic of post–Civil Rights intraracial class conflict by containing it within the body of a light-skinned black woman (and her darker-skinned antagonists). In this, both texts draw upon the same figurative association between class privilege and the whitened black body that we saw in Graham's reductive autobiographical narrative. Yet Morrison's and Lee's texts also contain moments that productively undercut this oversimplification, using darker-skinned (and sometimes male) characters to point us toward another way of thinking about the relationship between black class status and corporeality—namely, how and why bourgeois subjects, particularly in a post–Civil Rights moment, might wield the particular "blackness" of the body *against* the homogenizing effects of privilege.

Tragic Mulatta Reconsidered

The trope of the "tragic mulatta" in the African American literary tradition can be traced back to William Wells Brown's *Clotel* (1853), and as Eva Raimon points out, in its earliest incarnations this figure "provides a central literary site for black and white antislavery writers to work through questions raised by the highly charged subject position of mixed-race persons in antebellum society."[24] Particularly in the antebellum moment, the mulatta is, as the word's feminine ending indicates, gendered female; womanhood and its associated "sexual vulnerability" do important rhetorical work, instantiating the mulatta's particular tragedy.[25] Yet as we consider a modern or postmodern update of this figure—even as the racial detritus of the antebellum moment continues to circulate within and, to some extent, shape our present one—the mulatta's privilege, a privilege tied specifically to her light skin and other bodily markers of "amalgamation," becomes a central part of how she is understood.[26] The "tragedy" of the post–Civil Rights era tragic mulatta—and as may be obvious, here I assert a rough *metaphoric* equivalence between "light-skinned black woman" and "tragic mulatta," in spite of the fact that not all light-skinned women are of mixed parentage and vice versa—is a tragedy well tempered by a host of apparent advantages.[27]

Thus one way that we might reconsider the trope of the "tragic mulatta," in the post-soul moment, is as a figure caught between not two racial identities but between two very different experiences of her skin color—the pain of exclusion and the pleasure of privilege. Toi Derricotte articulates this contradiction in her poignant memoir, *The Black Notebooks,* confessing that she has felt "superior to other blacks" because of her appearance but noting also that "just as there is an internalized picture of a hated and feared dark person, there is also a picture of a hated and feared light woman, and she looks like *me.*"[28] This archetypical light-skinned black woman has historically been "hated and feared"—as well as admired and envied—because of a perceived association with the politics and unearned privileges of whiteness.

Toni Morrison's novel *Tar Baby,* which until recently had not received its due in critical attention, evidences what at first appears to be a similar kind of logic vis-à-vis social class.[29] Jadine, the book's female protagonist, is light-skinned and, seemingly by extension, an internationally known fashion model with a degree in art history from the Sorbonne and a certain disdain for black culture (she "lik[es] 'Ave Maria' better than gospel music," and Charles Mingus "puts [her] to sleep").[30] At one point in the text, Jadine's fair complexion is likened to the color of "a natural sponge" (131).[31] While few of *Tar Baby*'s critics have commented directly on Jadine's skin color, many have responded to the embrace of European culture that seems to accompany it. In much criticism of the novel, Jadine has been read as an overwhelmingly negative character, a textual representative of a destructive Eurocentricism, intraracial self-hatred, and estrangement from black authenticity.[32] This reception of Jadine is certainly gendered; as Trudier Harris notes, "Our negative reaction to Jadine . . . is predicated on [our] inability . . . to applaud the traits she has when they appear in feminine guise."[33]

Not all critics of the novel have read Jadine as quite such an obvious villain; some interpret her in far more neutral terms, describing Jadine as "cosmopolitan," "post-essentialist," "post-enlightenment," and "transnational," merely one of an equivalent "plurality of perspectives."[34] These interpretations in part reflect critics' increasing attention to the postmodern black subject and their accompanying recognition of intraracial differences, including those of class, that complicate "black" identity. These concerns seem paramount to Morrison herself; indeed, it is no coincidence that *Tar Baby* is the only one of Morrison's earlier novels set in its own present moment—other volumes in Morrison's twentieth-century oeuvre take varying levels of historical distance from the periods in which they are written—suggesting that the issues Morrison tackles in *Tar Baby* have contemporaneous relevance. And as Judylyn Ryan notes, in a novel purportedly "about" social "'contentions' between Black women and Black men," these contentions "fall largely outside the parameters of gender(ed) relationships or heterosexual romance, and within the domain of class antagonisms," signaling the text's broader interest in "connections between the 'conflict of genders,' 'cultural illness' and class conflicts."[35] Through Jadine, Morrison signifies on precisely the changing contours of black community in the post–Civil Rights era and the related expansion of the black middle class to which I alluded at the start of this chapter. Yet my interest lies less in the specifics of Jadine as postmodern (female) subject and more in Morrison's deployment of the corporal proximity/political complicity relationship implied in the trope of the tragic mulatta—a trope to which Jadine's character clearly alludes.

Morrison's text emphasizes that Jadine is very light-skinned, so light that after two months of tanning she is only the pale gold color of a sea sponge; in addition, Jadine does not "have to straighten [her] hair" (48). These corporeal characteristics seem meant to imply that Jadine has significant European ancestry, perhaps even a white parent. Indeed, Morrison's depiction of Jadine's appearance so convincingly suggests racial admixture that more than one scholar has described Jadine as "mulatto."[36] Yet *Tar Baby* also gives every indication that Jadine is *not* actually of mixed parentage, that her parents are both black Americans. Sydney and Ondine—servants to the retired candy heir, Valerian Street, and his much younger wife, Margaret—are Jadine's uncle and aunt, who raised her after her parents' deaths (118). Jadine is Sydney's "brother's baby girl" (283), and Sydney, Jadine's closest living relative, is the reddish-brown color of "mahogany" (35). Jadine's mother is never directly described, and certainly could be the source of Jadine's fair skin and straight hair, but it is clear in the text that she is not a white woman, given her appearance in one of the narrative's central images of black womanhood: the cadre of "night women" who haunt Jadine when she visits Son's southern birthplace, the all-black town of Eloe (258).[37]

Instead, *Tar Baby*'s Jadine seems to be noticeably light-skinned for no reason that can be linked to her immediate ancestry. Unlike Clare Kendry or Janie Crawford before her, for Jadine there is no obvious white man in the woodpile.[38] Not literally, at least. But of course, Jadine does have a white "parent" of sorts. Valerian Street, who is Jadine's patron, functions in the text as a kind of surrogate father, though their relationship recalls the way that white men have, historically, *produced* but not actually fathered black children.[39] This connection is particularly fitting given the ways that Valerian's actual heir, Michael, is paralleled with Jadine in the text. Michael is perpetually absent from the Street family table, fleeing his mother's clinging devotion and her prior abuse (209), rejecting his father's wealth by embracing socialism, while Jadine willingly occupies his place and supplants him in the daily routine and affections of Valerian and Margaret—she "sat next to [Valerian] more alive and responsive and attentive than even his own wife was" (204). Jadine accommodates Valerian in this way in spite of the fact that to do so she must be, literally, served by her own family.

Jadine, then, is light-skinned not so much because her body has been infiltrated by whiteness but because her mind has been. Morrison represents Jadine's racial alienation symbolically, via her skin color, using a familiar trope of black class privilege to signify Jadine's material advantages *through* her corporeal proximity to whiteness. In her portrayal of Jadine, Morrison anticipates and addresses issues of intraracial difference, particularly around class, that have continued to surface in other post-soul black fiction, including work by Danzy Senna, Reginald McKnight, and Michael Thomas, among others—all of whom tackle the problem of the black bourgeois subject through the vehicle of the body. Earlier than any of these texts, *Tar Baby* literalizes Jadine's cultural and social proximity to whiteness in her body; Jadine's body must be *penetrated by* whiteness for Morrison to adequately signify the character's class aspirations and her racial indifference.[40] By using light skin as a purely symbolic marker of Jadine's racial alienation, Morrison's post–Civil Rights era text updates the historical notion that privilege infiltrates and "denaturalizes" blackness—or, as Gideon, also known as Yardman, claims in this chapter's first epigraph, "Yallas don't come to being black natural-like" (155).

Morrison's Jadine might seem to be the author's comment on the newness of the post–Civil Rights black subject, but Jadine's relationship to this new, postmodern black subjectivity is wedded to a much older link between physical whiteness and socioeconomic advancement. Indeed, *Tar Baby* suggests that Jadine's privileged status has as much to do with the plantation system that empowered the earliest versions of the black elite as it does with the educational and occupational opportunities that were created by the Civil Rights and Black Power movements.[41] After all, Jadine owes her success almost entirely to Valerian's willingness to finance her expensive private education, not to, for instance, the free public institutions that she later urges Son to attend (267). It is hardly coincidental that Son describes Jadine's departure from the Street household as an "escape from the plantation" (219). Ironically, Jadine in turn sees Son as a kind of racial relic, noting when she first encounters him that "she had not seen a black like him in ten years. Not since Morgan Street [in Baltimore]" (126). "After that," for Jadine, is boarding school, college, and then travel to Europe, graduate study at the Sorbonne, and in each place "the black people she knew wanted what she wanted. . . . [W]hatever their scam, 'making it' was on their minds and they played the game with house cards, each deck issued and dealt by the house" (127). The repetition of "house" here, with its racialized connotation of "house Negroes," brings us back to the plantation and the question of how whiteness historically has intersected the privileged black subject—marked here not by economic standing but by *aspiration,* diverse dreams of "making it."

What if, however, we reconsider Son as a "new" black subject? His character is typically read as the embodiment of modern (read: traditional) black identity.[42] This reading of Son as a kind of textual representative of black authenticity is tied closely to his positioning as an itinerant, working-class figure, a country boy (158) whose only ambition in life is to recover his "original dime" (169). Morrison gives us clues, however, to how we might read Son's class position as well as his racial subjectivity in more complex ways. Not only does *Tar Baby* point to the racialized and gendered resistance behind Son's ambivalent relationship to white-collar employment and middle-class conformity—he "had two semesters of Florida A and M" (262) but considers anything but hard physical labor "teenager's work" (262) or the work of black men "turn[ed] . . . into white men" by ambitious black women (270)—but through Son's character the text highlights, as well, the limits of romanticizing both black labor and black poverty.

Son's involvement with Jadine complicates his nostalgia for what he remembers as an uncorrupted black Eden (Eloe), existing outside Western hierarchies of value: "She had given him back his original dime, the pretty one, the shiny one, the romantic ten-cent piece, and made him see it the way it was, the way it really was, not just a dazzling coin, but a piece of currency with a history rooted in gold and cloisonné and humiliation and death" (299). Son had wanted "some other way of being in the world" (166), a path of fugitivity that would sidestep this history, and which he finds as a literal fugitive from the law after killing his first wife, during "eight homeless years" as part of "that great underclass of undocumented men" (166). Yet Son's return to so-called civilization and his love affair with Jadine, a "heavy, grown-up love" that makes him feel especially vulnerable—"fresh-born, unprecedented, surrounded by an extended present loaded with harm" (218)—precipitates a moral and existential crisis for him, as he recognizes his own newly drawn implication, however unwitting and contingent, in the social structures he has sought to escape. I argue, then, that Son might best be understood as a *post*modern rather than modern subject, one whose desire for and pleasures in blackness war with his provisional but persistent infiltration by privilege. Indeed, in raising the possibility of this other kind of "new" black subject, *Tar Baby* also anticipates the class and color politics of Spike Lee's feature film *School Daze,* released some seven years later—which similarly begins with, and then undercuts, a black (female) body penetrated by whiteness as the cultural representative of black class privilege.

New School, Old Guard

In this chapter's second epigraph, a note included at the start of the script for *School Daze,* Spike Lee makes clear his interest in telegraphing intraracial class hierarchy through phenotype, and the legendary "Good and Bad Hair" musical number, arriving less than thirty minutes into the film, seems to reinforce this point. Of course, while Lee's written note is pointedly free of gender references, implying that these on-campus Haves and Have-Nots are both male and female, the "Good and Bad Hair" scene takes place in a stylized, even surrealist beauty salon and stages a lengthy fantasy battle between warring factions of black women. Lee's film thus seems to imply, in Wahneema Lubiano's words, that "aesthetics [are] formal matters of physical appearance in which women only participate."[43]

In the same essay, Lubiano goes on to assert that "*School Daze* is incapable of making the connection between what the men do and what they are showing as their aesthetics."[44] Lubiano's assessment of *School Daze* is consistent with an overall negative critical response in the film's contemporary moment. Critics writing in the late 1980s and early 1990s, when Spike Lee's popularity as a filmmaker had reached a kind of cult status, repeatedly disparaged this particular film, and Lee's oeuvre in general, as simplistic, essentialist, misogynist and homophobic.[45] Though I acknowledge the truth of these critics' appraisals of the film, in what follows I reclaim Lee's film as a productive site of intraracial class discourse; despite the film's flawed sexual politics, it offers an important analysis of black class hierarchies and the complex relationship between privilege and embodiment. As Toni Cade Bambara notes, this analysis is couched in *pageantry,* which structures not only the film's plotting and characterization but also shapes its address of the socioeconomic and political discord that the film effects, "in the sense that confrontations between the groups are theatrically staged moments rather than realistic debates about the issues."[46]

Viewed from a twenty-first-century vantage point, in which these moments of pageant-like staging might be mined for performative (as well as "performatic")[47] meaning, *School Daze* offers insightful commentary on the aesthetics of intraracial class politics. Counter to earlier critics, I would argue that this includes ample reference to male aesthetic performance. For instance, the homogenizing, militaristic sameness of the "light-skinned and husky" Gammites (pledges to fictional fraternity Gamma Phi Gamma), as well as their clean-shaven heads, advances a particular aesthetic message.[48] In the "pass the pussy" scene on the back steps of the frat house, when the Gammites chant this phrase at Spike Lee's "Half-Pint" character, their bald heads glowing uniformly yellow in the diffuse glare of the streetlight overhead certainly speak to the ways that male "Wannabees" also conform to skin-color hierarchies. Not coincidentally, given the ways that light-skinned as well as middle-class black men have been associated with effeminacy, this conformity takes place at a moment of sexual policing, indicating the imbrication of racial, sexual, and class identity as expressed on and through the body.[49] The ambiguous chant "pass the pussy" emphasizes the Gammites' performative participation in male heterosexual desire, even as it underscores the roots of that desire in homosociality and communal consumption of the female body.[50]

Lee's film offers a number of similar points of entry for analysis of male aesthetics and embodiment. But we need not dismiss the relevance of the women's aesthetic debate in the film simply because it addresses issues of "beauty" that apply uniquely to women's bodies. Instead, I would like to reconsider the "Good and Bad Hair" scene in *School Daze* as a moment of theoretical richness, one that tells us something about not just the "Wannabes" but the "Jigaboos" as well. In particular, I am interested in how we might think about the Jigaboos as privileged bodies, classed precisely in their performance of "naturalness" and their theatrical acceptance of the "nappy." Before turning to a closer reading of this scene, however, I want to consider a couple of related moments in the film that, perhaps even more so than the light-skinned, straight-haired female "Wannabees," raise the specter of the old black elite in *School Daze.* Placing these moments in dialogue with similar exchanges in *Tar Baby* will allow us to see where Lee's film reiterates and where it exceeds the "yalla"/"black" dichotomy that Morrison's novel raises.

Writing about the 1960s, Cornel West suggested in 1984 that "the young black student movement," which produced the politicized young blacks that would energize the Civil Rights era's black nationalist stage, "was not simply a rejection of segregation in restaurants . . . [but] was also a revolt against the perceived complacency of the 'old' black petite bourgeoisie."[51] This latter group, overwhelmingly reactionary in outlook, finds its fictional counterpart in *Tar Baby*'s characters Sydney and Ondine and its filmic representatives in *School Daze*'s "Wannabee" Julian as well as in the college's administration: President McPherson, played by actor Joe Seneca, and chairman of the board of trustees, Cedar Cloud, played by Art Evans.

Morrison's character Sydney, who describes himself as a "Philadelphia Negro mentioned in the book of the very same name" (163), sees Son, by contrast, as a "stinking ignorant swamp nigger" (100). When

Son, post haircut and bath, goes to the Childs' private servant quarters to apologize for the stir he caused in the household, Sydney deliberately positions himself as Son's social superior, using the material and educational markers of class to make the point: "My people owned drugstores and taught school while yours were still cutting their faces open so as to be able to tell one of you from the other" (163). Notably, Sydney uses achievement rather than ancestry to highlight his class superiority, showing himself to be a more recently arrived member of the black bourgeoisie than the "mulatto elite" that Jadine's character references.[52] Yet his oblique reference to African scarification practices suggests that Sydney sees not only Son but all non-U.S. blacks as faceless "primitives," indistinguishable because they supposedly exist outside of Western systems of value—an attitude borne out, as well, by his and Ondine's dehumanizing reference to Gideon as "Yardman." There is obvious overlap, here, with *School Daze,* and Julian's dismissal of Dap's activism on behalf of campus divestment from South Africa as "bullshit," insisting that "without question we are all *black Americans*"; he concludes the confrontation with, "I am from Detroit—Motown. So you can Watutsi your monkey-ass back to Africa if you want to."[53] In this scene, Julian emphasizes his own, and Dap's, Americanness in order to dismiss any perceived connection between Mission students and blacks elsewhere in the world. As Lubiano notes, for Julian "'Blackness' originates in and is concerned with United States geopolitical sites only."[54]

In *Tar Baby,* the absurdity of this self-righteous adherence to cross-national, intraracial hierarchy explains Valerian Street's decision to invite Son to dinner in the first place; the white man thinks to himself that "when he saw . . . Sydney and Ondine looking at the prisoner with faces as black as his but smug, their manner struck him as what Michael meant when he said 'bourgeois' in that tone that Valerian always thought meant unexciting, but now he thought meant false, but last night he thought meant Uncle Tom-ish" (144). While the "willfully innocent" (243) Valerian is hardly in a moral position to judge his servants for their bourgeois complacency, his social standing—outside and literally above the black class hierarchy that Sydney and Ondine so value—makes his observation fitting. As Morrison emphasizes, the positioning of everyone in the Street household—Sydney and Ondine in the servants' quarters, Margaret, Jadine, and later Son "up there" (100) in the main wing—is at Valerian's behest, solely a function of his whim as white patriarch.

Similarly, in the case of the fictionalized Mission College, members of the white Snodgrass family, whose wealth founded the institution and continues to support it, are the invisible powers-that-be who, behind the scenes and off-camera, pull the strings of the college's board of trustees and, by extension, its president. Given the long-standing relationship between white philanthropists and many historically black institutions, we might read President McPherson as another representative of the old-guard black elite whose power and status are "granted" by whites and who are therefore seen as reactionary by the new, more radical black middle-class students that West identifies. In *School Daze,* Dap is one of these radical students, chastised by the administration for staging public campus protests demanding the institution divest from South Africa.

Both Lee and Morrison represent the bourgeois old guard as darker skinned, perhaps to remind us of the complex history of black class privilege in the United States and thereby to unsettle the retrenched cultural association between embodied whiteness and class status. Yet the *metaphoric* association of class privilege and the black subject infiltrated by whiteness seems, if anything, at greater stake for these bourgeois figures in Morrison's and Lee's narratives. In both *Tar Baby* and *School Daze,* the old-guard black bourgeoisie and their analogues—which, as I have already noted, include the supposedly "new" Jadine—are *loyal to* whiteness, penetrated by its bourgeois investments figuratively if not literally. Hence Sydney and Ondine uncritically protect Valerian's property as if it were their own, and Jadine appears more devoted to her white patron than she is to her black flesh and blood, more willing to be pet than "daughter" (282).[55] In other words, for Morrison and Lee this version of the black bourgeois subject, occasionally dark-skinned, is inhabited by whiteness in subtler and perhaps more insidious ways.

Tar Baby and *School Daze* differ from a number of other African American texts of the period, however, in that they take seriously the possibility of a black bourgeois subject who resists such co-optation; in both cases, the black body is crucial to this resistance project.[56] Thus in the final section of this chapter I want to reconsider a few crucial moments in *Tar Baby* and *School Daze*—moments that signal another way of conceptualizing the relationship between the body and bourgeois status for the post–Civil Rights black subject.

Undoing Privilege: The Black Body's Return

Here, then, I return to the "Good and Bad Hair" musical number, one of the most commented-upon set pieces in Lee's film. We might note, to start, that both the Wannabees and the Jigaboos as groups of actresses are diverse in terms of skin color.[57] The very language of the song that the women sing emphasizes this: "talkin' 'bout good and bad hair / whether you're dark or you're fair." Hair, a phenotypic marker that can be manipulated far more easily than skin, thus becomes the primary battleground for the two groups—signaling that this conflict is an aesthetic one, based in performance rather than genetic inheritance. In other words, Lee's commentary on intraracial class hierarchy, when reexamined, allows us to think further about how "blackness" and "privilege" intersect *beyond* the body's literal penetration by whiteness.

The dialogue preceding the song and dance illuminates this more clearly. After encountering one another in the dormitory corridor, lead Gamma Ray, Jane, and Rachel, the lead "Jigaboo" and Dap's girlfriend, have the following confrontation, surrounded by their fellow "Jigaboos" and "Wannabees." I reproduce the stage directions and dialogue from the original script, because in this instance, with one exception, they do not deviate from the recorded version:

> *Jane gives Rachel a long, hard look. She then flips her hair at Rachel and the Gamma Rays follow suit.*
>
> DORIS: It's not real.
> DINA: Say what?
> LIZZIE: You heard.
>
> . . .
>
> RACHEL: It ain't *even* real.
> JANE: You wish you had hair like this.

DORIS: Girl, y'know you weren't born with green eyes.
LIZZIE: Green contact lenses.[58]

In the filmed version of this scene, "blue" eyes and contact lenses replace "green," likely an ad lib by the cast member playing Doris (Alva Rogers) but possibly also a pointed shift away from reference to the miscegenated black body. As Derricotte notes, green eyes, not blue, are a "hybrid characteristic—sign of the islands."[59] The switch to blue, whether deliberate or not, thus reinforces the possible *falseness* of the eyes' appearance. As such, by questioning whether the "Jane" character's light eyes and long, sandy blonde hair are "*even* real," the conflict emphasizes that the Wannabes make a choice to style themselves as "whiter" looking. Unlike Morrison's Jadine, whose material privilege is literalized and naturalized *within* her body, the Wannabees construct their privilege by manipulating the external appearance of their bodies in pointedly *un*natural ways—similarly, perhaps, to those Sisters of Ethos who wear "straightened" rather than "straight" hair.

More important for my purposes, however, this exchange reminds us that the Jigaboos, too, have choices and exercise a particular kind of class prerogative in embracing their "naps." The Jigaboo's choice to wear her hair "nappy" is a narrative instance of what I might call the *black bodily return*—an assertion or insertion of the "natural" body within the context of class privilege that is meant precisely to rearticulate black identity, a black identity in danger of being eclipsed by its own middle-class investments. Morrison's description of Son's dreadlocked hair gets us closer to understanding this move:

> Here, alone in her bedroom where there were no shadows, only glimmering unrelieved sunlight, his hair looked overpowering—physically overpowering, like bundles of long whips or lashes that could grab her and beat her to jelly. And would. Wild, aggressive, vicious hair that needed to be put in jail. Uncivilized, reform-school hair. Mau-Mau, Attica, chain-gang hair. (113)

Jadine looks at Son's nappy hair and sees an "uncivilized," "wild" blackness, a blackness that "needed to be put in jail." Morrison's inclusion of "Mau-Mau," a reference to Kikuyu rebels against the British colonial government in Kenya in the 1950s, reinforces that this "aggressive" hair must be understood racially, as the embodiment of a black subjectivity that refuses the "civilizing" imprisonment of bourgeois complacency. What does it mean for a middle-class black subject—particularly a female subject—to adopt this kind of bodily racial marker?

Perhaps a brief clarification is in order. The opening note that Lee attaches to the *School Daze* script insists that Jigaboos are the campus "Have-Nots," indeed, that they should be understood as "the black underclass" (185). In truth, however, the Jigaboos, too, are middle class, if sometimes newly so. The (not always) darker-skinned, kinky-haired "Jigaboo" is nonetheless *also* a student at Mission, distinguished from the working-class local black population by her situation within and not outside the college's gates. This becomes clear in the scene at a neighborhood Kentucky Fried Chicken, where the Fellas, led by Dap, are confronted by a group of local black men who express resentment at their relative privilege: "How come you college motherfuckers think y'all run everything? . . . We was born here, gone be here, gone die here, and can't find jobs 'cause of you." Later, after the confrontation escalates, the lead local, Leeds, adds, "Naw, I bet y'all do think y'all white. College don't mean shit. Y'all niggas, and you gone be niggas forever. Just like us. Niggas." Dap responds emphatically, "You're *not* niggers."[60]

Given that, as Imani Perry points out, the word "nigga" must be understood as both "an extension of the idea of the black everyman" and a "racial category *combined with* white supremacy, poverty, and social marginalization," it is clear that in this scene, Leeds posits that Dap and his friends—no matter how "white" their privilege makes them—can never escape the most oppressive and dehumanizing effects of blackness.[61] Dap's retort evidently refuses this interpellation, but as Margaret Thomas has pointed out, his abrupt shift to standard English (e.g., "you're not" rather than "y'all ain't") is an instance of code-switching that itself marks his class position.[62] Ironically, Dap's classed attempt to divorce both himself *and* his working-class interlocutors from the pejorative meanings associated with the word "nigger" also has the effect of distancing him from the fraternity of the black masses offered by the linguistic variation "nigga"; in both cases, his class privilege marks the site of a racial exclusion.

This literal face-off between the two groups of men is marked for us aesthetically; Dap, while not as dramatically styled as the female Jigaboos, nonetheless signals his allegiance to pan-African community via his kente cloth scarf and leather tam, adorned with cowrie shells—a relatively ironic symbol of African allegiance, given these shells' link to the slave trade—while the leader of the locals, a then unknown Samuel L. Jackson, wears his hair chemically processed.[63] The willing embrace of nappy hair is explicitly *not* a poor or working-class aesthetic prerogative in *School Daze*—nor in *Tar Baby.* Lubiano points out that in Lee's film, "the townies, who are working-class and, therefore, under some rubrics 'Blacker' than the middle-class college kids, are also the ones with the 'jeri curls' (generally recognized as evidence of aesthetic *disaffection* with 'Blackness') protected by shower caps."[64]

The "jeri-curled" locals in *School Daze* have their textual counterpoint in Alma Estee and her red wig in *Tar Baby.* To Son, Alma Estee's choice to cover her own dark, kinky hair and "midnight skin" with "a wig the color of dried blood" (299) constitutes a contrast as ridiculous as "an avocado with earrings" (299).[65] And, instead of allowing Son to remove the wig, she "jump[s] back, howl[s] and resecure[s] it on her head with clenched fingers" (299), indicating the intensity of her commitment to this "synthetic" (299) alteration of her appearance. Thus Alma Estee in *Tar Baby* and the "Local Yokels" in *School Daze* both represent a kind of working-class aesthetic that is neither an acceptable facsimile of or stand-in for whiteness, like Jadine and the Wannabees, nor a deliberate embrace of African phenotype and rejection of the racist standards of class privilege, like the Jigaboos. Indeed, the reason that the Fellas are so uncomfortable on the ride home from KFC is that they are forced to come to grips with their own privilege, as members of a middle-class group that has material advantages over local blacks precisely because they are Mission College students.

Similarly, Son's American citizenship affords him a kind of privilege on Isle des Chevaliers that persists in spite of Son's efforts to befriend the island's residents and is reflected in his own attitudes toward them. Witness, again, his attempt to remove the wig from Alma Estee's head, a gesture that he views as a mark of racial "fraternity" (299) but which is revealed as paternalistic precisely in Son's vocalization: "Oh, baby baby baby baby" he croons to Alma Estee as he reaches for the wig, indicating all too clearly the infantilizing posture of privilege he has assumed. Ironically, the character in Morrison's novel that many critics have read as the textual representative of black working-class authenticity is himself complicit—simply via his presence as invited guest in Valerian Street's house—with global hierarchies of human value that privilege him as a (black) American over Alma Estee, Gideon, and Therese. (I will return to questions of geography and transnational black/American privilege in chapter 3.)

Son's unwilling conscription into these and related *intra*national hierarchies—his contingent privilege—becomes clear even earlier in the narrative, however, when Jadine and Son return to the United States and Son, who has been away for eight years, is alarmed by how much racial circumstances have changed. African Americans whom Son expects to demonstrate unquestioning loyalty to black community are instead intersected by and invested in whiteness in multiple ways, causing him to question the meaning of his own allegiances. He eventually asks himself, "How long had he been gone, anyway? If those were the black folks he was carrying around in his heart all those years, who on earth was he?" (216–17). At first, the text suggests, he believes that his love for Jadine has "derailed his judgment," but he thinks better of that, concluding: "It was less an error in judgment than it was being confronted with *a whole new race* of people he was once familiar with" (217, emphasis added). Yet perhaps it is both. The people *are* new—many of them newly middle class, some newly assimilated to white American culture—but his love for Jadine does matter, precisely because, as the text makes clear, his association with her provisionally re-creates *him* as one of the "new" people in question.

Morrison highlights this fact in a scene during which Son is nearly brought to tears watching "Yardman"/Gideon working beneath him in the garden, as he stands in the window "clean, clean from the roots of his hair to the crevices between his toes" (140). Ironically, his thoughts turn to a familiar image of privilege, a privilege marked for him, until now, as white:

> He knew well the area into which his heart was careening—an area as familiar as the knuckle of his thumb. Not the street of yellow houses with white doors [Eloe], but the wide lawn places where little boys in Easter white shorts played tennis under their very own sun. A sun whose sole purpose was to light their way, golden their hair and reflect the perfection of their Easter white shorts. (139)

Standing in Jadine's room after using her shower, her shampoo, even her "natural sponge" (131), wrapped from "waist-to-thigh in an Easter white towel" (140), he is acutely aware of his own metaphoric distance from Gideon, his positioning literally above the older man, as well as his temporary incorporation by and participation in the privilege that he has, for much of his life, watched and desired from the outside.

This shift from excluded to included, however contingent, affects Son to such a degree that "he was as near to crying as he'd been since he'd fled from home. You would have thought something was leaving him and all he could see was its back" (140). Son recognizes himself as having gained, however inadvertently, access to the kind of advantages he has always envied white, "golden-haired" little boys; this includes his literal envelopment in "Easter white" cotton. In the new world of privilege that Son has entered, "Easter-white" cloth is associated not with the formality of the sacred—the annual Easter holiday, when the poor might acquire a new "Sunday best"—but with the informality of leisure (tennis shorts) and daily bathing (towels). Perhaps, then, what is leaving Son is his conviction about the black-and-white certainties of the world and his place in them. How to resist a newly achieved level of comfort and privilege so disorienting it can induce tears of loss, regret, and (survivor's) guilt?

For Lee's Jigaboos, taking defensive pleasure in their "nappy" hair is one way of performing, vocally and publicly, their resistance to the disciplinary hierarchies of privilege. In the words of the song, "I don't mind being BLACK."[66] This is more than, in the words of one of Lee's critics, a matter of being "politically correct"; it is a politicized and corporealized means of challenging the "sublimated public body" of (white *and* black) bourgeois culture.[67] Ironic, then, that in *Tar Baby,* Son eventually cuts the hair that "spread like layer upon layer of wings from his head" (132), dons a borrowed suit, and uses a much more conventional aesthetic to woo Jadine and to charm Ondine and Sydney. Before this transformation, still untouched, Son's hair literally "paralyzes" Jadine (132), renders her speechless (113). Morrison's prose represents, more coherently than Lee's images, the power of the "wild" black body to mute or literally to overpower the linguistic structures of bourgeois discipline. But Lee's Jigaboos, and his film overall, ultimately make the point more sharply—particularly given *Tar Baby*'s conclusion, which we might read as an indication of Morrison's pessimism about the possibilities for this new, post–Civil Rights black subject. At the novel's end, a despondent Son runs headlong into what Letitia Moffitt calls "the ambiguity of myth," lost on the darkened far shore of Isle des Chevaliers precisely because he feels trapped by his desire for Jadine into chasing her disaffected version of black privilege.[68] By contrast, at the end of *School Daze* the Jigaboos and their pro-black bourgeois politics have the final word, as the camera pans across the bewildered and humbled faces of Julian, Jane, and other central characters of the film while Dap shouts, "Wake up!"

Jadine and Son, as well as both the Wannabees and the Jigaboos, all are best understood as "new" black subjects, intersected and implicated in varying ways by material privilege—colliding products of the changing landscape of the 1980s and the post–Civil Rights era more broadly. In unpacking the trope of the "black" body penetrated by whiteness, both Lee's *School Daze* and Morrison's *Tar Baby* raise the question of why embodiment remains conceptually relevant in post-soul discourses of black bourgeois subjectivity. *School Daze,* in particular, offers us a way to rethink embodiment as a tool of *resistance* (rather than acquiescence) from within intraracial class hierarchy. In the next chapter I turn from texts tackling figurative questions around "whitened" black bodies to texts that represent such bodies in much more literal ways, attending to the embodied links between race, gender, and class privilege for the mixed-race and the "passing" subject. In *School Daze,* performing the "natural" body becomes a way of accepting the pleasures of privilege while simultaneously acknowledging and continuing to invest in the pleasures of blackness; the texts in chapter 2, however, are far more interested in ways that the "mulatto" body, often inadvertently, subverts and denaturalizes blackness, precisely via its privileged investments.

2 "Half of Everything and Certain of Nothing"

Cultural Mulattoes and Racial Property in *Black, White, and Jewish* and *Caucasia*

As whiteness is simultaneously an aspect of identity and a property interest, it is something that can both be experienced and deployed as a resource.

—Cheryl I. Harris, "Whiteness as Property"

If this *story of Venus* has any value at all it is in illuminating the way in which our age is tethered to hers. A relation which others might describe as a kind of melancholia, but which I prefer to describe in terms of the afterlife of property, by which I mean the detritus of lives with which we have yet to attend, a past that has yet to be done, and the ongoing state of emergency in which black life remains in peril.

—Saidiya Hartman, "Venus in Two Acts"

In 1989, Trey Ellis published his exuberant, naively optimistic essay "The New Black Aesthetic," which proclaimed the ascendancy of a generation of writers and artists who "grew up feeling misunderstood by both the black worlds and the white" but since "have liberated themselves from both white envy and self-hate" and taken their rightful places in the black creative vanguard.[1] Ellis's piece, a revision and extension of a college term paper, proved controversial. This was in part because of its narrow gender politics, which—despite Ellis's insistence that this vanguard was the epitome of the new—largely repeated the same marginalization and exclusion of women that had characterized the "old" Black Aesthetic of the 1970s, and in part because of its inability to address black class conflict in any meaningful way.[2] The "evasion of politics" identified by Eric Lott in his response to Ellis, what Lott then called "a refusal to spell out the bup/mass relationship," seems closely tied to Ellis's flawed but freighted concept of the "cultural mulatto," and is worth interrogating here at the start of this chapter on mulatto bodies, class, and racial property in turn-of-the-twenty-first-century post-soul narratives—specifically Danzy Senna's 1998 novel, *Caucasia,* and Rebecca Walker's 2001 memoir, *Black, White, and Jewish*.[3]

In this chapter I explore class-driven tensions between the metaphor of the "cultural mulatto" and that of the "real" mulatto—highlighting the still-permeable boundaries between figurative and literal notions of a privileged black body with, in Walker's words, "white inside." Racial "property" and privilege are at the center of my inquiry here, given the ways that Cheryl I. Harris's influential understanding of racial "whiteness" as property overlaps with and speaks to Saidiya Hartman's notion of contemporary black subjectivity as the "afterlife of property." These two conceptualizations of a kind of racialized capital, of race-*as*-(former)-property, both of which hail and implicate notions of materiality and privilege, collide in a very particular way in the (cultural) mulatto body. This body, which both possesses "whiteness" and is possessed *by* blackness, or rather by the history and the "ongoing state of emergency" and vulnerability that at least partially defines the "black" subject, is taken quite literally in Walker's text but is interrogated and deconstructed in Senna's.[4] Indeed, in this chapter I argue, ultimately, that while Walker's uncritical reliance upon the "truth" of the mulatto body serves to elide her memoir's investment in class and association of whiteness with material privilege, Senna's contemporary passing narrative highlights the costs of an embodied notion of racial subjectivity for a "black" subject whose body cannot be read as such. Her protagonist eschews the property of whiteness throughout the novel precisely because of its privileged investments, instead seeking to "belong" to blackness.

Before turning to these two narratives, I want briefly to unpack these notions of black and white "property" and then look a bit more closely at Ellis's notion of the "cultural mulatto," which masquerades in his essay as progressive but upon closer attention fairly easily gives up its troubled investments in racial biology and hierarchies of value. In this chapter's first epigraph, drawn from her foundational 1993 essay "Whiteness as Property," Harris writes of whiteness as both "an aspect of identity" and "a property interest," meaning that for those understood to be legally "white," "whiteness" can be both "experienced and deployed as a resource."[5] For Harris, a legally "white" person "'used and enjoyed' White whenever she took advantage of the privileges accorded white people simply by virtue of their whiteness—when she exercised any number of rights reserved for the holders of whiteness" (1734). As we will see, particularly in my discussion of Senna's text, in practice these rights include everything from the right to particular kinds of social access and visibility to the right to police and discipline other (read: black) bodies.

As Audrey Elisa Kerr notes, however, writing about colorism and the folkloric significance of the "paper bag" in distinguishing lighter skin colors from darker ones among African Americans, "Because white America went to such lengths to (supposedly) remain distinct and 'purely' white, comparable demarcations of the margins and borders of race have been tested internally as part of a rhetorical curiosity about whether whiteness can work for blacks as well as it works for whites."[6] This notion of whiteness *working* for black subjects—in other words, serving as a deployable resource even for those who are not "white"—has a particular resonance in the case of the mixed-race subject, who presumably has a biological relationship to "whiteness," usually one that is visible in his or her skin color and hair texture.[7] One question we must ask about whiteness as property, then, is: To what extent can whiteness also be the *property* of black or mixed bodies? How might these bodies similarly deploy whiteness as a resource—and to what ends?

The notion of whiteness as a property interest, a usable resource—perhaps especially if we can imagine that resource to be usable by black subjects—collides with Hartman's articulation of the black present as the *afterlife of property,* precisely because the black body *as* property continues to haunt our present moment. In writing about a dead slave girl, Venus,

Hartman is ultimately concerned with the limits and failures of the archive, and indeed, in "performing the limits of writing history through the act of narration."[8] Yet her point that "our lives are coeval with the girl's in the as-yet-incomplete project of freedom" speaks to the ways that blackness has historically operated as a sign or symbol of the less-than-human, of bodies that cannot possess even themselves.[9] The ontological conflict between black bodies as property and black bodies as *propertied,* bodies that under certain conditions have access to (material) privilege, is at the center of my larger inquiry in this project, but the case of the mixed-race black subject casts this conflict into a particularly literal relief, as the narratives that circulate around the "mulatto" body centralize the notion of that body's dual property interests, in both blackness and whiteness.

This duality is likely why Ellis finds the metaphor of the "cultural mulatto" so useful; the very usefulness of the metaphor, however, its biologically rooted simplicity, highlights its reductiveness and especially its inability to grapple with black class privilege. Ellis defines a "cultural mulatto" thus:

> Just as a genetic mulatto is a black person of mixed parents who often can get along fine with his white grandparents, a cultural mulatto, educated by a multi-racial mix of cultures, can also navigate easily in the white world.[10]

Yet while the phrase "cultural mulatto" may be a practical shorthand for a certain kind of "black" subject "educated by a multi-racial mix of cultures"—Ellis's use of the word "educated" here suggesting, if not insisting upon, a personal history of privilege and access for said subject—it also reifies categories of "black" and "white" in a way that simply returns us to biology. Although the phrase's emphasis on culture seems to sidestep biological race, the advancement of "cultural" as a modifier for "mulatto" suggests that the peculiar phrase "genetic mulatto" is a redundancy, that "real" mixed-race people are those in possession of a white parent. Ellis seems unaware of or uninterested in the ways both that so-called genetic mulattoes historically have had complex relationships to "blackness" (e.g., the "one drop" rule, black people as always already mixed race, etc) and that African American artists in generations prior to his own have claimed influences and been "educated" in cultures across the racial spectrum (see, e.g., Ralph Ellison's "The World and the Jug").

The class and gender politics of the term as Ellis lays them out are even more striking, however. There is a strange slippage in a subsequent passage from the essay, when Ellis moves between a celebration of cultural mulattoes' freedom from racial self-consciousness ("We no longer need to deny or suppress any part of our complicated and sometimes contradictory cultural baggage to please either white people or black") and a supremely self-conscious claim about race and class. Directly after his confident, collectivized refusal to please either blacks or whites, Ellis writes that "the culturally mulatto *Cosby* girls are just as black as a black teenage welfare mother," insisting that "neither side of the tracks should forget that."[11] For me this sentence raises a number of persistent questions, most of which seem to present obvious answers: To what extent does Ellis's formulation of "black teenage welfare mother" operate as a static, fixed sign for "impoverished black authenticity" that is granted, in Ellis's binary, no interiority, no complexity, and no possibility for dynamism? In this sort of oppositional framing, can a "black teenage welfare mother" ever herself be a cultural mulatto? If not, why not? And why is the best example Ellis can come up with for a "cultural mulatto" the fictional, fantasized "*Cosby* girls"? Why, indeed, are we talking about "girls" and women at all, in this contestatory moment in Ellis's argument? Ellis seems to have little problem bringing up actual black men by name in his piece, but in this strange moment of naming the stakes of who is "just as black" he switches over to two imagined (indeed, purely *imaginary*) female figures.

Ellis's rhetorical choices certainly reveal the importance of women's and girls' bodies in masculine contests over racial meaning and social power—and as Habiba Ibrahim reminds us, "multiraciality gains clarity through gender," so it is perhaps not surprising that Ellis reaches in the direction of the "*Cosby* girls" to make his point.[12] But these lines suggest, too, that if the black creative vanguard has indeed sloughed off "white envy" and "[black] self-hate," it has not yet come to as comfortable a place about its own material privilege. Thus Ellis uses the heavily class-inflected phrase "neither side of the tracks," which calls for a kind of truce across lines of social class—the begrudging acceptance of blackness by the "whitened" (cultural) mulatto and the similarly begrudging agreement, from poor and working-class black people, that Ellis and his fantasy proxies, the *Cosby* girls, are after all "just as black" as their less-privileged counterparts. Although Ellis tries for a parallel with "neither side of the tracks," the fact that one would never have to *argue* that a "black teenage welfare mother" was "just as black" as the fictional character Denise Cosby demonstrates the false equivalence and the poorly concealed class privilege of the "culturally mulatto" subject.

Keeping the material privilege of the *cultural* mulatto in view may allow us to better understand the nexus of privilege, power, and capital that historically has surrounded the "real" mulatto, and the way that both of these "mulatto" subjects occupy a vexed position vis-à-vis racial property. Particularly in the late 1990s, a moment of discursive upheaval for racial categorization—including, for instance, demands for a "multiracial" category on the U.S. census[13]—the question of to whom or to what the (cultural) mulatto body belongs is a particularly fraught one, taken up in varying ways by both Walker and Senna. Both of these narratives' attention to class, race, and corporeality highlights Hartman's "past that is not done" and points to the continued relevance of whiteness *and* blackness as forms of "property" that inhere in the body in figurative and literal ways.

Not Tragic

Rebecca Walker, the daughter of famed black novelist Alice Walker and Jewish attorney Mel Leventhal, writes early in her 2001 memoir, *Black, White, and Jewish: Autobiography of a Shifting Self,* "I remember coming and going, going and coming. That, for me, was home."[14] Walker longs for multiple lives and cannot find satisfaction in any one place:

> I am not rooted in the everyday. I move from place to place like a sybarite in search of pleasure, always thinking the final resting place will be just around the corner, at the end of this plane ride, behind the next door. I can never release myself from the mercurial aspects, can't allow myself to stand on some kind of ground. (167)

Walker insists, however, that this chronic sense of displacement, while certainly a function of how she grew up, and with whom, is not stereotypically tortured or sad. A self-described "Movement Child," she writes that she is "not a bastard, the product of rape, the child of some white devil," and goes on to state categorically, "I am not tragic" (24). Invoking the trope of the tragic mulatta in order to distance herself from it, Walker here insists, like Ellis, on the *newness* of her subject position, a hopeful, transgressive multiraciality made possible by the interracial coalition building of the early Civil Rights movement.[15]

Yet for all of this newness, throughout her memoir Walker does make recourse to a very old narrative of racial authenticity (or perhaps, inauthenticity), namely, that of the "impure" mulatta body. This "impurity" depends upon the authentic biological presence of whiteness *within* the mixed-race figure, and this sense of whiteness within recurs at many points in Walker's narrative. Indeed, Walker announces her interest in the biological on the very first page of the book, musing on the things that she has forgotten, "thousands of large and small omissions, bits of information I swear normal people have built into their DNA" (1). Aligning the notion of lapsed cognitive memory with a corporeal failure at the level of DNA, Walker thus begins her autobiography by highlighting her difference from "normal people," those who are not so "amorphous," who possess "the unbroken black line around [their] bod[ies]" that Walker believes herself to lack (2).

There is an interesting symbolic link here between the absence of "unbroken" blackness outside or around the body, literally a black surface or border, and the presence of whiteness within the body that Walker highlights repeatedly throughout her narrative. Discussing her maternal uncle and cousins' use of the word "cracker" to describe things she does that "they think are strange or weird . . . not black" (85), Walker writes, "a part of me feels pushed away when they say this, like I have *something inside of me* I know they hate" (85, emphasis added). She wonders whether her "great-great-great-great-great-great-great-grandmother, May Poole" (150), who was born a slave, would have seen Walker's light skin, the visible badge of her white ancestry, "as a sign of danger, the evidence of brutality" (151). She feels physically inadequate in the face of the "undeniable blackness" (239) of a woman in a photograph in a boyfriend's bedroom—a blackness as physical as it is undeniable, marked, for Walker, by the woman's "dark chocolate skin" and "perfectly formed thick behind" (239).[16] Thus, not only does this whiteness within deny Walker a protective cultural facade, as her performance of blackness is disrupted by behaviors deemed by other black people to be "strange," "weird," "not black," but her light complexion operates as a visual reminder that her body lacks an "unbroken black line" of dark skin, the "undeniable blackness" that presumably would have signified safety to her enslaved foremother Poole.

Walker again makes recourse to biological betrayal, to her body's internal makeup as a source of externalized, personal and racial alienation, when she writes: "There is an awkwardness to my body, a lack of grace, as if the racial mix, the two sides coming together in my body, have yet to reconcile" (255). Yet she notes with relief, in the next paragraph, that she can dance, that she has "rhythm":

> For black folks, "having rhythm" is like speaking a different language, and pity you if you don't know the words. "Poor thing," I myself have snickered about a mixed person with no groove, clinging to a rare, luxurious feeling of inclusion, "the mix just didn't turn out right." (255)

Curiously, ability to master the "language" of rhythm seems tied, here, not to so-called racial purity but to a fortuitous kind of impurity, a "mix" that succeeds rather than fails in particular ways. If Walker's mixed ancestry leaves her visually "awkward" and racially rootless, it does not leave her "groove"-less. Yet while she recalls dancing with both parents, she still concedes the truth of her black friends' and lovers' assertions that her rhythm is derived from her mother, her blackness; she despairs of the praise, the "rare, luxurious" sense of inclusion, which requires her to suppress her white ancestry. "But where does that leave me?" Walker writes, "Ashamed of one half, grateful for the other?" (256). These "halves" are far more than metaphoric, linked throughout this section to the corporeal, mixed-race awkwardness that prevents Walker from feeling "at home in [her] body" (255).

Given this recurrent concern with biology, it comes as somewhat of a surprise that when Walker's (black) lover asks her directly, "What does it feel like to have white inside you?" (304), Walker retreats into the constructedness of race. She reports, "My first response is, What is whiteness? And how can one 'feel white' when race is just about the biggest cultural construct there is?" (305). She goes on to note, "Is whiteness something I can feel on or in my body like a stomachache or a burn? No" (305). Here Walker refuses to articulate explicitly the notion of biological difference that she has raised, implicitly, throughout her narrative. And perhaps rightfully so; because race is "just about the biggest cultural construct there is," it should be clear that the racial alienation that Walker has subtly linked to her physical admixture is actually attributable to other, sociocultural factors that shape how identity is performed and interpreted.

In the case of Walker's incomplete or occasionally incoherent performance of blackness, one of these factors may well be material privilege. Walker associates her white, Jewish ancestry with her father's "totally bourgeois lifestyle" (208), the "white, rich, Jewish kids" (207) at her Larchmont high school, and the wealthy white adult residents of Larchmont, who, when she walks down the street with her younger half brother and sister, mistake her for "the baby-sitter, the maid, the au pair" (230). And Walker frames her emotional identification with her Puerto Rican friend Theresa explicitly in class terms: "[Theresa's] house . . . reflects how I feel inside much more than the calm, collected, solidly middle-class world of my father and stepmother and their new baby boy" (205). As Lori Harrison-Kahan notes, "Walker renounces her Jewishness in favor of being a 'Puertoriquena' because, in the world she inhabits, the most visible Hispanic population is working class and the most visible part of the Jewish population middle class."[17] Or, more accurately, upper middle class to lavishly wealthy; the Larchmont friend that Walker describes in the most detail, Allison Hoffman, lives in a house of "smooth gray stone and glass," which "from the outside looks like it should be in an architectural magazine," with a "Mercedes and Jaguar" parked in the carport (209). Uncomfortable with the entitlement that Allison exhibits, talking to her Latina maid, Maria, in a voice "a little too firm and dismissive . . . for someone our age to say to a woman so much older" (210), Walker instead seeks out "the mess, the drama, the darkness" (205) of Latinidad, embodied by Theresa—who in spite of Walker's feelings of kinship toward her, nonetheless looks "faded, haggard, and slightly green" (212) against the backdrop of Walker's own bourgeois home.

Like Ellis, Walker leaves these awkward issues of class and material privilege unexamined, instead allowing her so-called racial biology to stand in for a more nuanced consideration of how race and class complicate one another, how the presence of her beige body indeed disrupts the "calm, collected, solidly middle-class" and very white world of her father and stepmother, but also how continued access to this solidly middle-class privilege, and especially to financial support from her father's family, shapes Walker's interactions in both white and black spaces. In one instance, her "grandmother in Brooklyn" (read: her father's mother) sends her money to buy a bicycle after her mother refuses, which then becomes an emblem of Walker's regional and class difference from the kids in her mother's urban San Francisco neighborhood:

> Two girls, Sonja and Sandra, come down from the building up the hill. . . . Sonja is big. I don't know it then but everyone in her family is big, strong, meaty. She has her hair in plaits and has on these big burgundy overalls with jelly shoes and pom-pom socks. The pom-poms are yellow and blue, she must have on two pairs, one over the other. I don't remember Sandra too much, not her skin or her hair or anything in particular. Sonja is the one who tells me she is going to take my bike from me. Sonja is the one who asks me where I am from and am I new and says she should just take my bike so I could learn what it is like. I say, What *what* is like? (124)

Walker makes typical recourse to the body here, in this case the "big," "strong," "meaty" body of the working-class black girl, which sticks in Walker's memory (unlike Sandra, who remains a nondescript blur for both Walker and the reader) only because she poses a threat. The class dynamics of Sonja's resentment are clear, as Walker's "newness," her light skin, her shiny red bike, and the attention she receives from the "cute fine sexy [older] boy" (123), Michael, are all examples of her privilege over Sonja, a privilege driven as much by her access to wealth as her corporeal relationship to "whiteness." The memoir is written from Walker's childhood perspective, and Walker's apparent innocence in the moment of

Sonja's anger ("What *what* is like?") only highlights the stark contrast between the two girls' subject positions more clearly, as Walker must learn, often painfully, of the existence of—and her relatively privileged place in—social hierarchies of race and class the constraints of which girls like Sonja have long chafed under.

Walker reencounters this dynamic throughout her early teenage years in San Francisco with her mother, repeatedly being dismissed or attacked as a "yellow bitch" (108, 156) and simultaneously "attaching [her] self to people who hated [her] as an act of self-protection" (156). She avoids this dynamic in New York, with her father, by not just spending time with Latino friends in a part of the Bronx that seems miles away from her father's apartment in Riverdale, but by passing as a Latina: "The Bronx means . . . . walking around with my friends Sam and Jesus and Theresa and Melissa and being seen as I feel I truly am: a Puertoriquena, a mulatta, breathed out with all that Spanish flavor. A girl of color with attitude" (200). Yet she "can't imagine" her friends in her father's apartment, where "nothing . . . looks or sounds or smells like my friends' houses, . . . [nothing] would prove I am of color, that I am who I say I am outside of these walls" (202). And her concerns for her father's safety when he drives her "down the hill to Theresa's house" reveal a great deal about Walker's experiences with urban blackness, a space that has been far less safe for her than *el barrio*:

> He asks in that same way, Are you sure you'll be okay? And I think to myself that *I* am going to be fine, but will he? I belong because my skin says I do, because people don't question me, don't look at me and think of all the wack shit that white people do. They don't assume I have money or that I don't respect them. I can walk like I know, I can cock my head to one side and look at someone like they better step off, but my father? I worry that he's just another white man walking down the street, an easy mark. (202)

Walker's worry about her father here masks the ways that these very assumptions attach to her own body. The very skin that operates as a sign of belonging among her Puerto Rican friends, marking her as a "mulatta" with "Spanish flavor," is a sign of her position as privileged outsider in the

African American spaces she frequents on the other coast. Indeed, while Walker has already suggested that her maternal ancestor May Poole would have seen her light skin as "a sign of danger, the evidence of [white] brutality" (151), this dynamic, in which (black) people look at her and think of (white) privilege, assume she has money, assume she doesn't respect them, is clearly at play in the sometimes literally bruising interactions she has with poor and working-class black kids in San Francisco, who see in her light skin a "yellow bitch" who "thought [she] was better than everybody else" (156). Ironically, it is from one of these tormentors-turned-friends, Lisa, that Walker learns "to move like I know where I'm going, like I could be dangerous if talked to the wrong way, like I have brothers or uncles who would come out of nowhere to protect me if something should go down" (159)—in other words, to behave like "a girl of color with attitude." Walker's successful, gendered and raced, performance of this role thus depends upon her familiarity with and entry into spaces that initially view her with contempt precisely because of her class and color privilege.

We might also read Walker's relationship to education, specifically her high school education, as shaped by class privilege and access. In this case, her mother's increasing success as a writer enables Walker to attend an expensive private school once she realizes that she might leave her local public high school "know[ing] less than when [she] started" (251). The request she makes of her mother to attend private school is another moment that implicates the body simultaneously with class, this time calling attention to its adolescent vulnerability:

> I don't know where this comes from, really, this sudden exclamation, because it's not like I've been thinking about it and it's not like I know anybody my age who is actually in a private school. But I have just had an abortion at fourteen, and we don't read books in my English class, only endless mimeographed handouts, and Michael's friends in college work for minimum wage parking cars. (252)

While Walker's early experimentation with sex is framed in the book as a function of her mother's neglect ("Somewhere I feel like maybe I want my mother to find out that where I am may not be very safe and I want her to tell me to come home. I want her to tell me that I can't go so far away from her while I'm so young" [158]), Walker's abortion at only fourteen also suggests her figurative if not literal proximity to Ellis's "black teenage welfare mother." The distinction between Walker and that figure is, in part, a parent who has the resources to intervene. Walker's mother agrees without hesitation to "schedule an abortion" (249), protecting Walker from "hav[ing] a baby before [she] was old enough to take care of it" (251); she similarly agrees to look for a suitable private school, protecting her daughter from an economic future that involves "work for minimum wage" like the alums of her public high school.

Ironically, this *figurative* proximity to black poverty follows Walker and her mother into the interview at the paradoxically named "Urban," the "small, hippie private school" she and her mother choose (261); the headmaster, "without a hello, an introduction, a hi nice to meet you I'm so-and-so and your name is," opens his meeting with the two of them by saying "the first thing I must tell you folks is that there's just no financial aid available" (261). Walker takes a split second longer than her mother to recognize "the assumption, the train of thought he's following," namely, that "we're black and so we must need financial aid," but her mother's icy outrage carries them both out the door. As they exit, Walker considers a question with an obvious answer: "I'm thinking about . . . what it would be like if my big white father were here with us, and his white Volvo was parked outside. Would it be different then?" (262). Here, Walker's fantasy about her father's mitigating presence necessarily includes the white Volvo, because in *Black, White, and Jewish* the covering protection of whiteness is also and always already a class protection.

In these scenes, *Black, White, and Jewish* almost inadvertently highlights the class politics underlying Walker's racial alienation, an alienation that leaves her feeling not "at home" in her body (255). Yet even the solution to this alienation, as presented in the text, returns us to the corporeal, indeed, to the sexual:

> When I am under Michael in the dark, when I have my head under the covers and am sucking Luca's smooth, white penis, when Andre is stretching his hard, muscle-bound body over me as the fog seeps in the window above my head, when Ray Martinez grabs the back

> of my neck in the movie theater and pushes his tongue farther into my mouth, I feel all my fear and anxiety about being liked, fitting in, knowing where and who I am melt away. I feel I am finally just the soft part of who I am, the mushy part of Rebecca, the part underneath the hard outer layer whose face frowns and shoulders tense, who watches every move to know how to follow. Their attention is the salve that coats the wound, is the sound that drowns out all the people who don't like black white girls, who don't like white black girls, who don't like me, the skin on my body having determined this long before I even had a chance to speak. (256)

For Walker, sexual attention from boys and men releases her from her cross-racial anxiety about fitting in, from all those who categorize her by her skin as a "black white girl" or a "white black girl," a "half-breed race traitor" or "half-breed oreo freak" (271). It is unclear, however, how much this retreat into the "mushy part of Rebecca" is a way of avoiding the hard work of grappling with the meanings behind these labels, and their ties to various kinds of (bodily) privilege. Walker's youthful sexual activity seems to offer a safer or more socially sanctioned means of controlling her body's narrative. But it is unclear whether the costs of this manner of control are too high for her. By the end of her memoir, Walker asserts that "blood ties are less important, that all blood is basically the same," but also, finally, situates herself again "somewhere between black and white, family and friend" (322), noting "I am flesh and blood, but also ether" (322).[18] Taken together, these phrases call up her body, her mixed heritage, even as they seek to diminish its relevance—indeed, they suggest Walker's ultimate inability to turn away from the corporeal, which after all underlies the "shifting self" of her narrative's title.

"Black Like Me, a Mixed Girl"

Danzy Senna's fictional protagonist, Birdie, from *Caucasia,* is similar to Walker's younger self in that she is biracial and associates her white parent's origins with privilege. And although *Caucasia* is not a memoir, Birdie's observation that her mother's lineage is written into the very structures of Boston—"there seemed to be remnants of my mother's family everywhere—history books, PBS specials, plaques in Harvard Square" (100)—is remarkably similar to what Senna writes of her own famous mother (writer Fanny Howe) in her 2009 memoir, *Where Did You Sleep Last Night?*:

> I looked up and saw what I must have always known but had never really acknowledged: my mother's history—and therefore mine too—was written everywhere. A subway map to Quincy Market. An advertisement for DeWolfe Realtors. Before me was Harvard's campus, where my mother's father and forefathers had studied, taught, and presided. Just a few blocks up was my great-grandfather's ode to tobacco, engraved on a bronze plaque on the wall outside the century-old smoke shop Leavitt and Pierce. It was quite literally all around me: on street signs and statues, on subway maps and plaques.[19]

Senna makes this realization with a "rush of embarrassment, amusement, shame and pride, disgust and glee," because the vivid, material presence of her mother's history, of "privilege passed down through the ages" (16), brings with it awareness of a corresponding absence, "what was not there, the other half of me, my father's side" (13). As she goes on to note, highlighting the seemingly unbreachable void of this absence, "one side is unusually—even compulsively—documented, and the other is a black hole that, when you call into it—*Who are you?*—only swallows the very question" (17).

Indeed, this chapter's title is also drawn from Senna's memoir. "Half of everything and certain of nothing" is a phrase she uses to describe her father's uncertain ancestry, which involves not only multiraciality but also family secrets around his paternity. Senna's father had always believed that his father was a Mexican boxer, Carl Senna (the reason he is named Carl Senna Jr.), but as the memoir reveals, he may actually have been fathered by an Irish priest who had a secret relationship with his mother (Senna's grandmother) and who fathered several other children with her. Senna's father's origins are thus even more murky and couched in secrecy than she, or perhaps he, had believed; as she notes: "His is a tale as murky as the Louisiana swamp where he'd been born. He is neither a real Southerner nor a real Northerner. He is neither fully black nor fully Mexican nor fully white. He does not know his father; he has only a Mexican surname and a frayed news clipping showing a Mexican pugilist to possibly explain his light skin and mixed features. . . . Every descriptive statement you can make about my father can be contradicted by the sentence that follows. He is half of everything and certain of nothing" (124). This phrasing seems evocative of a larger state of being, one that Senna describes as somewhat universal to the American story—"It is, I realize now, my mother's side of the family that is the anomaly. . . . Most Americans have an experience closer to my father's regarding their ancestry. It is his family story in the end that feels more quintessentially American" (123)—but that we might apply to the (cultural) mulatto and to the post-soul "black" subject in a broader sense, a point to which I will return later.

While the Senna of *Where Did You Sleep Last Night?* thus seeks—through genealogical research and a kind of wandering pilgrimage South—to understand her father's individual history as a means of better understanding her own, *Caucasia*'s central character, Birdie, is forced into a much more literal search for her father, Deck, and beloved older sister, Cole, after the family is separated due to the radical activism of her mother, Sandy. Believing that Sandy has no choice but to go on the run for fear of prosecution by the "Feds," Sandy and Deck decide that she will take Birdie with her because of Birdie's racial ambiguity and ability to pass:

> The FBI would be looking for a white woman on the lam with her black child. But the fact that I could pass, she explained, with my straight hair, pale skin, my general phenotypic resemblance to the Caucasoid race, would throw them off our trail. The two bodies that had made her stand out in a crowd—made her more than just another white woman—were gone; now it was just the two of us. My body was the key to our going incognito. (128)

Crucially, here, though Birdie's skin color and hair texture mark a "general phenotypic resemblance" to whiteness, her darker coloring needs to be explained away via the last name her mother chooses for them: "'We're gonna have to use our imaginations. You know, make up a history for you. . . . You've got a lot of choices, babe. You can be anything, Puerto Rican, Sicilian, Pakistani, Greek. . . . And of course, you could always be Jewish'" (130). While much has been made of Sandy's claim that "Jews weren't really white, more like an off-white . . . the closest [Birdie] was going to get to black and still stay white" (140), I am more interested in the options that Sandy raises and then rejects.[20] Her easy rejection of her own initial litany of suggestions—Puerto Rican, Sicilian, Pakistani, Greek—cutting off Birdie's hesitant contribution to the conversation ("Italian, maybe? I like spaghetti") with the phrase "Jewish is better, I think" (130), begs the question of what makes Jewish "better."

The "tragic history, kinky hair, good politics" (140) that, Sandy assures her daughter, mean she's not *really* passing "for white, more like an off-white" (140) obscure the ways that Jewishness can be understood as both "whiter" and "wealthier" than the more recent immigrant identities Sandy first suggests. As Michele Elam notes, "Jews are persuasively associated with certain American myths of self-invention," and, indeed, "stand in closest relation to, and as a vehicle of, whiteness in part because they best represent . . . immigrant achievement and assimilation."[21] And the stereotypical and anti-Semitic association of Jewishness with the acquisition of money, what Andrew Killick calls the "most widespread anti-Semitic stereotype," is the implicit corollary to this association with (white) "achievement" precisely because of the material wealth to which Jews are perceived to have access.[22] Indeed, Sherry Ortner has argued that "to be Jewish is to be, in deepest essence, middle class (whether one is 'in reality' or not)" precisely because "class comes in racialized and ethnicized packages in America and . . . race and ethnicity are actually crypto-class positions."[23] As such, Judaism is a far more materially *appropriate* choice for Sandy's imagined foray across ethnic lines. Indeed, like Sandy's weight loss and her "auburn hair and horn-rimmed glasses," Jewishness—or more accurately, her daughter's supposed half-Jewishness and her own positioning as the widow of the "incredibly brilliant professor of classics" David Goldman (130)—operates as "another piece of her disguise" (139), a way of transforming Sandy from an outlaw associated with (black) radicalism into a "tall, statuesque, blue-blooded woman," (149), a more privileged and, seemingly by extension, *whitened* version of herself.

Sandy and Birdie, now renamed Sheila and Jesse Goldman, move first through a women's commune in upstate New York before settling, for a while, in New Hampshire. Here, as Brenda Boudreau points out, referencing Rebecca Aanerud, *Caucasia* highlights the "constructed," contingent, and contextual nature of whiteness, as the "tough," working-class New Hampshire girls that Birdie/Jesse falls in with are very different from the Boston Brahmin world that Sandy/Sheila has fled.[24] Still, class privilege, specifically white class privilege, paves the mother and daughter's way to acceptance in the town. Sheila secures their rented guesthouse from the wealthy WASP couple the Marshes, a college professor and his wife, by not only dressing the part but proving to them that she "spoke their language" (149), while Jesse's friendly, potentially sexual association with their teenage son, Nick ("You know Nick Marsh?" [221]), serves as her ticket into the group of "townie girls" led by Mona, a "blond girl" who lives in a trailer (signaling her family's white, semirural poverty) with her mother, "a young, wiry, chain-smoking factory worker with spiky black hair and a foul mouth" (226).

While I read Birdie and Sandy as having contingent, provisional access to "privilege" at this point in the text, the two do not, to be clear, have a great deal of money—instead, in terms of material resources, they are likely very similar to the trailer-dwelling Mona and her mother. Yet the new arrivals' class positioning nonetheless diverges from the townies' significantly, precisely because of Sandy's knowledge of and ability to engage in codes of elite self-presentation. Sandy uses bodily performances—thinness, conservative "preppy" clothing, and glasses—to signal her status and belonging among the wealthy, such that Walter Marsh privately avers, "I just can't figure them out. The mother hasn't a penny to her name, but you get the feeling she should" (194). His wife agrees: "I know what you mean. They're a funny pair, but they both just reek of class" (194). After overhearing this conversation, Birdie feels "a surge of pride" at their approval, though she knows Sandy would perceive the Marshes as "classist fucks, old-money snobs" (194). Ironically, Sandy, whose class *origins* are situated squarely within the "old-money" world she now views with such contempt, is able to leverage her insider knowledge of white wealth to gain advantages for herself and her daughter despite their temporary lack of means.

Mother and daughter's successful performance of (privileged) whiteness has profound effects on Birdie's sense of self, however. In New Hampshire, the black racial identity that Birdie has tried to cultivate—an identity that, as Ralina Joseph points out, itself was largely performative, based on "commercial signifiers, such as Jergens lotion [and] *Jet* magazine"—begins to disintegrate.[25] Birdie starts to forget what her father looks like; even as the cover story of "David Goldman" becomes clearer in her mind's eye, she loses her memories of Deck's face: "First his eyes, then his nose, then his mouth had faded until all I could see was the back of his head, his hands drumming on the steering wheel" (188). There is some irony, here, in Birdie's only remaining image of Deck being him turned away from her. Just as he never really seemed to see her when Cole was present (56), once she has "passed" into whiteness, her relation to Deck's blackness becomes one of seeking and never quite finding, of grappling with a sense of identity that proves constantly elusive.

Birdie's box of "negrobilia"—a collection of racialized objects, some pulled together by Deck and Cole before the family was separated, some added later by Birdie—similarly begins to lose meaning:

> At night I stared into my box of negrobilia, fingering the objects—the fisted pick, the Nubian Notion eight-track cassette, the Egyptian necklace, the black Barbie head—and tried to tell myself, "I haven't forgotten." But the objects in the box looked to me just like that—objects. They seemed like remnants from the life of some other girl whom I barely knew anymore, anthropological artifacts of some ancient, extinct people, rather than pieces of my past. (190)

These two failures—the failure of her memory and the failure of the individual items in the box of negrobilia to cohere into a narrative of Birdie's past, let alone of her blackness—accompany her physical and cultural assimilation into whiteness, a moment in which "the name Jesse Goldman no longer felt so funny, so . . . make believe" (190). The objects in her box of negrobilia become meaningless out of their original context, reduced to discrete and unrelated "remnants," and so, too, do her father's features, no longer part of a coherent whole but fragments that gradually disappear from her conscious awareness. Indeed, her inability to recall her father's face speaks to her own subjective disintegration, her intensifying "sense of watching herself from above" (190), looking at her own body "with the detachment of a stranger" (190). It would seem that her father's physical absence shapes her (in)ability to understand her blackness, as a literal product of his body. Earlier in the text, Birdie notes that while Cole, as the darker-skinned sister, has inherited their father's "kinky hair and small, round nose" (43), and indeed, that Cole's "mischievous curls" are "nappier" than her father's (56), the only bodily traits Birdie appears to have inherited from Deck are unrelated to phenotype: asthma and eczema (113). Still, both of these are chronic illnesses that disproportionately affect African American children, suggesting that Deck *has* racially marked Birdie, just in "invisible" ways.

What Birdie must grapple with in the narrative, and what Senna's novel pushes us as readers to consider, is what it means to inhabit a body that does not immediately reveal its racial origins, such that blackness itself—and in particular, the individual subject's relationship to racial vulnerability as signaled by his or her phenotype, what Ta-Nehisi Coates has called the "tenacious gravity" of blackness—seems to disappear, or perhaps to fall silent.[26] What steps into this silence, into the lack of visual evidence of the body's interior (*pace* Elizabeth Alexander) racial meaning, is whiteness. As Senna notes in an early interview, "What's become clear to me through my racial trials and tribulations is that at some point you do make a choice, not between white and black but between silence and speech. Do you let your body talk for you or do you speak for yourself?"[27] Senna's words not only equate whiteness with silence, and blackness with speech, but link silence to the white-skinned black body. While other texts examined throughout this book tend to understand the black body as a site of racial *articulation,* often with the enunciatory power to ground an otherwise shifting, materially privileged subject within blackness, *Caucasia* contends with a black body that misspeaks, and thereby silences, its racial investments. This silencing—and the concomitant whitewashing of her identity that comes with it—seems to trouble Birdie not simply because she is not allowed to *belong to* blackness, and to the black people she loves, but because of the property claims of whiteness within which she is enfolded instead.

In *Caucasia,* as in Walker's *Black, White, and Jewish,* so much of what "whiteness" is—in particular, the ancestral whiteness that stakes its claim on Birdie within and through her own body—is, or is situated within, material privilege. This is most directly articulated in the text through the character of Birdie's maternal grandmother, Penelope Lodge, who "traced her family line back to Cotton Mather, the Puritan prosecutor in the Salem witch trials" (99), and who "was proud of the Mather link and liked to remind [Birdie] of [her] heritage every time [she] came over" (100). Cole, whose black appearance severs her from Penelope's fantasy of a pure lineage, is never included in these episodes, despite the fact that Penelope is Cole's grandmother too: "I thought Cole was the lucky one because she was allowed to stay locked in the guest room watching television while I had to sit under the old lady's scrutiny, hands folded on my lap, listening to her tell me stories about how good my blood was" (100). The violence of this exclusion is not lost on Birdie, and when she returns to her grandmother's house several years later, seeking money so that she can travel to California to find Deck and Cole, she explodes with contempt for Penelope's racism:

> You and all your ancestors are the tragedies. Not me. You walk around pretending to be so liberal and civilized in this big old house, but you're just as bad as the rest of them. This whole world—it's based on lies. No wonder my mother left. I mean, it stinks. (365)

Echoing Walker's "I am not tragic," Birdie here speaks back to the racial condescension that leads her grandmother to describe Deck and Sandy's union, and the mixed-race black children it produced, as "tragedy in the making" (365).

Birdie's internal dialogue continues to indict Penelope precisely for the old woman's bigoted inability to get beyond the body and the "whiteness" she believes she sees in Birdie's face: "My grandmother had always loved me more than my sister. Or maybe it wasn't me she loved, but rather my face, my skin, my hair, and my bones, because they resembled her own. . . . She believed that the face was a mirror of the soul. She believed, deep down, that the race my face reflected made me superior. Such a simple, comforting myth to live by" (366). In offering this critique, Birdie speaks truth to power; the text reminds us of the grotesque contours of a belief system that enables Penelope to embrace one granddaughter on the basis of appearance while rejecting the other entirely on the same basis ("She had always referred to Cole as 'your sister' and my father as 'your father,' as if she couldn't bear to say their names, couldn't bear to admit their relation to her" [367]). Yet Penelope's immediate response to Birdie is unsatisfying; instead of withdrawing under the assault of Birdie's words or snapping back in mutual confrontation, she peers at Birdie, "genuinely concerned" (366), and recognizes the girl's feverish and weakened state: "You're sick. I should have seen it. You're sick" (366). While Birdie is indeed sick, "shaking and sweating" (365), this reading of her body by her grandmother still suggests that Penelope understands Birdie's speech as a kind of delirium. She is "sick," meaning not herself, not responsible for her resistant words and actions. Not surprisingly, Birdie rejects Penelope's pity, which seems to be just another way of staking claim on her "white" (read: fragile, innocent, protected) body.

Whiteness asserts its claim on Birdie's body at other points throughout the text, again in ways that highlight false narratives of white innocence and fragility while downplaying or ignoring the vulnerability of black bodies in proximity. In one instance, Sandy tearfully lectures Birdie, after another young girl's abduction and death in the area, not to go into Roxbury's Franklin Park alone, because "there are perverts, crazies, dirty old men, and they want little girls like you" (66). Even at her young age, it strikes Birdie as "odd" that Sandy "hadn't warned Cole not to go to the park, just [her]" (67). The text lingers over and emphasizes Sandy's words, "*Girls like you,*" a phrase that seems to apply only to Birdie, presumably because of her noticeable physical resemblance to the victim, "Luce Rivera," who is not described in the text except as "looking unsuspecting and utterly pure" (66). The irony of Sandy's warning to Birdie—and a clear parallel or through line between Sandy's unconscious racism and that of her mother, Penelope—is that Penelope echoes these sentiments when she discovers Sandy is sending the girls to Nkrumah, the Black Power school in Roxbury: "It's crazy, child abuse, to send your child into a neighborhood like that. She could be robbed or killed or anything!" (106). And like Sandy, who fails to warn her visibly "black" daughter, Cole, of the dangers of "perverts, crazies, dirty old men," Penelope's use of the singular "child" makes clear that Birdie is the only one whose attendance at Nkrumah constitutes abuse, precisely because of Birdie's "whiteness." As Birdie adds, "I noticed she hadn't asked about Cole. She didn't care what kind of school Cole was going to" (106). Cole's visibly marked "black" body devalues her and vacates any notion of her vulnerability, as a preteen girl, to sexual predators, even as Birdie's "white" body takes on a kind of hyper-value as potential victim.

A prior scene actually takes this racial logic to its most extreme conclusion, as Deck and Birdie are accosted by two police officers as they enjoy an afternoon together in the park while Cole is at home, sick. Despite both Birdie's and Deck's insistence that they are father and daughter, the police refuse to believe them, even pulling Birdie aside to say, "You can tell us kiddie. He can't hurt you here. You're safe now. Did the man touch you funny?" (61). What seems crucial to me upon reading this scene—more, even, than the way the text highlights Deck's vulnerability in this moment, his palpable fear of the police officers (60), his fruitless invocation of his status as tenured professor at Boston University—is the presence of an "older, well-dressed" white couple, walking a small gray terrier, the woman's hair "silvery blond," the man "wearing a trench coat and holding a cane" (59). This couple, revealed even in these minute details (leisure clothing that tends toward formal, purebred dog) to be upper class, watch Birdie and Deck long before the police get involved; indeed, they appear to have alerted the officers themselves to Deck's potential "crime":

> When I tilted my head slightly to the side, I saw again that strange couple with their gray terrier, pointing at me. I didn't move, just watched it happen with a lazy interest. They were talking to two men in uniform, the police on their beat, and then the four of them were trudging across the grass in our direction. (59)

In other words, the hand of white racial and class privilege has stepped in to turn the attention of the state toward a black body in need of disciplining and a contiguous "white" body in need of protection. The moment is telling in its revelation of whom, or whose interests, police actually serve.

Thus even when the law is unable to act—since Birdie will not confirm that Deck "touched her funny," will only reassert, however meekly, that he is her father, the police officers eventually desist—"the old couple didn't leave" (61). Instead, their surveillance continues until Deck and Birdie leave the park: "As we walked the distance across the grass to our car, I turned to see them still watching us" (61).

Birdie's instinct, partially stifled by her father, is to gesture rudely and shout at the couple; ultimately, her reaction speaks to the brutality of the mundane yet violative experience of being constantly watched, what Simone Browne calls "the facticity of surveillance in black life."[28] This intrusion destroys a rare moment of father–daughter connection and transforms Birdie and her father from relaxed and content with each other's company to fearful and "tense," all in the name of protecting an idea of whiteness as "utterly pure"—an idea that attaches to *her* body, because of her skin color. This is, of course, the violence that buttresses whiteness, that is necessary to enforce white racial and class privilege, a requirement of whiteness that Cheryl Harris calls the "absolute right to exclude." As Harris notes, "'whiteness' . . . is an ideological proposition imposed through subordination," specifically "the exclusion and subordination of Blacks."[29]

Throughout *Caucasia,* even as she passes for white in New Hampshire, Birdie remains aware of this violence and refuses to embrace it. When I teach *Caucasia* and ask students how they read her character's racial identification, a significant number of students (from across racial and ethnic origin spectra) insist that Birdie identifies as "both black and white," despite the recurrence of moments like this one in the text, in which Birdie deliberately resists "whiteness" and its repeated claims on her body. Birdie's active resistance to whiteness reflects what Joseph calls "*Caucasia*'s vehement argument . . . against the idea of black transcendence," instead insisting upon Birdie's continued relationship to blackness.[30] Such instances of resistance, which unfold with regularity in *Caucasia,* might be read as what I called, in chapter 1, *black bodily return,* the emergence of the body in a privileged context as a means of resisting that context and reasserting blackness. In Birdie's case, however, her white-appearing body complicates the possibility of her flesh alone offering such resistance—instead, Birdie's resistance to whiteness, and to privilege, is most legible when coupled with her voice.

There are moments, for instance, when Birdie's body seems almost involuntarily to rebel in the face of racist assault, as when she begins to wheeze asthmatically (recall her inheritance of asthma from her father) after her neighbor-turned-crush Nick Marsh tells her a racist joke (205). She reacts similarly, "breathing in little asthmatic wheezes" when her white girlfriend Mona wonders aloud if "black guys . . . . got big dicks, like everybody says" (248). She also, in this moment, feels herself "floating" (248) above the scene, in another instance of dis-integration that marks her refusal to accept "Jesse Goldman" as the truth of her identity—even as her embodied performance of "Jesse" becomes more and more real. Yet other moments signal this refusal of privilege more directly, as when Birdie not only rejects whiteness but forcefully, defiantly claims blackness. For instance, when Sandy's boyfriend Jim, after being let in on their secret, treats her father's existence with a condescension befitting his position as a white man who believes (after time spent living in Jamaica) that he knows and has *mastered* blackness—"'And yes'—he sighed, as if he were speaking to a small child—'I know your father is black. I know everything, kiddo'" (271)—Birdie retorts, "Oh, you *do* know everything? That my father's black? I feel so much better now. Did you know I was black too?" (272).

Indeed, Birdie's vocal excoriation of her grandmother's racial privilege near the novel's climax is explicitly applied, in the text, to all of the central white characters: "The words were aimed at my grandmother, but also at my mother, Jim, Mona, and the whole state of New Hampshire" (365). This proud resistance to whiteness marks Birdie as a "black" subject and is a moment of empowerment for her character even as her body is ready to collapse from illness. Indeed, Birdie's physical weakness in the scene, a weakness that her grandmother uses as pretext to dismiss her anger, might instead be understood as a racializing gesture or, again, a black bodily return, a moment when Birdie's blackness finds expression through her body's failure—insofar as "blackness" can be understood as a site of particular *power* because of its vulnerability, its proximity to a fragility that is truly human. I am thinking here of both Darieck Scott's analysis of "a black power that theorizes from, not against, the special intimacy of blackness with abjection, humiliation, defeat" and Coates's more recent words to his son, in *Between the World and Me*: "Part of me thinks that your very vulnerability brings you closer to the meaning of life, just as for others, the quest to believe themselves white divides them from it. The fact is that despite their dreams, their lives are also not inviolable. . . . You have been cast into a race in which the wind is always at your face and the hounds are always at your heels. And to varying degrees this is true of all life. The difference is that you do not have the privilege of living in ignorance of this essential fact."[31] Birdie's physical weakness in the moment of her resistant speech might thus be read as a redoubling of her *black* voice.

Before I turn to a conclusion, then, I want to consider another, final moment in the novel that signals Birdie's explicit resistance to whiteness, a moment when whiteness, as it so often does in this text, represents a specious narrative of innocence as well as a violent sense of entitlement (entitlement, especially, to the disciplining and compliance of black bodies). Shortly before Birdie finds the courage to flee New Hampshire in search of Cole, Jim takes Sandy, Birdie, and Birdie's friend Mona on a pleasure trip to New York City. Early on, while waiting with Mona in front of a museum, Birdie encounters a group of "black and Puerto Rican teenagers" dancing to "some kind of talking music" (read: hip-hop) that she hadn't heard in the six years she'd been away from the urban Northeast, an encounter that prompts her to trail "a few steps behind [her] mother, Jim, and Mona" on their way to lunch, "fantasizing for a moment that [she] didn't know them, that they were strangers" (262).

This subtle distancing becomes more extreme when Jim gets lost in New Haven the next night, on a failed quest to "show [Birdie's] mother a landmark near Yale, the school he had dropped out of once upon a time" (262). Jim circles "the same set of blocks four times," and one member of a "huddle of teenagers . . . sixteen or seventeen, three black kids" that they pass hurls a rock at the car's window, leaving "a small indentation, like a pellet wound" (262). Jim's reaction is swift outrage:

> Jim was struggling to free himself from his seat belt. He was breathing heavily.

> My mother said, "What the hell are you doing? Just drive, idiot."
>
> "No way," Jim said, wagging his finger close to her face. "I'm not taking that from a bunch of little fucking—" He didn't finish his sentence. He was out of the car then and storming toward the boys on the corner, with his hands on his hips. My mother got out of the car and stood at the side, watching. She ran a hand through her hair and cursed under her breath, "Oh, Jesus, he's stupid."
>
> Mona had gone pale. She looked as if she were going to cry. "Mrs. Goldman," she called to my mother, "what's he gonna do? Those niggers are gonna kill him."
>
> I punched Mona's shoulder hard and hissed, "Shut the fuck up. What do you know?" The reaction had been automatic, and I stared at my balled fist now, as if it were somebody else's. Mona gaped at me, open-mouthed, stunned. Then her face crumpled into a cry. (263)

In this moment in the car, as Jim, emboldened by a sense of (white) entitlement, storms off to confront the black boys, Mona and Birdie enact a kind of mirroring of the conflict taking place outside on the street. Mona figuratively finishes Jim's aborted sentence, by filling in the "niggers" to which he does not give voice; in response, Birdie hits her, a reflexive moment of retaliation for Mona's racism that triggers Mona's tears.

On the street, Jim succumbs to a parallel shock and dissolution when his own racist assault is met with similar resistance, down to the punch:

> "Who the fuck cracked my windshield?" Jim bellowed. "'Cuz you're going to pay for it. Now speak up!"
>
> "Can you believe this clown?" I heard one of the kids say.
>
> A stocky boy with braids walked up and stood close to Jim so that they were face-to-face. "Why don't you go home, man? You're not in your neighborhood now. Take your little wife and your little girls and get the fuck out."
>
> I thought it was pretty sound advice. But Jim shoved the kid so that he stumbled into his friends, who caught him. Then I heard Jim say, "Listen, kid, don't tell me where I belong. I used to live in Jamaica."
>
> There was laughter from the group, and it sounded almost jolly. But suddenly a punch was thrown. I don't know which of the kids

> did it, but I saw Jim hurtling backward and falling heavily onto the pavement. (263–64)

Ignoring the warning from one of the kids that his assumed racial privilege, the privilege to control and discipline their black bodies, is limited in this unfamiliar space, a place where he is not only lost but unwelcome ("You're not in your neighborhood now"), Jim asserts his right, as a white man, to colonize black spaces with his presence. His insistence on not being told "where [he] belong[s]" speaks to his belief that he can and should be allowed to move freely anywhere in the world, irrespective of whether he is welcomed by the "natives." His reference to Jamaica, a black nation with a specific history of exploitation by whites for marijuana-fueled leisure, makes this entitled position clear, and the boys' laughter in response, which Birdie at first mistakes for gaiety, reflects their derision and contempt for Jim's condescension.[32]

What most interests me about this scene is Birdie's reaction to Jim's comeuppance at the boys' hands: "I slid low in the seat. I was scared, but also embarrassed. Jim looked like a fool lying there, holding his face and groaning. I didn't want the teenagers to think I belonged with these white people in the car" (264). This strikes me as a provocative moment for a number of reasons. For one, the text is unclear on how Birdie's body figures into her embarrassment. Would she feel the same shame in a visibly "black" body, a body that could easily be identified as different from the "white people in the car," or is her mere *proximity* to Jim's foolhardiness the central issue? Clearly, seeing the black boys, Birdie identifies with them, not with Mona and Jim—as Birdie's narration goes on to offer, "it struck me how little I felt toward Mona and Jim . . . how easily they could become cowering white folks, nothing more, nothing less" (264). But Sandy's actions in the remainder of the scene suggest something of another potential role for whiteness and another way Birdie's character might relate to it, without embarrassment. I quote the passage at some length:

> But unlike [Mona and Jim], my mother didn't seem frightened at all. She was back to her old self as she jumped out, stormed up to the teenagers, and dragged Jim to his feet. She said as she led Jim roughly

> to the car, "All right now. The fun's over. Enough of this silliness." The kids were still mumbling obscenities at Jim, but appeared satisfied with the one blow. They didn't seem to know what to make of my mother, this tall white lady who didn't behave in the least bit ruffled by their bravado. She didn't say two words to them.
>
> She just shoved Jim into the passenger side, got in the driver's seat, and took off. . . .
>
> Jim cradled his face in his hands, and only when we were well on our way north did he look up. He glanced back at Mona and me. His top lip was cracked down the middle and was beginning to bleed.
>
> "I swear, I try to be liberal," he said to no one in particular. "I try really, really hard. But when you meet fucking punks like that, you start to wonder. I mean, Jesus, what did we do to deserve that? We're on their side, and they don't even know it."
>
> My mother turned to him. She wore an expression of extreme disgust. She stared at him for a minute. Then she shouted, "You didn't have to get out of the car, Jim. How idiotic was that? Trying to be a big man for a little crack in the window. They were children. Teenagers. Pranksters. I swear, sometimes your honky ass—"
>
> She ate the words she was on the verge of saying and turned back to the road.
>
> But Jim had heard enough. His face was the deepest crimson I had ever seen it. "What did you just say? My 'honky ass'? Who were you rooting for, anyway? Those ghetto thugs, or me? I mean, fuck, Sheila. Sometimes it's hard to tell with you." (264–65)

Clearly, Sandy in this moment is not "white," not in the way that Mona and Jim are. She evidences not a foolish bravado born of entitlement but actual bravery—calm in the face of potential disaster. She rescues Jim from his own idiocy, navigates the neighborhood that he could not, quickly finds the freeway entrance that had eluded him (265), and vocally resists his narrative of the black "punks" and "thugs" who refused to submit to his (white) authority.[33] And her evident disgust for Jim's thinly disguised "liberal" racism, evidenced in the epithet "honky," also argues for reading her as a kind of race traitor in this moment. Even Jim's

"Who were you rooting for, anyway?" response suggests that Sandy is not properly aligned with the "side" of whiteness. It is interesting, then, that Birdie describes Sandy here as "back to her old self." Her behavior recalls that of the fat, "wild" Sandy who had rejected her blue-blooded ancestry to marry a black man and work as a radical activist. Indeed, despite Sandy's failures as a parent, her seeming inability to understand Birdie's racial consciousness and frequent reference to only Cole as her "black child" ("It was as if my mother believed that Cole and I were so different. As if she believed I was white, believed I was Jesse" [275]), Sandy is the novel's only character that suggests any redeeming possibilities for whiteness—although these possibilities exist only as that whiteness actively resists its own hegemonic power.

Yet Birdie, rather than personally embracing even this version of whiteness, as we might expect her to do as a mixed-race subject, instead continues until the conclusion of the novel to understand herself as black, or more accurately, as simultaneously black and biracial. As she looks at another biracial child on a school bus in the final pages of the book, Birdie's words to describe her—"She was black like me, a mixed girl" (413)—are telling. This simultaneity, the both/and of "black" and "mixed," replaces expected notions of black/white biracial self-identification, which assume the mixed body will understand itself to be "black *and* white."[34] In this characterization of Birdie's racial identity, Senna's novel recalls Naomi Pabst's analysis of mixedness as a category of difference *within* blackness, like gender and sexuality, ethnicity/national origin—or class.[35] Reconceptualizing mixedness as a subjectivity that exists within blackness deescalates questions of racial authenticity, particularly as these are tied to specious ideas about racial biology and the "white blood" circulating within the mixed subject that necessarily claims her away from one sort of racial property, Hartman's black *afterlife of property,* in order to place her body under the covering protection of another, very different property interest. This sort of property, or perhaps more accurately this set of properties, are those that, via violent exclusion, inhere in "whiteness." And particularly for a pale-skinned mixed body such as Birdie's, whiteness as property remains perpetually at the ready to make its claim on her.[36] That the character speaks back to this claim in her particular way in the text, a way that defies narrow notions of biological mixture and instead remains concerned with black *interiority,* allows us to think more deeply about the power within structures of racial identity, particularly for the "mulatto" subject.

By returning to the outmoded word "mulatto" here, I mean to point us back to Ellis's concept of the "cultural mulatto" by way of reaching toward a conclusion. Where do Walker, Senna, and the questions of whiteness, blackness, and material privilege raised in their texts leave us in understanding the post-soul black subject? It would be easy, perhaps too easy, to understand only the characters in other texts touched upon in this book—Bertrand Milworth in *He Sleeps,* J. in Colson Whitehead's *John Henry Days,* Monk Ellison in *Erasure*—as, specifically, cultural mulattoes, given that in each case both of their parents identify, and are identified, as black. But if race is "just about the biggest cultural construct there is," then wouldn't Walker, and Senna's Birdie, *also* be "cultural" mulattoes? Indeed, Birdie's rejection of the conventional understanding of mixed-race as "white and black" in favor of "black and mixed" suggests that the most crucial figure in the phrase "cultural mulatto" is not "mulatto" but indeed, "cultural." If, as Patricia Williams argues, "In the United States, being 'black' virtually always means some mixture of African, Native American, and European ancestry"—and it is worth noting here, quiet as it's kept, that being "white" in the United States often does too—then not only should the very notion of the biological mulatto lose coherence during any conversation in which the constructedness of race has been acknowledged, but the question of how we understand race at all should attend more closely to who or what one claims than to the body's meaning.[37]

The fact that it often does not, that we not only still rely upon biology in our consideration of race but also invoke it even in the terms—like "cultural mulatto"—meant to dismantle its power, suggests that even after questions of cultural authenticity and racial belonging have presumably been resolved, the specter of the "authentically" raced *body* may haunt us. And because class privilege is operationalized in the racial body, because whiteness-as-property has *material* consequences even for black people whose lived experiences are shaped, as well, by the afterlives of (chattel) property, the question of which bodies belong to blackness is always, at least in part, a question informed by our sometimes shifting and provisional class performances, and one that speaks to larger moments of subjective incoherence.

"Half of everything and certain of nothing"—Senna is hardly the first to make an argument about the essentially mixed or multiracial, "mongrelized" American national identity, and it seems no coincidence that what makes her father's story "quintessentially American" is both the known and unknowable details of racial mixture *and* the instability, secrecy, and fundamental unknowability of the subject/self. We might consider how and why this sense of unknowability attaches to a specifically American context and whether—or how—the resultant complexities of identity are both bound by and excessive to the figurative and literal spaces of the United States. In the next chapter, I employ the theoretical frame of black geography to consider two other turn-of-the-twenty-first-century post-soul narratives, novels that depict the gendered complexities of race and class abroad. The contrasting backdrops of, on the one hand, sub-Saharan Africa and, on the other, Western Europe provide particularly dramatic foils for these two works' exploration of privileged subjects in non-U.S. contexts and the ways that the black (American) and bourgeois dilemma might, in fact, travel.

3 Mapping Class

He Sleeps, Black Girl in Paris, and the Gendered Geography of Black Labor

> The history of black subjects in the diaspora is a geographic story that is, at least in part, a story of material and conceptual placements and displacements, segregations and integrations, margins and centers, and migrations and settlements. These spatial binaries, while certainly not complete or fully accurate, also underscore the classificatory *where* of race. Practices and locations of racial domination (for example, slave ships, racial-sexual violences) and practices of resistance (for example, ship coups, escape routes, imaginary and real respatializations) also importantly locate what Saidya [*sic*] Hartman calls "a striking contradiction," wherein objectification is coupled with black humanity/personhood.
>
> —Katherine McKittrick, *Demonic Grounds*

I begin the third chapter of *Black Bourgeois* with these words from Katherine McKittrick's arresting work on black women's geographies of struggle because they highlight the centrality of *place* to understandings of racial subjectivity—a perspective that is crucial to the two novels this chapter will examine, Reginald McKnight's *He Sleeps* (2001) and Shay Youngblood's *Black Girl in Paris* (2000). The "*where* of race" is central to both texts, as each sends a putatively middle-class protagonist outside the United States, with poignant and unexpected consequences for each character's racial and gender positioning. While one character's geographic privilege seems to eclipse, or at least to muddle and obfuscate, his blackness in a context where he has imagined racial solidarity, the other's sense of racialized precarity becomes heavier—moving her away from the freedom she had sought—under the weight of her spatially informed disadvantage. And in both texts, the protagonist engages with the spaces around him or her on explicitly gendered terms, often via a spectacularly, even violently, gendered body.

Yet this book is ultimately a project about class—specifically, about how late-twentieth- and early twenty-first-century African American fiction narrates the paradox of the black and bourgeois subject. How do post–Civil Rights or post-soul texts like *He Sleeps* and *Black Girl in Paris* navigate the dilemma of black subjectivity, both proud and vulnerable, colliding with the presumed—but also restrictive and incomplete—protection of privilege? In this chapter I consider how the answer to this question might be illuminated through particular attention to space and place.

I continue to argue in this book that class cannot be understood *apart from* race and gender, even as it does not remain fully submerged to those categories. The quotation from McKittrick that opens this chapter, raising as it does Hartman's "striking contradiction" between the "objectification" and the "humanity/personhood" of black people, is thus crucial to my discussion here for two reasons. First, I find this passage intriguing for the familiar duality it evokes in a different disciplinary register—McKittrick's spatial reading of Hartman's "striking contradiction" in Western history between black personhood and black dehumanization resonates with what I have highlighted in this project as the simultaneity of (black) flesh and (bourgeois) body. From a geographic vantage point, McKittrick's words remind us that the black and bourgeois dilemma is one piece of a larger paradox, the paradox of blackness itself, suggesting that the complex duality of black subjectivity, articulated over a century ago by W. E. B. Du Bois through the concept of double consciousness, remains with us across multiple spheres of black life in the (post)modern world.[1]

I am also, however, intrigued by the question that goes unasked in the above quotation. Namely, how does *class* exist in space? If there is a "classificatory *where* of race," is there a similar *where* of class, or of class privilege in particular? And how does the where of class intersect with the where of race, particularly as middle-class black American subjects leave the confines of the United States? McKittrick has raised the concept of class in relation to traditional geography, "formulations that assume we can view, assess, and ethically organize the world from a stable (white, patriarchal, Eurocentric, heterosexual, *classed*) vantage point"—but as should be evident, I am interested here in disrupting the neat association between whiteness and material privilege by thinking about how black subjects move across and through these often opposing ideological and political positions.[2]

In previous chapters, for instance, with characters such as *Caucasia*'s Sandy and *Tar Baby*'s Son, I noted that class privilege can be contingent upon circumstance and often should be understood as mutable and shifting, particularly for black subjects. This mutability is informed, for such characters, by their spatial and geographic positioning; in this chapter, however, I want to expand upon this idea of class's *spatial* contingency by examining how the where of class operates across diasporic and international boundaries, and how this classed sense of space might work in concert with racialized global geographies of both domination and resistance. McKnight's and Youngblood's turn-of-the-twenty-first-century fictional narratives are crucial to this inquiry; these works remind us via black American mobility not only that "power and privilege are embedded in the ability to cross national borders and geographic lines" but that such movement can shape, albeit often temporarily, the class positioning of black subjects as and after those borders are crossed.[3] In other words, because place is so integral to these two texts, analysis of them helps us to imagine not only how racialized space might be classed but also how and why different racial spaces actively *class* particular subjects.

These questions seem particularly germane to *He Sleeps* and *Black Girl in Paris* because both novels set their primary story arcs in historically discrete periods and overseas locations that temporally and spatially *defamiliarize* black American subjectivity, thereby making possible new ways of reading blackness and black class privilege across space and time. Writing of an earlier generation of black writers in the mid-twentieth century, Eve Dunbar has suggested that "in some deep sense there is no escape from 'the region of blackness' out of which these African Americans write"; these newer works by McKnight and Youngblood prompt us to ask whether a similar inability to escape a particular, paradoxical sense of black subjectivity continues to obtain decades later.[4] In other words, *He Sleeps* and *Black Girl in Paris* push us to question how and why the black and bourgeois dilemma might remain a conundrum even for the black expatriate of the post-soul era.

It seems important to note at the outset that I am not a geographer; indeed, my work's general theoretical investment in *embodiment* might be construed, critically, as a form of what McKittrick and Clyde Woods have called "bio-geographic determinism."[5] Yet such determinism is hardly my goal. To argue, as I have in previous chapters, that class might be understood as not just one's (fixed) position in an economic hierarchy but as bodily performance, contingent upon context and deeply interwoven with increasingly complex and constructed identity categories such as gender and race, is in fact to remain open to the idea that blackness is "socially produced and shifting" and to apply a similar openness to the categories that coconstitute blackness.[6] My aim in this chapter, then, is to bring an abiding interest in questions of class performance and the contested "territory" of the black and bourgeois body into productive conversation with broader ideas about place and space, paying attention to what McKittrick describes as "the close ties between the body and the landscape around these bodies (the traces of history)."[7]

If it is the case that "often . . . the only recognized geographic relevancy permitted to black subjects in the diaspora is that of dispossession and social segregation" and that in the face of such a "spatializing [of] our imaginations, any sense of black "affluence, professionalism, class, dress, and education sometimes slip[s] away" in favor of "racial-bodily stereotype," then the questions that animate this project on the black and bourgeois dilemma in post-soul fiction might be usefully extended to considerations of how some post-soul texts self-consciously speak to dilemmas of race, gender, and class by manipulating geography—mapping black and bourgeois bodies across space and place.[8] I am interested in the ways that, even as they tell very different stories, both McKnight and Youngblood represent space in their texts as both an ideological product and an active producer of those who move through it. McKnight ultimately uses place to critique a particular kind of black middle-class obliviousness and investment in American exceptionalism by emphasizing the geopolitical underpinnings of privilege for African American subjects, while Youngblood resituates her protagonist in a locale that disrupts her already precarious middle-class status—removing the modest class protections that she enjoys in the United States—to interrogate the notion of privilege and its relationship to race, to creativity, and to gendered labor. In different ways, both novels raise the question of whether and how the black and bourgeois dilemma might *travel* with transnationally mobile African American subjects.

Privilege and Terror in *He Sleeps* and *Black Girl in Paris*

He Sleeps and *Black Girl in Paris* share a number of structural features, despite also diverging, narratively, in several ways—a divergence that will become more important in the latter part of this chapter. Both texts are, as I have already noted, turn-of-the-twenty-first-century works published within one year of each other (*Black Girl in Paris* in 2000, *He Sleeps* in 2001). More curiously, both of these early twenty-first-century texts are set firmly in the twentieth century, specifically in the mid-1980s—and both deliberately absent their protagonists from the continental United States. The "black girl" of Youngblood's title, twenty-six-year-old aspiring writer Eden, travels to Paris in September 1986, while McKnight's thirty-four-year-old African American protagonist, Bertrand, a PhD student, travels to Dakar, Senegal, on a Fulbright fellowship to research urban legends in the spring of 1985.[9]

Thus both novels present black creative or intellectual figures who journey abroad during a politically complex period in recent history—the Reagan era, which, as I have already argued in chapter 1, was a moment of expansion for the U.S. black middle class even as it also constituted a moment of repression and restriction for the black poor and working class after the Civil Rights and Black Power movements.[10] This period in history, the early to mid-1980s, is also a moment during which, despite a Cold War–driven politics of isolation among Western world leaders including Ronald Reagan and Margaret Thatcher, black thinkers continued to advance a sense of the complex interconnectedness of African-descended peoples around the globe, even as they acknowledged that these diasporic connections contained "disunity, misrecognition, differences, and disjunctures."[11] The structural similarities between *He Sleeps* and *Black Girl in Paris* vis-à-vis the temporal position of their characters, as well as those characters' geographic dislocation from the United States, thus point to the turn of the twenty-first century as a moment when older post-soul black artists are both beginning to look back—to the 1980s as a related but distinctly different period within the post–Civil Rights era—and turning outward, beyond the borders of the United States, to consider how post-soul blackness moves globally.

The black and bourgeois dilemma—a sense of racial vulnerability that persists despite the presumably covering protection of class privilege—influences both Bertrand's and Eden's journeys out of the United States, although these journeys subsequently take radically divergent paths. Nods to this classed and raced paradox are evident in both their protagonists' class positioning and the signal role of racial terror in both narratives. *He Sleeps* follows Bertrand, an African American doctoral candidate in anthropology (158) who has traveled to Dakar to complete his thesis research. And while Bertrand's immediate circumstances, as advanced graduate student and lecturer, preclude us from identifying him as particularly privileged economically, his chosen occupation—college professor and scholar—is certainly a middle-class one. Further, the text makes clear his middle-class origins. Bertrand is raised in suburban Colorado Springs, in "the white world" of "small Colorado towns . . . dry air, fir trees, Chinook winds that scale down the mountains" (178). He attends "parochial school" (89)—signaling parents with the financial means, and motivation, to pay for private education and the pedigree that is presumed to come with it.

By contrast, Eden's class status in *Black Girl in Paris* is more ambiguous. Eden describes herself as a "girl born into a poor family" (28), the adopted orphan daughter of two older adults who were orphans themselves:

> When I was four years old my parents told me that I was an orphan. My parents were orphans too. They found each other in church one

> Sunday. Hermine was a big-boned, sturdy, pecan-colored woman, with green eyes and gray hair she kept braided and wrapped around her head. She taught Prior Walker how to read the Bible, and in return he worshipped her. . . . She was a seamstress in a blue-jean factory, and he was the custodian at a bank. (15)

Eden's mother and father are employed in blue-collar occupations involving low-status physical labor such as cleaning and factory work. Instead of bourgeois, then, on the basis of occupation and material resources alone, we might read Eden's family of origin as working class or perhaps as part of the working poor. And describing both Eden and her parents as *orphans* also symbolically denies the family access to generational wealth—recalling the way that class status for black people is so often both aspirational and perpetually in progress. Yet it would be an error to misread an adult Eden as poor or even working class in status based on these circumstances.

As we learn, Eden has always aspired to a life of the mind, a goal that her parents did what they could to support: "When I was thirteen my parents gave me a typewriter, for which they had made many sacrifices" (20). She earns a college degree and, before scraping up the funds to move to Paris, makes her living as an archivist: "Before Paris, at university, I studied English literature, and all it was good for in the end was a job as a librarian" (21). The "library" in which she works, however, is "the basement of a dead man's house" (28), specifically the Villa Louisa, "known locally as the Dimple Mansion, built by the richest black man born into slavery." The house "had become a museum and a memorial to a family of successful African American entrepreneurs" (22). This description of the Dimple family operates as a reminder, in Youngblood's narrative, of how mutable class has been, historically, for black people—one might be born a slave but end up a millionaire, just as one might be, like Eden, "born into a poor family" but become a middle-class college graduate. By situating Eden as an employee of—and *placing* her within—the Dimple Mansion, Youngblood both gestures toward this history of class mobility and aspiration and sets up a contrast between Eden as humble librarian and the outsized wealth of the Dimple family. This positioning is the first moment in the novel in which space and place somewhat obscure Eden's middle-class status. Yet Eden's modestly compensated but professional work, giving tours and working to catalog the vast collection of Dimple artwork, papers, and ephemera, clearly marks her as a skilled, middle-class worker despite her origins.

We might also consider how even the training Eden's parents provide speaks to middle-class *aspiration*: they raise her to observe what we might now call "respectability politics," which scholars have pointed out are frequently indicative of black American middle-class mores and strictures of decorum.[12] Eden's parents teach her to be respectable in a number of ways, both through direct disciplining of her sexuality and gender performance ("Don't let boys touch you. . . . Be a sweet girl" [21]) and through a series of indirect messages about proper (and improper) comportment that she absorbs through differing versions of the black church—one that she encounters with her "holy" (20) and restrained parents, another with her mother's exuberant best friend and adopted "aunt" to Eden, Aunt Victorine.

As Eden notes, at her parents' church, First African Baptist Missionary Church, "the service was orderly, the hymns hushed, and . . . nobody cried too loud or shouted that the Holy Ghost had them by the collar" (17–18); at Aunt Vic's church, by contrast, the Church of Modern Miracles, there was a "three-piece band—drums, electric organ, and electric guitar—and several ladies in the front row who shook tambourines and their ample hips and tremulous breasts all through the service" (18). Eden, whose strong voice leads her to be put in the young people's choir at Aunt Vic's church, is also brought by Aunt Vic to perform "at the age of six in juke joints on dirt roads for miles around almost every Saturday night" (18). Eden notes, "If Mama hadn't found out when I was thirteen, I might've become a star on the dirt floor circuit" (18). In other words, Eden learns a particular kind of middle-class (or middle-class-aspiring) church-girl decorum from her parents' congregation but observes an entirely different aesthetic and cultural approach to worship in Aunt Vic's church, where "People shouted [and] . . . were possessed by the Holy Spirit, who took over their bodies, shaking them with emotion and filling their eyes with tears and their throats with hallelujahs" (18). This version of worship is a fleshly and passionate one, evincing an aesthetic that seemingly extends to (or draws from) the secular, blues-driven performances that Eden is coached into on Saturday nights.[13]

Yet once Eden's mother becomes aware of Aunt Vic's circulation of Eden as performer, instead of being punished for her years of youthful labor as a budding blues woman on the "dirt floor circuit," Eden's talents are contained and disciplined into a more class-appropriate outlet: "I started taking classical voice lessons from a mean old Creole woman who used to be an entertainer. Her long black curls left greasy spots on the collars of her old-fashioned quilted pastel dressing gowns" (18–19). Not only do the lessons themselves shift the genre of music from blues to classical, itself a class marker, but the teacher's "Creole" identity and "long black curls" mark her as a higher-class carrier of culture and bearing. Eden's mother prefers that a teenaged Eden study music in this way rather than through performances in low-class ("dirt floor") outlets for money and attention. Of course, such performances also likely raised moral and practical concerns for Eden's religious mother. Performing as a minor in front of adult crowds, particularly as "Aunt Vic taught [her] to lift the hem of [her] dress and dance at the end of the song like Josephine Baker" (18), Eden could well be risking not just her reputation but her safety. Yet it is difficult to tease such concerns completely apart from the apparent class breach effected by her performances, particularly given the classed nature of the remedy (e.g., formal voice lessons rather than additional time in church or prayer at home).

Considering Eden's parental training in concert with her education, then, I argue that Eden—despite her parents' working-class livelihoods—can and should be read as a black middle-class subject. Or perhaps it might be closer to describe Eden as a black middle-class subject *in the making,* the product of her parents' aspiration and her own self-creation, from orphan to librarian to—she hopes—writer. This, despite the fact that her sojourn to Paris repeatedly emphasizes how little money she actually has. In fact, I want to suggest that Youngblood's narrative situates Eden in Paris in order to strip her *temporarily,* via her spatial positioning, of any of her class protections. This has the effect not only of re-creating Eden's character as an impoverished "starving artist" but also of granting her a critical vantage point from which to view both the geopolitical and economic circumstances within which creative and intellectual labor happens, particularly for black women. Unlike Bertrand, whose geospatial positioning in Dakar reinforces his own gendered privilege, Eden's location in Paris—and the attendant destabilization of her class position—enables her to see both her blackness and her gender critically and through the eyes of an emerging artist. This geographic shift, and accompanying shift in Eden's material circumstances, allows *Black Girl in Paris* to question the relationships between privilege, gender, labor, and creative voice.

Importantly, we can read not just class privilege but also a paradoxical sense of corporeal vulnerability as foundational to both Bertrand's choice to travel to Dakar and Eden's decision to travel to Paris. If we understand both characters as middle class, we must also take note of the ways that both characters, despite this positioning, perceive themselves as perpetually susceptible to racial terror. The persistence of this racialized sense of vulnerability for Bertrand and Eden runs counter, in many ways, to black expatriate narratives and mythology from earlier periods in American history, which have suggested that other parts of the world, and Europe in particular, might serve as a kind of safe haven for black American artists and writers fleeing U.S. racism.[14] Thus we might understand *He Sleeps* and *Black Girl in Paris* to be speaking to a newer, post–Civil Rights or post-soul sensibility about place—one that refuses to understand any locale around the world as a space of safety from anti-blackness. While a figure like the eponymous (and perpetually coming or going) protagonist of Andrea Lee's *Sarah Phillips* gestures in this direction, as when a racist insult from her French boyfriend makes clear that "the bright, frank, endlessly beckoning horizon of the runaway had been, at some point, transformed into a complicated return," Youngblood's and McKnight's texts, both published some fifteen years after Lee's, offer more explicit attention to black vulnerability's global reach.[15]

In the case of Bertrand, his deep-seated fear of racialized violence is only revealed near the end of the novel, as he explains a long-standing mystery within the text, the mystery of why he had been so invested in "privacy" that he refused to cohabitate even with his own wife:

> Private, private, I had to be private. . . . I let all these stories mess with my mind. I remember this young couple who were murdered out on Gold Camp Road, back when I was in high school. Black boy, white girl, both sixteen. They were out hitchhiking, not far from where the girl lived, near Cheyenne Mountain. Some guy picked them up, drove them down Gold Camp, shot them dead, and cut off their ears. . . . I was sixteen myself, when I read that story, and it made me feel that our homeland, our whole fucking country, is full of people like this. The whole goddamn planet. So I suppose I learned to believe that people like us need to be quiet and careful. (208–9)

What Bertrand here describes is a lingering trauma, persistent fear born of his sense of identification with another "black boy," sixteen years old like himself, who is punished violently for his association with a white lover. The punishment involves not merely loss of the boy's life but mutilation of his (and his girlfriend's) body, with the violent removal of the couple's ears signaling a strange kind of refusal of their engagement as human beings—after all, the killer does not cut out their eyes, tongues, or even genitals, but attacks an organ that represents the human ability to listen, to hear not only each other but the world that surrounds them.

The fact that Bertrand extrapolates from this story a sense that the United States is "full of people like this" is hardly surprising, given the history of racial terror in this country—particularly around the perceived sexual threat of black boys and young men toward white women, from Jesse Washington to Emmett Till and beyond. "All these stories" that "mess with" Bertrand's mind are not, after all, apocryphal, but a horrifying fact of black life in America. Yet his addition of "the whole goddamn planet" signals his belief, or his fear, that this virulent hatred of blackness is not confined to the borders of the United States and instead lurks within whites everywhere in the world. This, then, speaks to Bertrand's decision to travel to West Africa, which he sees as a place where he as a black man might find respite in *anonymity.*

Like Bertrand, Eden is traumatized by racist violence during childhood. Her first-person narration in *Black Girl in Paris* notes that "the spring before I arrived in Paris, the city was on alert" (4) due to a series of terrorist attacks in Europe, including a commercial airplane exploding over Athens. Yet Eden reacts to the potential danger of traveling into Europe with world-weary cynicism, as a black American whose childhood was framed by Civil Rights–era violence:

> *I was no stranger to terrorism . . .*
>
> I was born in Birmingham, Alabama, where my parents witnessed the terror of eighteen bombs in six years. During that time the city was nicknamed Bombingham. When the four little girls were killed by a segregationist's bomb at church one Sunday morning in 1963, I had just started to write my name. I still remember writing theirs . . . *Cynthia . . . Addie Mae . . . Carole . . . Denise . . .* Our church sent letters of condolence to their families. We moved to Georgia, but I did not stop being afraid of being blown to pieces on an ordinary day if God wasn't looking. (5)

Just as an adolescent Bertrand identifies with the sixteen-year-old "black boy" who is murdered, a three-year-old Eden identifies with the four young black girls killed in the bombing of the Sixteenth Street Baptist Church. In each case, learning of the death of another black child or children defines the character's childhood in ways that continue to resonate in his or her adult life. As Bertrand goes on to note, for instance, "I didn't live with you, Baby, because I thought they'd track us down, chuck rocks through our windows, burn crosses on our yards" (210). He refuses the marital intimacy that he craves (he "loves to hear the sounds of marital sleep" [85]) for fear of being systemically targeted by racists. By contrast, an adult Eden, survivor of years of post-traumatic stress over the racist terrorism of her childhood, seems to seek out the terrorism that France promises precisely because she has turned her fear inward, into depression and even suicidal ideation: "Bombs were exploding all over the city the fall I arrived, and that made tickets to Paris cheap and suicide unnecessary" (7). Unlike black artists and writers before her, Eden travels to Paris not—or not simply—for creative freedom, or freedom from American racism, but also because the terrorism happening in the "City of Light" feels depressingly familiar.

If both characters are shaped by their class positioning and their experience of racialized vulnerability, both also temporarily reposition themselves through travel. Yet this travel does not, ultimately, free or protect them from embodied precarity. By journeying to an impoverished, postcolonial West African geopolitical site, Bertrand inadvertently *de*-emphasizes his racial hypervisibility as a black person among whites and emphasizes, instead, his spatial and material privilege as an (African) American among Africans. Eden, by traveling to a wealthy European city with little money and few of the institutional and structural connections that Bertrand has (i.e., his Fulbright fellowship), voluntarily abandons much of her own relative material privilege, in the process emphasizing her blackness and her womanhood—both of which operate in concert with her *chosen* poverty to compound her position of disadvantage. For both characters, this re-situation offers the possibility of new perspective on their racial and gendered identities, but each must first arrive at a kind of corporeal violation—for Eden, a desperate brush with prostitution and sex work under the influence of a lecherous, wealthy white man; for Bertrand, a "very crude, very sloppy circumcision" (207) at the hands of a group of Senegalese men—in order to precipitate their new sense of vision. In these two texts, the physical "territory" of the (sexualized) black body thus remains vulnerable to, even terrorized by, the geographical territories within which that body resides.

"Everybody Not Free": Gender, Labor, and Privilege in Dakar and Paris

He Sleeps is told from Bertrand's point of view and, in addition to conventional third-person-limited narration, includes a postmodern assemblage of texts that Bert ostensibly produces throughout his time in N'Gor Village, a small community just outside of Dakar: letters to his sister, best friend, and wife; transcripts of phone calls and imagined conversations; and most important, entries in his journal. As the novel opens, readers learn via one of his letters that a Senegalese family, the Kourmans, has unexpectedly begun living in the other two rooms of the large house he is renting. The drama of the novel takes place largely in Bertrand's mind, as his life in Dakar—which begins as a series of gendered conflicts with Senegalese men over dominance—is increasingly taken over by both the Kourmans's presence and the sudden onset, for Bertrand, of frequent, vivid, sometimes sexual dreams.

These dreams are all the more shocking for him given that, as he claims, "never in all my thirty-four years have I ever dreamed" (30). He has also never been sexually or romantically involved with a black woman, a peculiarity of his character that shapes his interactions with women throughout the text. His wife finds condoms in his suitcase before he leaves for Dakar and believes he intends to end his lifelong flight from black women while on the continent; his deep but unacknowledged attraction to Kene Kourman is made all the more fraught by Bertrand's confused desire to imagine her as "his first, his only, the corporeity of his dreams" (77). By the novel's conclusion, Bertrand's life is utterly upended; Kene's husband, Alaine, accuses Bertrand of sleeping with Kene, something Bertrand cannot remember doing but cannot quite deny. The novel reveals that Kene "gave" Bertrand the dreams by talking to and touching him as he slept (170). At the novel's climax, Bertrand, who is almost constantly asleep—a situation that the novel emphasizes for both its figurative meaning in and literal complications for Bertrand's life—is put on trial for the crime of his alleged dalliance with Kene, found guilty, and punished by Alaine with a forcible circumcision.

This brief synopsis captures only some of this novel's complexity. Only at its conclusion does *He Sleeps* make clear that Bertrand's motivation for traveling to Dakar has a great deal to do with his desire to escape the sense of racialized, bodily vulnerability that accompanies black subjectivity in the United States. The notion that journeying to Africa, in particular, would alleviate the fear of racist violence that plagues Bertrand, however, comes up a bit earlier in the text—but as the novel continually makes clear, Bertrand's fantasy of "Africa" has little to do with the reality of the continent, and especially the specific geopolitical location, Senegal, where he ends up:

> There is something about this path leading to the summer home [the location of the tribunal] that reminds him of the way he used to imag-

> ine Africa before he actually came here. . . . The path is resplendently green and wild, flitting with birds by day, rustling with bats at night. In short, it is the African jungle he'd carried in his mind's eye since childhood, *not so much a place of mystery but of vanishing.* But it is the only such strip of land he has seen in his short time here. The Senegal he's come to know in these five months is semiarid, mostly rolling grassland, interrupted now and then with naked baobab trees and patches of red earth that reminds him of his stepfather's native home of Harlem, Georgia. (180, emphasis added)

For Bertrand, the imagined Africa of his childhood—a stereotypically verdant and "wild" tangle of natural splendor and animal life—is a place not of mystery, as indicated by white fantasies of Africa such as Conrad's *Heart of Darkness,* but rather of "vanishing," suggesting that what appeals to Bertrand about Africa as a location is the possibility that he might lose himself there, his blackness no longer a highly visible exception in a "white world" (178). Yet the next lines of the passage undercut Bertrand's vague and exoticizing fantasy with specificity, a highly particular description of the wide-open Senegalese landscape as "semiarid . . . rolling grassland"—hardly the fertile hiding place that Bertrand has dreamed of—and a reference to "red earth" that serves as a reminder of, rather than an escape from, the black American experience as one grounded in both southern landscapes and urban carcerality (Harlem, Georgia).[16]

We might, in fact, consider Bertrand's dreams themselves as offering a kind of alternate geography in *He Sleeps,* mapping Bertrand's *unexamined* inner reality, and his unconscious or unacknowledged desires, especially as these diverge from the actual landscapes he traverses in Senegal. I emphasize *unexamined* because Bertrand makes clear that he does not experience his dreams as a product of his own consciousness or as something he has deliberately crafted. He understands himself, rather, as a passive victim of the dreams' content, signaling both Kene's role in triggering his dreams and also his lack of self-awareness: "'I had always suspected that people were talking about something they'd invented, imagined. I always believed dreams took one's will. But this thing *happened to* me" (22). Not surprisingly, when Bertrand seeks advice from his research assistant, Idrissa, as to the meaning of one of his dreams, Idrissa's response is to point out Bertrand's own lack of conscious awareness: "'Dreams always mean the same thing,' he said. 'Means you're asleep'" (33).

The dream at the center of Bertrand and Idrissa's exchange is the very first dream that Bertrand has in the novel. In the dream, he travels up a mountain and through a decay-filled swamp with his two brothers-in-law (his lesbian sister's two ex-husbands) in the direction of his parents' house, ending up in his "father's garden," a garden that grows fruits in "shapes like breasts and penises, elbows, brains, faces" (29). This points to his unconscious fantasies about Africa as a literal Eden and to his journey there as one that would cement bonds of brotherhood and provide for him "solid ground" where he might "plant" his "bare feet in the soil" (29) and cleanse himself of the "swill" and "muck" (28) of American racism. This may be Bertrand's unspoken dream of Africa, but the novel repeatedly exposes how what Bertrand seeks, in his mind's eye, from his new location in Senegal, is very different from the spaces and places he actually finds there. Indeed, the contrast between Bertrand's expectations of Senegal as an African American and the reality of his experiences reveals how, as Michelle Ann Stephens has argued, "empire . . . is the context shaping all black travels, displacements, and even engagements with various forms of internationalist discourse throughout the twentieth century."[17] The diasporic brotherhood Bertrand seeks contains within it a colonizing impulse that turns on not only his geographic and material privileges but also on his problematic understandings of black American, and African, masculinity.

Not surprisingly, class privilege is one way that Bertrand is immediately marked as an American, and an outsider, in Senegal. Even without knowing his circumstances, strangers in Dakar make assumptions about his financial status; shortly after he arrives he is surrounded by a group of teenage boys who demand, "'Merican bruddah, you godt money?" (34). Bertrand recalls, "they weren't poor, even I could see that. Western clothed, . . . they dripped oil milk fat honey" (34). The fact that these boys demand money from Bertrand although they "weren't poor" implies a global power differential in which Bertrand's status as (African) American traveler is automatically equated with economic excess—an excess so great that he is expected not to notice, or to acknowledge, the relative privilege of his Senegalese interlocutors. Bertrand is asked to play the role of "wealthy American" to the boys' (literally) assumed poverty, in the process participating in a monetary exchange that plays on the supposed kin relationship—"'Merican bruddah"—between himself and his Senegalese hosts. As Bianca Williams notes, "the classed differences associated with the 'American' in 'African American,' and the subsequent access to class and geographic mobility," trouble the presumed "unity or . . . sameness of diaspora."[18]

There is resonant overlap here between McKnight's fictional narrative of one black American's experience in Senegal and the later, nonfiction account of another black American's experience in Ghana. Saidiya Hartman's 2007 *Lose Your Mother,* a text that weaves memoir, travelogue, and history into critical analysis, tells a similar story of solicitation, also couched in the slippery language of kinship: "As I climbed the muddy incline leading to the entrance of Elmina Castle, a group of adolescent boys approached me yelling, 'Sister!' 'One Africa!' 'Slavery separated us.'" These boys hand Hartman well-worn letters proclaiming their brotherly feelings for her and asking her to help, presumably financially, with their "need of pencils and paper." Hartman goes on to note: "It was a hustle, and we were all aware of this; nonetheless, we assumed our respective roles." These roles of patron and supplicant, beggar and benefactor, imply a pecuniary relationship that Hartman recognizes as inimical to the family affinity that the boys affect: "But how could these scruffy adolescents love me or anyone else like me? You could never love the foreigner whose wealth required you to inveigle a handful of coins."[19] For Hartman, as for Bertrand, lip service to diasporic "brotherhood" cannot adequately conceal the structures of economic exchange and uneven access that shape this interaction.

This incongruity perhaps explains why, in *He Sleeps,* Bertrand has similar problems even from those with whom he is more intimately involved. The fellowship money that he uses for his living expenses is considered a small fortune by many in Dakar, and as a result the Senegalese people Bertrand becomes close to also read him as affluent—a perception that both corresponds to and exceeds his actual material resources in the

United States. After all, in many ways he is "rich" by Senegalese standards, as are most Americans, even if by U.S. measures his lifestyle as a graduate student is more than modest. As Hartman is chastised by a fellow black American, a permanent expatriate living in Accra, "You're still sitting pretty compared to most. Do you know how many families could live on your Fulbright fellowship?" (28). Because he is unable to reconcile or even acknowledge this contradiction, Bertrand is unable to connect fully with any of the Senegalese men close to him, as money and status always create a barrier between them.

For instance, even though the man who will become Bertrand's assistant and confidant, Idrissa, refuses a tip from him when they first meet, because he recognizes Bertrand as a scholar, not a tourist, their subsequent relationship is complicated by the fact that Idrissa is both Bertrand's employee and his guide to the Senegalese cultural marketplace. In one crucial exchange, Bertrand believes that Idrissa has gotten him a good price on his rented room, but when Alaine Kourman discovers how much Bertrand is paying, he accuses Idrissa of cheating his American employer: "He's take advantage of you" (69). Confronted by Bertrand, Idrissa is unrepentant and resentful of Bertrand's dependence on him: "You told me that . . . the university was paying you, and this other foundation, too, who pay you. I didn't think it was your own money" (80). Idrissa's comment highlights the way Bertrand's money is viewed by his Senegalese acquaintances as a kind of windfall rather than "[his] own," earned, money. Indeed, in many ways Bertrand's intellectual work—not perceived as labor in the conventional sense—situates him outside of the economic system in which many of the Senegalese men who surround him operate, creating further distance between them.

Ironically, however, given his anger on Bertrand's behalf, Alaine himself also "take[s] advantage" of Bertrand financially. Alaine, who appears solidly middle class by Senegalese standards—he was educated in France and now has a civil service job—manipulates Bertrand into buying a new refrigerator for the house and into paying Kene extra money for weekly supplies. Bertrand deeply resents these efforts but is paradoxically unable to refuse Alaine's requests. As Bertrand writes in his journal, "I remember every franc he's robbed me of, how frequently he's lied to me: There *was* coffee in the house last Monday. He did have the money for the water bill. He did forget my quinine tabs, and he does owe me the eleven thousand CFA. But do I stand up to him? I do not" (31). Bertrand sees his own behavior as weak, even imagines himself as "the new Mrs. Kourman" (68) because he is unable to stand up to his housemate.

Differing conceptions of masculinity are at the center of this conflict. Bertrand follows a Western model predicated upon "rugged individualism" and defensive displays of bravado, imagining himself as what Paul Smith, referencing film icon Clint Eastwood, has called the "rebellious, maverick, sometimes Promethean hero," or what post-soul critic Mark Anthony Neal defines as the "Strong Black Man," while the Senegalese men that Bertrand encounters privilege interdependence and mutual respect—hence Alaine's seemingly emasculating treatment of Bertrand as a younger brother, a member of his family (68).[20] Despite his dream of finding brotherhood in an African Eden, when Bertrand is actually treated as a brother, with accompanying real-life demands and responsibilities, he is taken aback, suggesting his American inability—or refusal—to adapt to the cultural norms of his actual environment in Senegal.

In addition to his conflict with Alaine, Bertrand's Westernized approach leads to numerous other misunderstandings in his interactions with Senegalese men. One central example is his encounter with a local man named Doudou, whose home Bertrand visits during an ultimately disappointing search for Senegalese palm wine. Indeed, Bertrand's expectations of this native African wine, which he had "craved . . . ever since [he] read Amos Tutuola's novel *The Palm-Wine Drinkard* in college" (97), again reveal the extent to which his perceptions of "Africa" are informed by fantasy and even misinformation and foreshadow the subsequent interpersonal conflict. The very fact that Bertrand's interest in palm wine is piqued by a work of fiction indicates the manner in which his expectations of West African culture are grounded in invention, in what E. Frances White calls the "collective political memories of African culture" that African Americans "construct and reconstruct" for our own purposes.[21] That Bertrand is in Senegal seeking a beverage more common to Nigeria (where Tutuola's novel is set) is also significant, here—to Bertrand as an

(African) American, perhaps these two countries appear interchangeable in spite of their divergent cultures and histories.

Although he describes Tutuola's fantastical novel as "so strange, like a dream"—again suggesting that the dreamscape of Africa is more real to Bertrand than its actual geography—and although Tutuola "never attempts to describe the taste, color, or smell of palm wine" (97), Bertrand nonetheless bases his beliefs about the wine's magical properties on the improbable adventures of the novel's central character. Bertrand muses to himself, "It would be cold as winter rain. It would be sweet like berries, and I would drink till my mind went swimming in deep waters" (99). Not only does Bertrand expect to encounter a sort of delicious and heavenly nectar, but he expects that drinking it will lead him to new levels of mental profundity. These expectations parallel his expectations for West African culture more broadly—as he imagines that his first "taste" of that culture will confer a physical or emotional "sweetness," and an intellectual depth, to him as middle-class (African) American consumer.

Indeed, this connection is made explicitly earlier in the narrative when, during another of his particularly vivid dreams, Bertrand converses with a journalist whose racially ambiguous features "never fall together" (64); his "wide nose festooned with freckles, tired cat-green eyes, rust beard, small ears, short 'fro" (64) signal black American hybridity, but a hybridity that to Bertrand's mind reads as "disjointed flashes" (64), not the presumably pure African coherence he craves. The journalist discusses Senegal with Bertrand in the language of both American cultural consumption and geographic occupation: "Strike out on your own. Take it in; drink it up. You'll like it. Can't help but. It's home, homey. Drink deep, young man" (64). The linguistic parallel between "drink deep, young man" and the old American saw "go West, young man" invokes a spirit of exploration and the colonizing sense of West Africa as uncharted geographical territory, while the man's insistence that "it's home, homey" (use of the slang term "homey" here calling attention to Bertrand's black Americanness) suggests that Bertrand will automatically feel comfortable and at ease within the culture of his presumed ancestors—entitled, as an American, and empowered, as a black man, to consume that culture with confidence. This cultural assumption extends to palm wine, which Bertrand believes will taste delicious to him.

Yet the reality of palm wine not only falls short of Bertrand's sweet fantasies, but it also turns out to be "*awful,*" even "impossible to drink" (107). Notes Bertrand after his first taste, "If you could make wine from egg salad and vinegar, this palm wine is pretty much what you'd get" (107). Instead of an initiation into the "deep waters" of Senegalese or broader West African culture and experience, Bertrand is confronted with his own difference from them. He is shocked by the wine's sour, "sulfuric" bouquet (107), quite literally its *foreignness.* Of course, Bertrand's negative perception of the palm wine has been colored by what he as cultural outsider imagines it should be. The implicit imperialism of this standpoint is what puts Bertrand at odds with many of his Senegalese acquaintances, including Doudou.

Throughout the following scene, which spans several pages in the middle of the novel, Bertrand seems unable to understand this Senegalese man's hostility toward him, although it is directly related to Bertrand's status as outsider to and scholar (but not student) of Senegalese culture. Almost immediately after meeting him, Doudou challenges Bertrand's academic work, highlighting the political meanings that historically have been embedded in the anthropological study of culture: "Omar tells me you're an anthropologist. . . . The study of primitive cultures" (110). Doudou goes on to comment, with some sarcasm, "I knew an anthropologist once . . . who told me I should be proud to be part of such a noble, ancient, and primitive people" (111). Here Doudou critiques the exploitative and racist notion that black Africa is savage or "primitive." He also, however, criticizes the paternalistic attitudes of figures like the unnamed anthropologist, who condescends to instruct the Senegalese on the relative value of their culture, even as he sets up a hierarchical relationship between "noble" savage and Western modernity, intellect, and technological advancement.[22]

Bertrand's response, however, in broken French, reveals his inability or refusal to grasp the meanings behind Doudou's statement, and particularly ignores the condescension of teaching "primitive" peoples that their culture has value: "Maybe . . . he trying to tell you that primitive . . . I mean, that in this case primitive mean the same thing as 'pure'" (111). Here Bertrand takes the same paternalistic position vis-à-vis his African acquaintances, implicitly defending his fellow anthropologist's use of the loaded term "primitive" by euphemistically associating it with purity. "Who studies your people?" Doudou responds. "Do you have anthropologists milling about your neighborhood? Do they write down everything you say?" (112). Doudou here points out the essential power imbalance that exists between (black) American academic and African "native." His question might bring to mind, for us as readers, the ways that African Americans have, indeed, been the objects of anthropological inquiry. Yet in another ironic reminder of Bertrand's class privilege, his inability to respond substantively—instead of answering Doudou's question, Bertrand begins with a patronizing "Look, I know how you must [feel]" (112) before again being interrupted—suggests his estrangement from the impoverished black communities that have most often been similarly investigated. In this instance, class and region supersede the shared racial affinity that Bertrand assumed would exist with his Senegalese host. Instead, in Bertrand's role as black American scholar of Africa he stands in for an entire history of Western exploitation of the global South, for the sake of knowledge.

Reiterating this point of view, another Senegalese man present during the exchange states hotly, "I get offended. I get very offended. You write us down. You don't respect us. You come here and steal from us" (112). In response, Bertrand claims that he is "trying to help all black people by recovering our [lost] things" (112). Bertrand's "trying to help" argument here, and his use of the first-person-plural possessive, "our," suggest that he sees himself as a "native" anthropologist, that is, an anthropologist who studies his own cultural group, often "for the explicit political benefit of those co-natives under study."[23] Yet Bertrand, as a black American, is not truly a "native" to West African culture. Worse, he cannot seem to recognize his outsider status or the multiple arenas (geographical, national, ethnic, and material) in which his identity is not only marked differently from the Senegalese men's but also monetarily privileged over theirs in historically informed ways. In Hartman's words, "Who else but a rich American could afford to travel so far to cry about her past?"[24] Indeed,

Bertrand seems unaware that his very investment in staking a claim upon a mythicized, lost African inheritance marks him with the "sense of not belonging and of being an extraneous element [that] is at the heart of slavery"—in West Africa, a signal of his status as outsider.[25]

Thus even when Bertrand tries to rearticulate his black identity in the face of the men's hostility, his efforts only highlight what the Senegalese men see as a fundamental difference between them. This is clear in Doudou's reply: "Things lost? . . . That must mean you're not pure. . . . [Y]ou think you can come here and bathe in our primitive dye, legitimize your blackness to the folks back home" (113). Given Bertrand's fantasies of palm wine, the way that he imagines a taste of the liquid will send him to "deep waters," we might well take Doudou's words as an accurate description of Bertrand's motives. But rather than expressing contrition after being thus called out for his misstep, Bertrand attempts to turn his own status as privileged American "Other" against his adversary. In response to Doudou's hostile reference to his cultural impurity, Bertrand himself highlights the narrative analogy between palm wine and African culture, this time via a rejection of that culture, in his attempt to insult Doudou: "'Want some palm wine?' I said to Doudou. 'It really tastes like crap'" (113).

The exchange culminates with Doudou asking Bertrand: "How does it feel . . . to be a black toubob?" (113). *Toubob,* a Wolof word that can mean both "stranger" and "white," is here rightly taken by Bertrand as a counterinsult, especially after he tries to clarify in which sense Doudou is using the word, and Doudou replies aggressively, "In Wolof, 'toubob' is 'toubob' is 'toubob'" (113). In other words, Bertrand's status as Western "stranger" here reduces him to whiteness; such an accusation is particularly painful for a middle-class African American man whose connection to black identity is already tenuous at home. These interethnic and international clashes foreground global narratives of racial identity and their relationship to material privilege, as well as Bertrand's simultaneous discomfort with his position as a "rich" American and related lack of consciousness about the political ramifications of his anthropological work in Senegal. In this black—African but not American—context, the black and bourgeois dilemma fractures, not into safety but into a parallel alienation. Just as it might in a working-class black American context, Bertrand's black flesh accompanied by privilege fails to signify clearly to his Senegalese hosts, and the racialized belonging that he had imagined Africa would offer eludes him. In Senegal, his bourgeois status is only emphasized by the geographic privilege that accrues to his Americanness; both lead to his dismissal as a toubob, or stranger, and suggest, ultimately, that Bertrand's idyllic dreamscape can never become his reality.

Youngblood's *Black Girl in Paris* is a *Künstlerroman,* an artist's coming-to-voice novel, about a young black woman, Eden Walker, who leaves everything she knows behind in order to travel to Paris and become a writer. Throughout the text, Eden is seeking to come into herself, creatively, and to follow in the footsteps of her idol, James Baldwin, in some way; she hopes even to meet and perhaps learn from him, and to find her writerly voice. As she notes on the first page of the novel:

> James Baldwin, Langston Hughes, Richard Wright, Gabriel Garcia Marquez and Milan Kundera all had lived in Paris as if it had been part of their training for greatness. When artists and writers spoke of Paris in their memoirs and letters home it was with reverence. Those who have been and those who still dream mention the quality of the light, the taste of the wine, the joie de vivre, the pleasures of the senses, a kind of freedom to be anonymous and also new. I wanted that kind of life even though I was a woman and did not yet think of myself as a writer. (1–2)

While for Eden Paris's significance rests in the site as the home of her artistic development, the reverence with which she speaks of and imagines the city is akin to Bertrand's imagined sense of Africa in *He Sleeps*; in both cases, a real geopolitical location takes on a far more potent symbolic meaning in the fantasy world of the protagonist. Eden and Bertrand *imagine* Paris and Dakar, respectively, as places to be free, "anonymous and also new," yet both characters find that the real places they encounter are far different from their fantasies.

After her father's sudden death of a heart attack (30), Eden, inspired by the freedom fantasies of her Aunt Vic ("she talked about [Paris] as if it were a made-up place" [17]) and driven by her own dreams of "a kind of life different from the one [she] was living" (19), scrapes up money for a plane ticket to Paris and arrives there with a few hundred dollars and plans of working to keep herself afloat. These plans grow increasingly complex and desperate as Eden discovers how difficult it is to live outside of the modest class privileges she possessed in the United States. At the novel's end, after becoming so strapped for money that she flirts with both prostitution and performing in an "erotic art film" (228), Eden finally finds her voice as a writer—coincidentally, before she actually encounters James Baldwin, on the penultimate page of the novel and during her "last day in Paris" (235)—and spends weeks holed up in a tiny room triumphantly writing down her story.

The title of the opening section of Youngblood's text, "museum guide," begins a pattern that continues throughout *Black Girl in Paris* of naming each section of the novel for the job or role that Eden holds during the period that section details; in this way, *Black Girl in Paris* is structured by Eden's labor. Notably, this extends to emotional labor, as three of the nine sections of the text—"traveling companion," "lover," and "thief"—detail Eden's various romantic entanglements in ways that highlight how much effort each relationship demands of her. Yet whether affective or physical, paid or unpaid, this story of Eden's labor is far more compelling, and risky, for her character in Paris than it is in the United States precisely because of the way she is stripped of class protections in her new environment. Eden cannot work in middle-class, salaried employment while in Paris, because "stricter immigration rules" in the mid-1980s made it nearly impossible to get a "carte de séjour, an official work permit issued by the French government" (60).[26] While she enacts a plan to find work anyway, her French friend Delphine warns her, "If you are caught working without a permit you could be deported" (61). Thus, unlike Bertrand's experience in Dakar, Eden's experience in Paris is one of sharply increased material precarity, as she must seek work that is off the books, paid in cash, and offered by individuals rather than institutions, in some cases individuals who themselves have limited funds to pay her—highlighting what LaShawn Harris calls "the complexities, danger, and unsteadiness of underground work."[27]

Eden's first paid work in Paris, for instance, is as a model for an impoverished painter and Holocaust survivor, Monsieur Deschamps. This is the first of several jobs Eden takes that reduce her to her body; as she says of the experience of working as an artist's model generally, something she did once while in college: "I took off my robe and became a body, an art exercise, a statue" (68). It is worth noting that when Eden does such labor in the United States, it is not because she needs the work to survive but as a last-minute favor to her professor:

> When I was in college I was asked by my art history professor if I wanted to make extra money modeling for an evening art class. One of the regular models had not shown up and they were desperate (67).

By contrast, both of the times Eden works as an artist's model in France, her own financial need guides her choices. She seeks out and answers Monsieur Deschamps's ad for a model because "I had only two days to find a job or I would soon be sleeping on a park bench or trying to sell my clothes from a blanket in the métro" (57). The imagined, even romantic quality of Eden's hypothetical destitution here marks this as an early moment in her journey in Paris; by the time she again works as an artist's model near the end of the text, after stints as an au pair, poet's helper (in-home nurse, assistant, and "maid" [129] for a physically incapacitated writer), English tutor, and even (inadvertent) thief, Eden is the one who is nearly "desperate" for money: "I would not have been lying naked on a sofa in an almost empty apartment in the chemin du Casse Pieds if I had not been hungry and the artist were not paying me so well" (225–26).

Like early post-soul character Sarah Phillips's game of Galatea with her French boyfriend Henri and his friends, in which Sarah "stood naked on a wooden box and turned slowly to have [her] body appraised and criticized," this positioning of Eden as nude model—embodied object—in Paris has a particular, fetishized history.[28] It recalls Khoisan woman Sarah Baartman, "Born in South Africa in 1789 [and] . . . exhibited on stage and in a cage in London and Paris" from 1810 until her death five years later, under the name "Hottentot Venus."[29] She was dissected by Georges Cuvier after her death, and her brain, skeleton, and genitalia remained on display at the Musée de l'Homme in Paris until the mid-1970s. Her tragic story remains that of an "icon of the black female sexualized savage."[30] This history haunts Eden's turn as a nude black woman on display in France; indeed, Baartman might be understood as more of—or at least just as much of—an artistic forebear for Eden than Baldwin is, despite

Eden's desire to trace her creative lineage through only her "literary godfathers" (4).

The freedoms those figures (specifically James Baldwin, Richard Wright, and Langston Hughes) find in France are much more difficult for Eden to access as a black woman. As Jennifer D. Williams has noted, "The ease with which . . . a black woman's performance of Galatea conjures the Venus Hottentot casts doubt on travel-as-freedom, by exposing racism's inescapable boundaries."[31] In fact, these boundaries are not only those of race and racism. As with Bertrand's tense conflicts with Senegalese men in *He Sleeps,* often over money—conflicts shaped by differing conceptions of masculinity—Eden's encounters in *Black Girl in Paris,* particularly those related to her labor, are explicitly *gendered.* And despite her expectation that relocating to Paris will free her from systemic racial and gendered oppression, these gendered encounters almost always evoke a long and familiar history of whites devaluing and exploiting black women's bodies and labor. After her short-lived stint as a model for Monsieur Deschamps, who lets her go because he cannot afford to pay her, Eden places ads around town, at "the American Church, the British Council, and the American Embassy":

> *American Girl Seeks Employment as Au Pair, Typist, Private Secretary, House Painter, Companion. Experienced. Reasonable rates.* (87)

With the possible exception of house painter, the positions that Eden lists in the ad are all low-paying, low-status, gendered work, and this gendering is reinforced by the word "girl," which Eden uses "because all the other ads said it, and 'woman' in that context seemed too, well, womanly" (88). This is no coincidence; the nature of the work Eden seeks depends both upon the notion of this low-paid work as temporary and contingent, the sort of work that an inexperienced "girl" might do without opening her employer to charges of exploitation, and upon a history of infantilizing and disrespecting such workers, especially men and women of color.[32]

Indeed, given the racist history of the word "girl" (and "boy") in the U.S. South, in which black adults in service roles were infantilized by whites, it is no surprise that Eden recoils when the infirm English poet who hires her as a caretaker says casually, "my girl will let you in" (124). Notes Eden, "I hope that the girl she is referring to is her daughter"—

though, of course, she is not the poet's daughter but a maid, a "French girl wearing a uniform of a simple gray dress with a plain white collar" (125). Eden is well aware of the history that attaches to the notion of being a laboring "girl," described and used as a kind of possession. In speaking of the aged poet, Elizabeth, Eden acknowledges not only that "my people have a history of service to her people" (122) but also that "her skin is pale and privileged, mine is brown and sweaty from labor in her house" (122–23). The poet herself projects upon Eden's body a history of black enslavement and possession, imagining herself into a fantasy of absolute power over Eden, a perversion of the power that an able-bodied Eden holds over Elizabeth given the latter's illness and infirmity: "She said to me once that in glory days I would have been presented to her as a gift, like a toy at Christmas . . . and she wouldn't have had to pay so dear a price" (123).

Eden wants to refuse this positioning of her black body as laboring object, but she cannot do so completely; instead, she allows her long-desired situation in the city of Paris, and her need for rent money and food, to compromise her presumed principles:

> I don't want to be anybody's girl. My mother worked for white people all her life so I wouldn't have to, she constantly reminds me. I don't want to disappoint her, but I have not met James Baldwin, written a novel, or fallen in love. I want to stay a little longer in this place, and for that I am willing to do many things. (124)

Notably, *place* here provides the justification for Eden's embodied compromises, her willingness to labor in ways that her parents' hard work and class aspiration—and her own college education—would otherwise make unnecessary for her. Eden chooses to participate, via her continued labor, in the poet's fantasy of her as her "girl" because of the pull of her own fantasies and desires—to meet James Baldwin, to write a novel, to fall in love—dreams that she believes can only come true for her in Paris. Eden ultimately continues to work for the poet until Elizabeth shares what has drawn Eden in all along, James Baldwin's location in the south of France.

At other points in the text it is only the threat that her labor—already profoundly physical and embodied—will turn specifically sexual that motivates Eden to set strict boundaries on what she will do for money.

Throughout the novel, even as she is willing to engage in many different kinds of informal labor to survive, she is unable to set aside "childhood lessons of religiosity, chastity, . . . and other tenets of respectable politics" to accept "extralegal employment [sex work, in particular] that was incongruent with learned and expected family and community values."[33] For instance, when Eden hears from a Swedish au pair of a nanny position with a French family that pays 8,000 francs (110), she inquires, only to realize that in addition to childcare and cleaning responsibilities that amount to those of a "full-time slave" (116), the position involves sexual exploitation by Monsieur Fabre, who is "usually very fond of the au pair" (118). Upon Eden's arrival at the Fabre home, the door is answered by a "very pretty, petite dark-skinned woman" (113) in an ill-fitting maid's uniform who speaks only "rapid Spanish" (113) in response to Eden's queries. Eden later observes her "holding on her lap a baby that looks like her own" (117). As Madame Fabre mentions in passing that "there are some aspects of the job that may strike you as unconventional" (117), Eden begins to understand the sexualized pressures of the position: "I thought of the pretty young woman in the kitchen and wondered about the baby on her lap. I was sad to have found that I wasn't so far from home after all. No thank you, Madame Fabre, I'd rather eat mud" (118). Eden's refusal of this offer paradoxically speaks both to her privilege as a middle-class black American, still invested in respectability politics—since Eden's ability to decline the job, and with considerable disdain, positions her above the less fortunate "dark-skinned" woman in the kitchen—and to the racism and sexual exploitation built into domestic labor both in the United States and globally, to which Eden's presence in France makes her, ironically, more vulnerable. As Eden observes, the specifics of the job and the lingering presence of a previous victim in the person of the current maid, remind her that in Paris she is not "so far from home" as she might have hoped.[34]

Ironically, the position Eden here refuses turns out not even to offer the generous pay that she had imagined; during the interview, Madame Fabre tells Eden that the pay is only 5,000 francs per month, and responds to Eden's gentle inquiry about the rumored 8,000-franc salary, "You misunderstood" (117). Clearly, a position that would merit 8,000 francs per month when performed by a white, Swedish woman is not so lucrative when Eden is the potential hire. Recalls Eden, "I remember my mother's stories of being turned down for jobs or being refused housing or being offered lower wages because she was black" (117). Once again, Eden's potential labor reveals that her positioning, even in France, is not "so far from home"—just as happened to her mother in the U.S. South, Eden finds that her blackness leads to an immediate devaluing of her laboring body.

This devaluing has everything to do with the way her racial origins are marked on her flesh; Eden's narration includes the line "I was born in America, but you could look at me and see a map of Africa" (88). Because "Africa" is mapped onto Eden's black body, any privilege that would normally accrue to her as an American abroad—the sort of geopolitical privilege that Bertrand unwittingly relies upon and is ultimately punished for in Senegal—does not operate in the same way, or at all, for Eden in Paris. The Welsh au pair who was employed by the American family immediately before Eden tells a story of following "American tour groups" on her days off and managing to "blend in": "she would often be asked to join them for meals and invited onto their large buses for tours of the countryside" (151). These experiences are unavailable to Eden: "I could not blend in so well. My skin marked me, set me apart even though I was the American" (151). Just as the black and bourgeois dilemma fractures for Bertrand in the black-but-not-American context of Dakar, it fractures, and is refracted, differently for Eden in the white-but-not-American context of Paris. Her black skin obviates any privilege that might accrue to her as an American abroad, compounding the disadvantage of her temporarily diminished material circumstances, in her Paris life as a (laboring but) starving artist.

In addition, the "map of Africa" that marks Eden's body precludes her ability to find refuge in Paris from American-style racial terror. Instead, the vulnerability of her black flesh travels with her to her new environment. Eden becomes involved with Ving, a white American jazz musician raised in New Orleans, with whom she falls in love in defiance of her upbringing and her sense that such a pairing constitutes "disloyalty to the race" and a reenactment of the "master-slave relationship" (150). Unlike

Bertrand, who has never been with a black woman, Eden's foray into interraciality is a first for her, something she believes is possible precisely because she is in Paris and there is "no one to judge [her] actions"—she is "a free woman and could choose whom and what [she] wanted" (150). On a date, however, walking home from a jazz club late at night, Eden and Ving are accosted by four young Frenchmen who call out insults ("*T'as vu, le pédé qui promène son chien noir.* Look at the queer walking his black dog" [164]) and throw empty beer bottles at them. Eden is violently reminded of the anti-black environment—notably bolstered, here, through a concomitant homophobia—she thought she had left behind in the United States: "Not far enough away to escape a familiar kind of humiliation. No translation was necessary" (164).

The text frames Eden's reaction to this incident as precisely a question of class standing and privilege, erased or made irrelevant in the face of racist violence—the black and bourgeois dilemma made manifest in the streets of Paris. Eden remarks:

> "Everybody not free, somebody somewhere is a nigger tonight." My father's words blazed in my memory. Those men hadn't cared that I was American, college-educated, and Christian; all they saw was the color of my skin. Back home, I still wouldn't be able to hold Ving's hand without inviting comment or threat. What made me think I could be free? (164)

Eden is "American, college-educated, and Christian"—middle-class, and ostensibly privileged both geopolitically and in terms of her religious beliefs—and yet she is reduced to the derogatory terms "*Salope. Putain. Chien Noir* (Bitch. Whore. Black dog)" in these men's eyes. Thus the thousands of miles between Paris and the space of "back home," where there is no question that her interracial relationship would render her unsafe, seem to disappear in an instant, and Eden's location becomes a familiar one of *un*freedom. Notably, her sense of herself as unfree is haunted by the warning voice of her late father, whose words point out both the historical price of so-called freedom—in Western conceptions of liberty, "somebody somewhere" must be the "nigger" in order for others to perceive themselves as free—and the irony that Eden's location-based sense of herself as a "free woman" has proven largely illusory. No matter where she is in the world, she brings the "territory" of her black body and the "traces of history" that accrue to it.[35] The *where* of black class privilege quickly becomes, for Eden, nowhere at all.

Respatializing the Black and Bourgeois Subject Abroad

At the conclusion of the tribunal evaluating whether Bertrand has slept with Kene, Bertrand is found guilty. His own journals are used as evidence against him (196), and while the group concludes that Kene manipulated Bertrand to her own ends, this manipulation is less important to the group of men judging Bertrand than his own seeming complicity: "Yes, Kene used charms, but the question is, did she need them?" (200). Bertrand's final, frenzied attempt to counter the accusations not only proves fruitless but returns, obliquely, to the fear of racial terror that motivated his journey away from the States in the first place:

> I dream that I flip through the pages with my sweaty hands and look for a passage that I think would help me. I can't find anything. Everything I read seems to suggest that I really did want the man's wife. I did, and I didn't. What I really wanted was to be in a relationship that the world wouldn't despise. (201)

Bertrand's desire for Kene, in other words, like his desire to "vanish" into a fantasized African jungle, is in truth a desire for both racial anonymity and an accompanying geographical asylum. Kene represents "the corporeity of his dreams" (77) because he imagines—naively—her black body as safe harbor for his own, just as he has imagined Africa more generally as a place where his blackness would mark neither hypervisibility nor invisibility but rather a sort of collective safety that Bertrand, raised in a "white world" (178), has never known.

As the tribunal concludes, however, Bertrand's body is deeply in danger; not only does he come to understand that "they have [his] life in their hands" (203)—a realization that precipitates first a desperate attempt to escape and then a disingenuous confession "to everything" (203)—but his punishment is a crude circumcision, performed against Bertrand's will by the aggrieved party, Alaine. While this circumcision is again framed as a question of masculinity ("I could have made you a woman, but I decided to make you a man. Go in peace" [204]), it nonetheless operates as a violation and a deadly threat against Bertrand's life. When Bertrand fights to break free from the men who hold him down for the act, Alaine's friend Allasambe warns, "Berdt, if you struggle, he might miss and kill you" (204). Thus, Bertrand's sense that the space of Dakar, or of West Africa more broadly, might provide a safe haven for him as endangered black American is shattered by this disfigurement of his body. The circumcision, enacted by the very community he imagined could protect him, is a sexualized violation accompanied by the not-so-subtle threat of actual death.

The end of Bertrand's story suggests that his journey from the United States to Dakar has ultimately done little to assuage his deep-seated fear of racialized violence. In fact, the "sleeping sickness" that he is only beginning to overcome as he recuperates in a hospital at the conclusion of the novel—alluded to in the work's title, *He Sleeps,* and throughout the story, as both narration and other characters reveal that Bertrand "sleep[s] all the time" (207)—suggests a deeper meaning for Bertrand's somnolent lack of awareness. Bertrand sleeps because he is unwilling to face the truth of his existence as a black American subject. Even at the end of the text he believes that to recognize and admit to himself the depths of American racism—like that of the "White Knight" who writes to a college friend of Bertrand's, a white woman who preferred black men, that he could only "think about [the black man's] King Kong dick in her white pussy" (209)—is somehow to embrace its logic: "You can't be aware of a thing without in some small, subtle, deeply subconscious way believing it, no matter how it may contradict truth or mother wit" (210). Bertrand's groundless shame, his irrational belief in the truth of the "White Knight's" fantasy that interracial couples were "only walking cunts and cocks" (210), reveals that he, still, sleeps.

Eden, by contrast, arrives at self-awareness, and something we might call empowerment, by the end of *Black Girl in Paris*—despite also enduring a sexualized crisis of embodiment. She is not violated in the same way that Bertrand is, but her body, and particularly her body as commodified and sexualized object, becomes increasingly at stake in the text, culminating in circumstances that she finds not only humiliating but dangerous. The book's penultimate chapter, "artist's model II: vence," describes Eden's final paid position in France, her second turn as an artist's model. Here she works for an older, wealthy white painter named Jake, whom she recognizes as "bad news" (228) the first time he casually touches her: "I felt a chill run down my spine. It felt like a warning, but I brushed it aside" (227). Still obsessed with fulfilling her own dreams of finding a writerly voice in France, Eden once again accepts an exploitative situation in order to stay in the country just a bit longer. Shortly after meeting her, Jake invites her to be part of an "erotic art film" for extra money, again a sexual boundary that she is unwilling to cross: "He called them erotic but they were nasty any way you looked at them. . . . Erotic to him meant women humiliated, submissive, spread open for his pleasure" (228). And while Eden refuses this request of Jake's with the narrative aside "He knew I needed money, but I was not as desperate as that" (228), the text has already highlighted Eden's desperation via an apparent willingness, only a few short weeks before she meets Jake, to enter into prostitution.

In "thief," the chapter of the novel immediately preceding "artist's model II: vence," Eden's friend and unconsummated queer love interest, a young Bajan woman, painter, and hustler named Lucienne, teaches her "how to get by" with a list of prescriptions under the heading "how to be a whore (if all else fails)" (201). In fact, in the chapter preceding "thief," titled "english teacher," Eden is relieved to discover that a man she thinks is soliciting her for sex ("We crossed the street and soon came to a small hotel. He started inside. I stopped in my tracks, realizing the kind of place it was and the kind of girl he thought I was. I started to cry" [184]) actually wants to hire her to converse with him in English (185). Yet despite her dismayed reaction, Eden has followed the man to his hotel knowing that he might be seeking a prostitute ("I didn't want to understand what the man was asking for" [183]) precisely because she "needed money so badly" (183) and the man had promised to pay her. Thus the novel presents, chronologically, a gradual and progressive breakdown of Eden's limits as her financial circumstances deteriorate. Despite her efforts to hold on to agency, Eden's increasingly literal embodiment of the fantasy status of "starving artist," as she is stripped of her material privileges in Paris, makes her black and female flesh more and more vulnerable to exploitation and potential violation.

Indeed, this moment in *Black Girl in Paris* recalls another post-soul text, Z. Z. Packer's 2003 short story "Geese," in which Dina, another young, precariously classed black woman, travels abroad, in this case to Japan, and eventually finds herself financially desperate, unable to survive except via sex work.[36] Both Packer's and Youngblood's texts remind us that for black women abroad, particularly in non-black spaces, the racist history of framing black women's bodies as hypersexualized commodities makes prostitution and other sex work the always available solution to material precarity, a solution that is also, often, a crisis. By the time Eden becomes one of "Jake's girls" (229) she has avoided having to "choose" prostitution but believes herself to be in physical danger of a different sort:

> I wondered what my mother would think of her little girl if she saw me stretched out naked, mauled by the eyes of a drunken hairy beast. I wondered if she would have understood why I wanted to meet Baldwin so badly. Nothing had prepared me for that moment in that dusty room with cobwebs lacing the corners. At first I wondered if I would have to do battle with him and run naked down the marble staircase and into the square below filled with plane trees, old pensioners, and tourists sipping beer through straws. (229)

Eden fears being raped by Jake, but she also is reminded, in this moment of fear, of her mother's judgment, the class training in respectable decorum that Eden's very presence on Jake's sofa disrupts. Yet this class training has not "prepared" her for actual racialized and gendered precarity, precipitated by her assumed poverty—a precarity that she is willing to "battle" through for the sake of her writerly dreams. Here, again, Eden recognizes that her mother's approval, and being "respectable," cannot supersede her desire to find herself as a writer. When a friend of "Jimmy's" stops by Jake's home for a beer and reveals that Baldwin "was not well, that he was not in St. Paul De Vence just over the hills from where we were sitting . . .

but that he was in Paris working on an upcoming theater production of *The Amen Corner*" (231), Eden's stunned "panic" motivates her to leave Jake's sexualized exploitation behind for good. Instead, she "slip[s] away unnoticed" and returns to her desk, as "between [her] tears words began to bloom on the page, one after the other" (231).

Crucially, this moment in which Eden finds her writerly voice is framed as one of geography—of *mapping.* Eden writes to understand the where of her life up to this moment:

> The maps I'd made were guides to my interior. I remembered all the places I'd been, all the things I'd seen, and I caught them in my imagination. Jimmy was with me and Langston too. I wrote to understand where I had been, where I was going, to make sense of the world that had led me to the small room on the edge of the abyss. (231–32)

And although she finally realizes that "There was power in the pen" and even that "I didn't need Jimmy to tell me that" (232), Baldwin remains for her a powerful symbol of the *where* of writerly freedom. Not coincidentally, when she encounters Baldwin on her last day in Paris, his inadvertent gift to her is also a map, this time a literal one. After Baldwin, visibly ill, "frail and weak" (235), recognizes her need for his benediction and gently embraces her in the street, he departs with his aide in a taxi. A waiter from the restaurant he has just left rushes out and hands Eden something Baldwin had left behind—a map of London, with "words . . . scrawled across the lines of the map like directions" (236).

Eden, who at the start of the novel is unable to think of herself as a writer, instead imagining herself as a cartographer ("*I was a mapmaker*" [2]), by the conclusion of the text comes to understand that "a story is like a map" (227), both in its rendering of worlds we know and its status as guide to worlds we have not yet seen. It is no coincidence that the map she inherits from Baldwin is of London, not Paris—hinting, perhaps, at another destination for Eden the newly minted writer. Baldwin's "small and wild" (236) words scribbled across the map operate as markings across space and time, guidelines for Eden's passage into creative maturity.

Thus we might view Eden's negotiation of space in Paris, and her literal mapping of the city and her own experience of it through her writing, as what McKittrick calls a "respatialization"—of questions of European mastery, colonial power, and even writerly voice. McKittrick notes that "if practices of subjugation are also spatial acts, then the ways in which black women think, write, and negotiate their surroundings are intermingled with place-based critiques, or, respatializations."[37] Eden's mapping of Paris via her labor poignantly underscores the price that she must pay to come to voice:

> "You have to make sacrifices to be an artist," [mentor and onetime lover] Indego had said the last time I saw him.
>
> *I will keep one of the blurry photographs* [taken by Jake] *to remind me of my sacrifice. Though my flesh will remember and though my flesh will fade away, my mind will remember.* (229)

Eden carries her sacrifices with her, in her very flesh, but recognizes that such corporeal sacrifices are only valuable if she can carry them in her mind, as well, and use them in her work. In this way, Youngblood's novel reminds us of the price black women pay for their own and others' liberty. Bertrand, despite beginning to "stay awake for longer periods of time" (207), remains asleep to many of the spatial and geopolitical systems that privilege him in the Senegalese context, unable to critique these systems as they affect him and those around him—indeed, he instead readily occupies a colonizing position via his work as a budding anthropologist, one seemingly unable to turn his critical gaze inward. But Eden's coming to writerly voice is a spatial as well as affective transformation—"I had found a path on my interior map and learned to follow it"—that allows her to understand that the freedom she has been seeking must be earned through her own and others' sacrifice:

> *story by story*
> *mile by mile*
> *let the sound of the voices carry you the distance*
> *welcome.* (236)

For Eden, the physical journey to Paris precipitates an *interior* journey through a landscape of her own conscious making, one that—unlike Bertrand's unconscious dreamscape—is mindful of the multiple and intersecting geographies and communities that constitute her as middle-class black writer and black American woman abroad.

In the next chapter I turn to another early twenty-first-century post-soul text about a writer, this time an established one: Percival Everett's *Erasure,* a work preoccupied with questions of both interiority and futurity. Everett's text forces us to question the very logic upon which the ontological opposition between black and bourgeois rests, and challenges the notion of a raceless future.

4 Interiority, Anteriority, and the Art of Blackness

Erasure and the Post-racial Future

> What does it mean for a black feminist to think about, consider, or concede the concept of futurity?
>
> —Tina Campt, *Listening to Images*

> Imagining a racial future in the black interior that we are constrained to imagine, outside of the parameters of how we are seen in this culture, is the zone where I am interested in African American creativity. "The black interior" is not an inscrutable zone, nor colonial fantasy. Rather, I see it as inner space in which black artists have found selves that go far, far beyond the limited expectations and definitions of what black is, isn't, or should be.
>
> —Elizabeth Alexander, *The Black Interior*

At the conclusion of *Black Skin, White Masks,* Frantz Fanon repudiates racial history—"the body of history does not determine a single one of my actions"—in order to claim freedom as a "man of color."[1] The phrase "body of history" can be read at least doubly, as both the collected events of the past and the representative black body in and on which those events are understood to cohere. The slippage in meaning that "body of history" suggests, between a body of historical evidence and a fleshly body who is tasked, socially, with wearing that other body's stigmas and traces, occurs throughout *Black Skin, White Masks,* but especially in the chapter "The Fact of Blackness," as when Fanon speaks of Negro identity as "the burden of that corporeal malediction" (111) or notes "I was responsible at the same time for my body, for my race, for my ancestors" (112), or writes, in response to those familiar, repeated refrains of "Look, a Negro!" that "my body was given back to me sprawled out, distorted, recolored, clad in mourning" (113).

I invoke Fanon here, at the start of this chapter on Percival Everett's 2001 novel, *Erasure,* both for what Fanon recalls to us about a black past—written on and borne by the black body, a body that, as Sharon Holland notes, "is the quintessential sign for subjection, for a particular experience that it must inhabit and own *all by itself*"—and for how Fanon's repudiation of that past limns and limits a potential black future.[2] The question of black futurity, and of black temporality more broadly, has in recent years been taken up across a number of disparate topical and disciplinary critical texts in black studies, though what many of the most intriguing have in common is their situatedness within and emergence from black gender and sexuality studies.[3] These works, on the whole, push back against the suggestion that black subjects must move *past* blackness—past, specifically, that black "body of history"—in order to fully inhabit any future space/time.[4] Instead, they are alert to what the hope of futurity, or the "not yet here," might make possible for black subjects, particularly in light of what Kara Keeling calls "present institutions and logics" of anti-blackness within which "a black future looks like no future at all."[5]

For Tina Campt, who opens her concise meditation on black quotidian photography, *Listening to Images,* with the question posed in this chapter's first epigraph—"What does it mean for a black feminist to think about, consider, or concede the concept of futurity?"—the question of the future is not only "inextricably bound up in the conundrum of being captured by and accountable to the historical impact of the Atlantic slave trade on the meaning of black womanhood in the Americas" but is also trapped "*in the* [present-day] *shadow of the persistent enactment of premature black death.*"[6] She goes on to articulate the difficulty of theorizing black futurity "in the face of the bleak facticity of this present and that past."[7] If Fanon's words ask us to renounce the black "body of history," Campt emphasizes the ways that this body—read across its multiple meanings—remains insistently in view, a *presence* in the present that haunts and disrupts the notion of a black future.

Arguably, these difficulties continue to plague any investigation of black futurity in the twenty-first century. I am especially interested in Campt because of how she articulates black futurity, despite this "bleak facticity," as a space enabled by present-day action and imagining—an understanding that she reaches through the idea of *tense*: "To me it is crucial to think about futurity through a notion of 'tense.' What is the 'tense' of a black feminist future? It is a tense of anteriority, a tense relationship to an idea of possibility that is neither innocent nor naive."[8] *Anteriority* is key, here; it signals a tense attentive to the painful weight of both past and present but also sensitive to what is to come as more than mere fantasy. Campt goes on to note that what she calls black feminist futurity "strives for the tense of possibility that grammarians refer to as the future real conditional or *that which will have had to happen*. The grammar of black feminist futurity is a performance of a future that hasn't yet happened but must."[9] For Campt, then, what makes a future both black and feminist is its insistence upon *possibility*—upon living now in a way that will create the conditions necessary for an otherwise future to emerge.

I am interested in thinking Campt's notion of anteriority in concert with what Elizabeth Alexander describes in this chapter's second epigraph as black *interiority,* that "inner space in which black artists have found selves that go far, far beyond the limited expectations and definitions of what black is, isn't, or should be."[10] We might put these two ideas in conversation by considering how interiority can create the conditions for anteriority—or, put differently, how anteriority as a *tense* of possibility is enabled by interiority as a *space* of possibility. Campt locates the "realization" of black feminist futurity in "the everyday imagining practices of black communities past, present, and future"; Alexander frames the black interior as a space of internal creativity that allows us to imagine ourselves "outside of the parameters of how we are seen in this culture."[11] In other words, the black interior is a space that allows for the "imagining [of] a racial future," the articulation of black selves beyond "what black is, isn't, or should be."[12] There is a striking resonance between this interior space, a space *of imagining,* and a black feminist and queer futurity dependent upon "imagining practices," practices that might "envision that which is not, but must be."[13] The "power to imagine beyond current fact," to give voice and vision to a black anterior, is a power found within a black interior. Futurity and interiority are thus linked in crucial, if not always self-evident, ways.

Everett's *Erasure* is neither a particularly queer nor an avowedly black feminist text; instead, it is a text preoccupied with both material privilege and black (cis-hetero-masculine) creative voice. Nevertheless, I find it useful to read the novel in concert with—and sometimes against—these meditations on black feminist and/or queer futures. Not only do such critical approaches all raise, in different ways, the question of the black body, its inescapable presence, its failings and its vulnerabilities, and its forward movement, both as it emerges from the past and as it, presumably, transitions from past to present to hypothetical future, an interest also taken up in Everett's text; in addition, the conversation I have outlined here between anteriority and interiority takes on special resonance in relation to *Erasure* precisely because the novel also raises questions of *tense* and futurity even as it seems to foreclose those spaces of imagining that might make a black future possible for the work's protagonist.

Erasure offers a particularly sharp rendering of the corporeal metaphor, the black and bourgeois dilemma, I have been outlining throughout this book—the notion that a tension between the privileged black body's effacement and its stubborn recurrence lies at the heart of various narratives of black bourgeois subjectivity, a tension that highlights the persistent vulnerability of the black body, even in the face of privilege. In *Erasure* this tension is made literal, as the corporeally alienated bourgeois personhood of the protagonist, Monk Ellison, is gradually overtaken by the performance of a "black" body that is and is not his own. The insistent presence of this body in *Erasure* radically transforms Monk's financial circumstances, but it becomes an existential albatross around his neck precisely because of its circulation as entirely projected, and vacant, surface. The particular constraints of this bodily performance—especially its pointed indifference to black *interiority*—ultimately highlight both the unseen possibilities of blackness and the imaginative failures embedded in the notion of a "post-racial" future.

Black Skin, White Mind

Erasure tells the story of Thelonius "Monk" Ellison, a writer of erudite but unsalable literary fiction (his most recent effort is, in his own words, "an obscure reworking of a Greek tragedy") and a putatively "black" man who "do[esn't] believe in race," who "hardly ever think[s] about race."[14] Others seem to do the thinking for him:

> I have dark brown skin, curly hair, a broad nose, some of my ancestors were slaves and I have been detained by pasty white policemen in New Hampshire, Arizona and Georgia and so the society in which I live tells me I am black; that is my race. (1)

Monk's resistance to this imposed racial identity appears obvious, but he nonetheless responds to an agent's advice that he "could sell many books if . . . [he] settle[d] down to write the true, gritty real stories of black life" with a retort that seems to stake a peculiar kind of temporally based claim on his own authenticity: "I told him that I was living a *black* life, far blacker than he could ever know, that I had lived one, that I would be living one" (2). As I will explore later in this chapter, these words, appearing on the second page of Everett's novel, signal that there is perhaps far more to Monk's sense of racial self than his initial disavowal ("I don't believe in race") might suggest. Indeed, the odd shifts in tense—was living, had lived, would be living—suggest a coterminous relationship between present, past, and future that will prove particularly relevant to the notion of black futurity circulating in the novel.

"*Black* life" or no, both Monk and his body of work are accused repeatedly of being "not black enough" (43). In a moment of frustration with this circumstance, Monk pens a scathing parody of a "black novel," a retelling of Richard Wright's *Native Son* titled *My Pafology,* which he signs with the pen name Stagg R. Leigh. Shopped around by his agent without qualification, the parody, much to Monk's chagrin, secures a lucrative publication deal and eventually garners the attention of a Hollywood producer, who offers "Stagg" several million dollars for the film rights. Monk abruptly becomes as much of a sellout as narrative foil Juanita Mae Jenkins, whose runaway bestseller *We's Lives in Da Ghetto*—a stereotypically "black" story inspired by the middle-class, Akron-raised Jenkins's "visit [to] some relatives in Harlem for a couple of days" as a child (53)—is in part the impetus for Monk's own parody. Forced by *My Pafology*'s financial success to move through the world as Stagg, Monk's character becomes increasingly unstable in the final third of the book, finally unraveling in *Erasure*'s final pages as *My Pafology* (now renamed *Fuck*) wins a prestigious book award, ostensibly for being "the real thing" (261).

Monk Ellison as a character is decidedly middle class; he may be even more accurately described as part of the black elite given the long history of educational and professional attainment affixed to his surname: "I grew up an Ellison. I had Ellison looks. I had an Ellison way of speaking, showed Ellison promise, would have Ellison success" (151). Monk's paternal grandfather and uncle, father, brother, and sister are or were all medical doctors. Like Colson Whitehead's Benji Cooper, his family owns a beach house (as well as a boat).[15] Yet this class privilege seems only partially responsible for Monk's alienation from blackness, something he has experienced since childhood. Instead, his *intellect* marks him as different, "awkward, out of place . . . like [he] didn't belong" (21). In effect, for Monk the classed tension of the black corporeal has devolved into a kind of literal Cartesian dualism in which his "special mind" (9) operates distinctly from his black body, though both seem capable of betraying him in "black" contexts.

Monk recounts, for instance, playing basketball at age seventeen, "making safe pass after safe pass"—itself a way of being on the court without engaging, appearing to participate while "not so much playing the game" (133)—when he is thrown the ball while distracted by his reflections on Western philosophy, a fact that he reveals to a teammate in the aftermath of his disastrous missed shot:

> "He [Hegel] was a German philosopher." I watched the expression on his face and perhaps reflected the same degree of amazement. "I was thinking about his theory of history."
>
> The order of the following comments escapes me now, but they were essentially these:

> "Get him."
> "Philosophy boy."
> "That's why he threw up that brick?"
> "Where the hell did you come from?" . . .
> "You'd better Hegel on home." (134)

In a parallel incident at age fifteen, Monk arrives with a friend at a party in "a part of Annapolis [he'd] never visited before," where "the music was loud and unfamiliar, the bass thumping" (22)—signaling, like the basketball court, a racialized, "black" space, and one that also prioritizes being present in one's body, in this case in order to dance. Before even entering the house or stepping onto the dance floor, Monk is ridiculed for his nickname ("What the fuck kind of name is *Monk*?" [22]) by two black teenagers named Clevon and Reggie, whose failure to recognize the cultural reference to jazz great Thelonious Monk contained within the nickname "Monk" immediately signals their own, and likewise Monk's, class positioning.

Clevon and Reggie assume "Monk" is short for "monkey," a particularly awkward *chosen* name for a black person given historic racist associations between black people and primates. Monk, for his part, fails to correct this assumption—"Right at that second I didn't want to tell him my real name was Thelonious" (22)—claiming the name "Theo" in hopes of avoiding further ridicule. Of course, he fails at this goal as well, and spectacularly so. He finds himself on the dance floor with a pretty young girl named Tina, and Clevon and Reggie cruelly expose his body's involuntary but inconvenient intrusion:

> Her breasts were alarmingly noticeable. Her thighs brushed my thighs and as it was summer I was wearing shorts and could feel her skin against mine and it was just slightly too much for my hormonal balancing act. My penis grew steadily larger through the song until I knew that it was peeking out the bottom edge of the left leg of my pants. Tina became aware of it and said something which I couldn't make out, but included the words "baby" and "all right." Then someone switched on the lights and I heard the voices of Clevon and Reggie saying, "Look at Monkey's monkey." (24)

Monk's bodily exposure here, in a "black" context, makes him vulnerable, and his immediate instinct is to flee. He runs in the direction of privilege—"down the street toward the Capitol"—and ends up at the city dock, with his brother on the Ellison "family boat" (24). Monk differs from Bertrand, the protagonist of Reginald McKnight's *He Sleeps*—who suffers a similar bodily shaming as an adolescent—in that his body's betrayal, and the associated humiliation, is not reduced to a problem (immediate or sustained) with black women.[16] Indeed, "Tina" in the anecdote seems to offer only tolerance and discretion; Clevon and Reggie, however, broadcast and multiply Monk's embarrassment, suggesting that Monk's physical awkwardness in black settings has to do with masculine performance among peers.

This gendered racial performance is driven by language, and specifically code-switching, something that Monk, for all his facility with codes of textual signifying (13), cannot master:

> I watched my friends, who didn't sound so different from me, step into scenes and change completely.
>
> "Yo, man, what it is?" they would say.
>
> "You're what it is," someone would respond.
>
> It didn't make sense to me, but it sounded casual, comfortable and, most importantly, cool. (166–67)

Aware that such performances are just that—"to my ear, it never sounded real coming from anyone" (167)—Monk is nonetheless haunted by his inability to signify racially, convinced that his awkwardness "was the defining feature of [his] personality." And the progression from class-inflected language performance to gendered bodily failure remains straightforward: "*Talks like he's stuck up? Sounds white? Can't even play basketball*" (167). It seems no coincidence that later in the text the rival for short-lived consort Marilyn's affections is also named Clevon and that Monk's awkwardness in the face of the other man's black male "cool" brings Monk directly back to his adolescence: "The sound of it, *going home to Mother,* in front of Clevon made me want to die. I felt like I was a teenager again. When I was gone, he would laugh and then ask her what kind of name was Monk?" (180).[17]

Of course, the "sounds white" in the italicized lines above remains crucial to understanding how Monk's privilege and related racial alienation operate, as it signals the metaphoric relationship between the black middle class and "whiteness"—the sometimes optimistic, sometimes problematic social position of the "cultural mulatto." As I noted in chapter 2, Trey Ellis's use of the term pointed to creative influences from both sides of the racial divide, of which Monk's interest in Western philosophy, music, and art provide ready examples, but as with a number of racially inflected abstractions, *Erasure* also offers a somewhat perverse extension of the cultural mulatto metaphor *in* Monk's person. Indeed, we learn later in the novel that Monk was born after his father's adulterous affair with Fiona Hanley, a white British nurse whom he met in Korea. Some of Monk's dissimilarity from his siblings is attributed to this relationship, at least figuratively—Monk, his father's favored and favorite child, conceived after his return from the war, is cast as a kind of symbolic product of his father's affair. His "difference" is thus linked intellectually to a kind of whiteness, or more accurately, to cross-racial reconciliation and desire. This is true even as the *actual,* secret product of that affair, his half-white half sister, Gretchen, is decidedly not privileged in the same way that he is—indeed, she might be understood as peculiarly *disadvantaged.* Her "difference" from her white family of origin, a difference that seems to be as marked as Monk's if not as openly acknowledged, has not served as any kind of capital, either within or outside the family's boundaries. Monk and Gretchen—whose name subtly suggests her wretched existence as an impoverished single mother and now grandmother, a fatherless outsider whose cousin "knew she had nigger in her" (240)—are textual doubles and mirror images of one another, images distorted as they cross a racial line. Gretchen's "white" poverty and Monk's "black" privilege have little to say to one another, though ironically both sets of circumstances can be traced back to the presence or absence of Monk's father.

And Monk's father is, finally, the key to Monk's racial alienation, precisely because—convinced of Monk's difference, his "special mind"—he trains Monk to think, and to perform intellectually, in a "purposely confusing and obfuscating" (32) manner, a training that even Monk recognizes to be a kind of violence against the possibility of (familial if not racial) belonging. Egged on by his father into expounding upon *Finnegans Wake* at the dinner table, for instance, an eighteen-year-old Monk "looked at Mother and my siblings and felt sick, like I had been seduced into slitting their throats" (185). He later reflects:

> I didn't enjoy being so set apart and I was well aware, painfully aware, of the inappropriateness and incorrectness of Father's assessment of me. . . . [H]ow bad [siblings] Lisa and Bill must have felt. They were far more accomplished than I at the time (and later). I had done nothing yet. I viewed my father's favoritism as irrational and saw myself as being saddled with a kind of illness, albeit his. (185–86)

Monk's father turns him into an exception, whose unusual intellect marks him as impossibly different from—and, by his father's unspoken estimation, better than—his siblings, an intimate estrangement that comes to serve as a reference point and point of origin for his broader, racial estrangement. It should perhaps not surprise us that Van Go Jenkins, the protagonist of *My Pafology* and, arguably, another alter ego or textual id for Monk, ultimately murders his father—Monk's resentment of his father's exceptionalizing treatment simmers just below the surface of the narrative, like the "rumble or hiss" (154) of his father's submerged volcanic temper. Scholar Imani Perry calls racial exceptionalism "the practice of creating meaning out of the existence of people of color who don't fit our stereotypic or racial-narrative-based conceptions."[18] While her focus is the meaning made by those who would conclude that racism is no longer relevant because of the successes of a select few, it is worth considering that the meaning Monk makes for himself throughout *Erasure* is crafted out of his own learned sense of himself as "awkward" racial exile.

Monk's exceptionalist sense of himself as insufficiently "black," as irreparably "different" from the Clevons of the world, is particularly relevant considering simultaneous gestures in the text toward Monk's longing for *racelessness,* for an escape from race that even his exceptionalism seems unable to grant him. Monk is a bourgeois black man who doesn't "believe in race" (2), precisely the sort of "educated Negro" Fanon describes in *Black Skin, White Masks*:

> The educated Negro, slave of the spontaneous and cosmic Negro myth, feels at a given stage that his race no longer understands him.
>
> Or that he no longer understands it.
>
> Then he congratulates himself on this, and enlarging the difference, the incomprehension, the disharmony, he finds in them the meaning of his real humanity. (14)

Yet Monk's learned racial awkwardness fails to free him from race, and as the text progresses it becomes clear that his character can only be tied ever more tightly to blackness. As Perry notes, while "exceptionals are deprived of a history by virtue of their identification as . . . 'different,'" such figures "are still bound by their bodies to the American race game."[19] For Monk, the body that links him to American racial narratives turns out to be the body of *text* that he produces under the name "Stagg R. Leigh," a body of text born out of Monk's own corporeal rage against the "black" literary machine. Just before he begins writing the book that will change the trajectory of his creative and personal life, Monk contemplates Juanita Mae Jenkins's face on the cover of *Time* magazine: "The pain started in my feet and coursed through my legs, up my spine and into my brain," causing his hands to shake as he "remembered passages of *Native Son* and *The Color Purple* and *Amos and Andy*" (61). And the textual body that results, his parody *My Pafology,* implicates and animates a host of other bodies in the novel. In the next section I will consider whom *My Pafology* brings to life as well as how and why such creations are accompanied by Monk's own destruction—if not his death, then certainly his disintegration.

"Suicide—of a Generational Sort"

My Pafology, while situated within *Erasure* as an impulsive act—growing out of Monk's righteous anger at a publishing industry and a reading public without the critical discernment to appreciate his obscure brand of creative production as appropriate from a "black" author—is also linked in the text to Monk's palpable financial exigencies. In the pages immediately prior to his penning of the parody, the text reveals that "money was tight" (55) and that Monk, while he cannot quite bring himself to accept the "slave wages" (139) being offered by American University for adjunct teaching, is in somewhat dire financial straits in the wake of his sister's untimely death ("Young doctors have a lot of debt" [54]) and his mother's gradual succumbing to Alzheimer's. In spite of the socioeconomically privileged status accorded Monk and his family in the text, particularly in flashbacks to Monk's youth, we learn here that "My mother had some savings, but she was not wealthy" and that "what had been my father's office was a money drain" (54). Again Monk's father, the enigmatic black patriarch who created Monk and cast him out of racial community, effects, with his absence, Monk's financial dissolution—just as his absence from Gretchen's life seems to force her impoverished circumstances. In producing and selling *My Pafology,* the work "on which [he] knew [he] could never put [his] name" (62), Monk makes a pecuniary decision that counters the intellectual and creative principles his father has instilled in him: "You don't sign it because you want people to know you painted it, but because you love it" (32).

Perhaps it shouldn't surprise us, then, that when Monk contemplates his choice to accept the terms of sale on his black parody-cum-novel (Random House acquires the book for a $600,000 advance), he begins for the first time to consider seriously his own suicide—what he fittingly calls "my making my own death" (139)—signaling the more complex psychic and social death that this transaction ultimately sets into motion. This larger "death" is effected *through* the name that Monk ultimately signs: "Stagg R. Leigh." This name, which evokes the folkloric figure of the black anti-hero Stagger Lee, or Stagolee, is Monk's ironic nod to the idea of an "authentically black" writer, one who is assumed by the reading public to have privileged access to the "true, gritty real stories of black life" (2). But how does giving life to such a figure effect Monk's dissolution? The suicide that Monk contemplates at the moment of Stagg's emergence—"stopping always at the writing of the note" because he didn't want "[his] silly romantic notions shattered by a lack of imagination" (139)—speaks, as well, to a fantasy of *racial* death, one with troubling consequences.

The title of this section references Sharon Holland's words in *The Erotic Life of Racism* about (post)racial movement: "To move forward in this moment, given all that has happened, would surely be like committing suicide—of a generational sort." This quotation is evocative in relation to Monk's imagined suicide precisely because Holland's words tie a kind of (post)racial futurity to collective death, specifically the death of the "black" body, a death that must, to some of us, feel like suicide.[20] Holland, in her reading of Paul Gilroy, raises the question of whether getting *beyond* race might "involve a vision of the self that does not include the messy materiality of the body," or perhaps more accurately, one that excludes "a materiality that mires the body in a location it might not want to occupy."[21] Monk's palpable distaste for the way his life has been constrained by race, the way his "dark brown skin, curly hair, [and] broad nose" have trapped him in the racialized "location" of (insufficiently) black man, suggests that he is eager to achieve this sort of subjectivity *beyond* blackness. At minimum, however, Everett's novel encourages skepticism toward this hope of racial transcendence, given that Monk's displacement of his body's "messy materiality" onto the imaginary figure of Stagg R. Leigh not only seems to bind Monk ever more tightly to black excess but also effects just one death in the text—Monk's own. This "death" is not a physical one, for Monk, but a psychic and creative one. It suggests that a raceless "self" divorced from its racial "body" cannot survive—or, perhaps more fittingly, cannot *cohere.*

Stagg R. Leigh, for Monk, is a self-consciously fictitious figure, a figment of racism's narrow imagination—but more than that, he is a kind of specter or phantom (a *spook* in multiple senses of that term) whose hollow figure haunts and threatens to eclipse Monk's own creative voice. Stagg personifies the racialized misapprehension that finds Monk's work (mis)shelved in the "African American Studies" section, a move with both physical and fiscal consequences:

> I became quickly irate, my pulse speeding up, my brow furrowing. Someone interested in African American Studies would have little interest in my books and would be confused by their presence in the section. Someone looking for an obscure reworking of a Greek tragedy would not consider looking in that section any more than the gardening section. The result in either case, no sale. That fucking store was taking food from my table. (28)

The rage that registers in Monk's body at this moment—heightened pulse, furrowed brow—relates directly to his sense that this mischaracterization of his work adversely affects his bottom line. Thus, for Monk, signing *My Pafology* with the name Stagg R. Leigh not only functions as angry acknowledgment that in seeking the "real, black" author and text the publishing industry and most readers have reduced black literature to stereotypical parody and black authorship to a kind of falsehood, a mask or performance embodied by the pseudonym; it also registers Monk's resentment that these performances are seemingly the only ones that *sell.*

We might read this as an indictment of the literary establishment and of African American literature as participatory in that establishment, with its expectations for and endorsement of black stories of extreme poverty and suffering; *Erasure* as a metanarrative that includes a book-within-a-book makes this critique evident and, as I have already noted, extends its critical eye to the tastes of the reading public and the way these tastes and expectations implicate and compromise literary artists. In his analysis of Everett's text, Rolland Murray uses the term *incorporation* to describe the "dynamic mutuality between commodity culture and the liberal [academic] institution"—including the African American literary works now championed and canonized within such institutions—that Everett's narrative highlights, pointing out that "Monk creates a second identity for himself largely because the literary market marginalizes him."[22] As Murray observes, *Erasure* is preoccupied with the fact that narrow representations of racial authenticity tied to naturalized "urban poverty" have attained significant fiscal value, which places Monk, the cash-strapped artistic purist, in a moral bind and brings Stagg to life.[23] Murray's reading of *Erasure* as a commentary on incorporation is persuasive; I am equally interested, however, in how *Erasure* presents Monk's creative and personal disintegration in the face of Stagg's emergence as a kind of black and bourgeois cautionary tale.

Instead of embarrassing or offending publishers by calling out their racism, Monk finds to his dismay that the industry takes the name and the fantasy of "Stagg R. Leigh" at face value. Very quickly, "Stagg" takes on a life of his own in the text, becoming not a sardonic warning of the excesses of racist fantasy but a sort of predetermined role that Monk must perform. As Monk notes, "the irony" is "beautiful": "I would not be economically oppressed because of writing a book that fell in line with the very books I deemed racist. And I would have to wear the mask of the person I was expected to be" (212). In other words, Monk escapes his mounting financial pressures by creating a work that fits into a market view of black identity he despises—and as a condition of this already fraught escape, he must also step into the shoes of the authorial persona he has attached to it. Offered more than half a million dollars as an advance for the *My Pafology* manuscript, Monk at first simply "becomes" Stagg on the phone with the editor at Random House (156), but when a Hollywood producer offers several million for the film rights on the condition that Stagg appear in person at a meeting, Monk dons sunglasses and a stoic persona and shows up to lunch (216).

Crucially, Stagg's appearance coincides with a shift, for Monk, from "middle class"—with the attendant financial demands and uncertainties that accompany that status for a post-soul black man with his training and familial obligations—to "rich" (223). Monk's newly exalted economic status, directly a result of his inhabiting of "Stagg," points to the way that certain easily legible black bodily performances have been rewarded, financially, in the post-soul moment—examples from reality television and other spaces in popular culture abound, including, for instance, the massive financial rewards that accrue to certain hip-hop artists and athletes for their renditions of black (hyper)masculinity. Everett highlights the performative difference between these sorts of "rich" but securely "black" figures and the deracinating class status that Monk occupies by birth, his elite pedigree that has always had as much to do with position, social standing, and comportment—in other words, class *culture*—as with money, in a scene where Monk attends the late-in-life wedding of his family's longtime maid, Lorraine.

After a tense conversation with Lorraine's future son-in-law, who resentfully calls Monk's family "rich" because they have "servants" (as Monk corrects, "Only Lorraine") and because "you're telling me you're not working and it doesn't matter" (194), Monk glances at the baseball game on TV and reflects, "Leon would have no trouble with my having money, no matter how much a figment of his imagination it was, if I were that ballplayer. The problem was the one I had always had, that I was not a *regular* guy and I so much wanted to be. Can you spell *bourgeois*?" (195).

Ironically, however, as Monk becomes more willing to play the role of Stagg, what he perceives as a personal inadequacy—his *bourgeois* inability to be a "regular (black) guy"—is increasingly obscured by the excesses of the "black" mask that he wears. Through Stagg, Monk finally finds the "cool" persona, legible to all as sufficiently and appropriately "black," that has eluded him for his entire life. The unintended consequence for Monk, though, is ultimately a complete loss of self.

Not coincidentally, Everett, via Monk, repeatedly invokes Rinehart from Ralph Ellison's *Invisible Man* in this section of the text; as he wonders how far he will take the ruse, Monk thinks "I might in fact become a Rhinehart [*sic*], walking down the street and finding myself in store windows" (162), and later, as he physically prepares to meet Morgenstein, the Hollywood producer, the section begins "*Aint you Rine the runner?*" (216). The allusion is crucial for what it recalls to us about surfaces and interiors. Rinehart, whose very name suggests a figure of all surface and no substance—the rind is the heart—is a phantom just as Stagg is, and Monk becomes as invisible as Ellison's narrator the more he assumes Stagg's mask.[24] While Rinehart's shifting identity serves as a kind of inspiration to Ellison's narrator, however, a model for how to comfortably occupy multiple subject positions, Stagg offers no such relief for Monk; instead, Monk's psyche begins to disintegrate under the pressures that performing as Stagg exert upon him. The more he must contort his "*bourgeois*" body into Stagg's "black" shape, the more his own black interiority is compromised and, indeed, erased entirely.

This disintegration begins at the moment Monk agrees to begin passing as Stagg, agreeing to Morgenstein's request that Stagg meet him for lunch. Monk first loses his ability to understand his brother's language ("I watched his lips and realized I understood nothing he was saying" [213]) but quickly escalates to a noticeable hallucination while speaking with his mother's new doctor:

> Then the fat doctor was my [dead] sister Lisa. She leaned back in the chair and lit that imaginary cigarette and said my name. I allowed my awareness of my hallucination to serve as evidence that I was not in fact insane, but I had to note that coming on the heels of my brother's linguistic show I was a bit concerned. (215)

It is more than a coincidence that this striking signal of Monk's coming mental dissolution happens as he speaks to his mother's doctor about her rapidly deteriorating condition. Monk's mother's progress toward complete mental incapacitation from Alzheimer's—at this point in the text she has finally gotten sick enough for Monk to commit her—serves as a strange kind of foreshadowing for Monk's own textual transformation. The doctor predicts that Monk's mother will "lose her abilities to think, perceive and speak," and that "her personality will disappear" (142). And the peculiar incongruity of his mother's progress once this decline has begun ("The irony was that as her mind failed, her body became healthier" [223]) relates particularly well to the changes that Monk will undergo, as his own mind and "personality" are gradually eclipsed by Stagg, a figure who is all body, all (black) surface, "black from toe to top of head, from shoulder to shoulder, from now until both ends of time" (245). This is a body whose racialized "health" indeed seems to depend upon a concomitant mental failure, the breakdown of Monk's creative and social voice.

Monk muses, "Had I by annihilating my own presence actually asserted the individuality of Stagg Leigh? Or was it the book itself that had given him life? . . . What would happen if I tired of holding my breath, if I had to come up for air? Would I have to kill Stagg to silence him?" (248). These queries—which highlight the novel's preoccupation with relationships between literal and literary bodies, as well as textual and social death—are not idle ones. Nor is the related question that Monk seems unable to articulate: "If Stagg survives, can I?" In this chapter's final section I consider the question of (Stagg's) life and (Monk's) death, and how the suicide that Monk both disavows and threatens throughout *Erasure*—his self-erasure, if you will—is brought into being by his artistic choices and speaks to a relationship between racialized subject and work of art.

A Gravestone Certainly

Numerous seemingly random inclusions—imagined conversations between historical figures, meditations on the nature of trout and the character of a piece of furniture—pepper the text of *Erasure*. The novel's fragmented structure, explained in its very first line with the conceit that the narrative is itself the text of Monk Ellison's private journal, highlights its postmodern investments while allowing Everett a means of commenting, in ways both subtle and direct, on the philosophical questions circulating in the mind of the protagonist and suggested by the trajectory of his story: What is art? What is the responsibility of the artist? By what measures can a work of art be deemed "authentic"? Circulating through these musings, however, is another question: What is blackness—particularly for a bourgeois, "educated Negro" such as Monk?

Early on in the text, prior to the penning and publication of *My Pafology,* Monk's "notes for a novel" include imagined conversations between, first, German sculptor and pacifist Ernst Barlach and German-Swiss painter Paul Klee, commiserating over the Nazi distaste for their art ("They are calling me a Siberian Jew . . . and they are burning any books which contain pictures of our work" [37]), and then Adolph Hitler and Dietrich Eckart. In the latter conversations, Hitler and Eckart complain about Judaism and other threatening incursions to the German national scene, specifically on the terrain of the arts and cultural production—a creative landscape clearly linked to the political one ("They will destroy German culture if we let them" [38]). Notes Monk, "I must admit to a profound fascination with Hitler's relationship to art and how he so reminded me of so many of the artistic purists I had come to know" (39). Ostensibly, these artistic purists are the same ones who refuse to accept Monk's writing as sufficiently "black," whose narrow conception of a "black" novel Monk understands as nothing short of fascist. But Everett positions this scene just before another in which Monk, while on a flight, skeptically reads a favorable review of Juanita Mae Jenkins's *We's Lives in Da Ghetto* and becomes so visibly agitated that he garners attention from his seatmate: "'Is something wrong?' the woman seated beside me asked" (40). While Monk claims to have been inspired by the anti-abortion zealots picketing outside his sister's clinic (eventually responsible for her murder), whose faces are "washed with hate and fear, wanting so badly to control others" (39), his own palpable outrage over Jenkins's success marks him, too, as an "artistic purist"—albeit one whose ideals are soon compromised by his own monstrous creation.

Indeed, in the later portion of the book, Monk's musings on art shift into a more cynical register as he reflects upon his own hypocrisy, his status as a "sell-out" (160). Crucial to these musings are questions of market value and creative ownership, and the fraught relationship between the two. For instance, he imagines a conversation between Willem de Kooning and Robert Rauschenberg regarding Rauschenberg's famous 1953 *Erased De Kooning Drawing*:

> *de Kooning: You put your name on it.*
> *Rauschenberg: Why not? It's my work.*
> *de Kooning: Your work? Look at what you've done to my picture.*
> *Rauschenberg: Nice job, eh? It was a lot of work erasing it. My wrist is still sore. I call it "Erased Drawing."*
> *de Kooning: That's very clever.*
> *Rauschenberg: I've already sold it for ten grand.*
> *de Kooning: You sold my picture?*
> *Rauschenberg: No, I erased your picture. I sold my erasing.* (228)

The question of who is artist in this exchange is crucial, but so is the fact of the drawing's sale. Does the erased de Kooning drawing become Rauschenberg's "work" at the moment he signs his name to it, or at the moment the drawing is "sold"? Given that the drawing is "already" sold in this exchange, the order of these two points in time is not at all clear. The link between this conundrum and Monk's is fairly direct. In a sense, "Stagg" has taken the canvas (body/body of text) upon which Monk's obscure and insufficiently or illegibly *raced* artistic vision was drawn, erased/*re-raced* that vision, and has *already sold* the lot for three million dollars. Is *My Pafology* Monk's work, then, or Stagg's? Is Monk's body Stagg's, or his own? Monk may be the architect of the Stagg R. Leigh/*My Pafology* ruse, but given subsequent events, it becomes less and less clear in the text that he is the artist.

Instead, as Monk feels his own creative and subjective integrity succumbing to pressure from *Stagg's* expanding artistic and financial successes—book advance, movie rights, and finally the major book award, chosen by a selection committee on which, in a final irony, Monk as bourgeois, black academic is tapped to serve—he (Monk) functions increasingly *as* a work of art, though more the "discarded art, shunned art, bad art, misunderstood art, oppressed art, shock art, lost art, dead art, art before its time, artless art" that remains even once a given piece has been "thrown out of the museum" (227). The analogue to the performative utterance that cannot be undone even with such a throwing or casting out of (artistic) community—"*this is a work of art*"—is one that applies to Monk himself: *this is a black man.* Yet that blackness, insofar as it attaches to Stagg, not Monk, seems to imprison Monk in its artifice. Stagg's "black" body—which is and is not Monk's own—is a figurative creation, as much a "work of art" as *My Pafology/Fuck.* Which is to say, it is a work of art that labors to become one with, and thereby destroy, its creator. After he has insisted to the publisher that the title of *My Pafology* be changed to *Fuck,* Monk greets his agent's skepticism with "This thing is in fact a work of art for me. It has to do the work I want it to do" (221). But this shift from *My Pafology* to *Fuck,* ostensibly a creative choice on Monk's part, also marks a shift of his person from subject to object, as he gradually *becomes* Stagg—a performative shift toward what Uri McMillan calls "*objecthood*" that, for Monk, because it is largely involuntary, remains *not* a "way towards agency . . . [but] a primal site of injury."[25]

Consider Monk's dream in the final chapter of the novel, just at the moment that it becomes clear to him that *Fuck* will win the book award despite his protests. In the dream, Monk hides from Nazi soldiers while watching those soldiers chase an unidentified woman carrying the van Gogh painting *Starry Night*—only to discover, when the soldiers slash the painting across its face and he begins bleeding profusely from his stomach, that he has become the painting (255). Despite his awareness that he is dreaming and his repeated affirmation "This is a dream," he cannot wake from the scene, which escalates when the painting is set aflame and "the heat [he] felt made [him] scream out" (256). Like his inability to awake from the "dream" of Stagg's increasing success, Monk senses his own power and agency slipping away as Stagg's seems to expand, and Monk, as Stagg, feels the *heat* of increasing attention (read: public scrutiny). In addition to this reading, we might also understand this portion of the dream as a comment upon the vulnerability of the black body to racialized violence, as Monk's bleeding stomach and his feeling of being burned alive make reference to lynching—the Nazi soldiers standing in for the lynch mob and reminding us of the state's frequently tacit approval of, if not involvement in, the spectacle of blackness brought to violent extralegal "justice." It seems no surprise that later in the dream the music changes from "Horst Wessel" (the Nazi Party anthem) to "Stars Fell on Alabama"—this shift marks a return to the American racial context and the geopolitically specific white supremacy that informs Monk's own understanding of blackness, particularly Stagg R. Leigh's blackness. And at this point, Monk is unable to answer the final soldier's question, "*Wie heißen Sie*? (what is your name)" (256). Is he Monk, or Stagg? (Or, as the dialogue at the end of the novel seems to imply, is he Van Go?)

Starry Night is a particularly suggestive choice to embody Monk's person, given that it both depicts the view from van Gogh's room at the asylum where the artist checked in after famously mutilating his ear—potentially tying Monk and black embodiment more broadly to mental dissolution—and refers visually to an expansive cosmos that might be read as a reflection on spirituality, death, and the afterlife. This latter aspect of the painting speaks, if obliquely, to a wide-ranging sense of human possibility, a cosmic profundity tied to blackness not only by the painting's dream rebirth as Monk's body but also by the protagonist of *My Pafology/Fuck*'s name, "Van Go Jenkins." Monk's dreamscape sense of himself as the painting seems unaware of this latter, expansive potentiality, however; he remains trapped, instead, in the painting (and in his body) as mere physical object.

Similarly, Monk has never truly believed that *My Pafology/Fuck* is a "work of art," not in any way consistent with his father's training about what art should be. That his agent calls his claim about the parody as work of art "bullshit" (222) is fitting, particularly when read against Monk's words at an earlier point in the novel, the moment just before he agrees to Morgenstein's financial offer. After explaining the material and creative difference between a painting and a chair ("The canvas occupies spaces and the picture occupies the canvas, while the chair, as a work, fills the space itself" [208]), Monk goes on to note:

> The novel, so-called, was more a chair than a painting, my having designed it not as a work of art, but as a functional device, its appearance a thing to behold, but more a thing to mark, a warning perhaps, a gravestone certainly. (208–9)

Monk perceives the book as an object, not an idea (though de Saussure reminds us that even a chair is only legible to us, linguistically, as an idea of itself), a marker—indeed, finally, a gravestone. But *whose* death does *My Pafology* mark?

Not just the novel, but its "author," Stagg, are Monk's creations, born out of his reaction to what he perceives as the unfair imposition of race on his work. Monk intends Stagg, and the parodic text that "Stagg" produces, to highlight the folly of race and thereby free him from it—to serve as a "gravestone" for a certain kind of racist reasoning; instead, Stagg's increasingly "real" presence ensnares him (Monk) further within race/racism. In other words, in his attempt to move "beyond" race, Monk allows for—breathes life into, literally—a particularly constricting notion of what blackness is, and this notion becomes his prison. As Monk notes: "I was a victim of racism by virtue of my failing to acknowledge racial difference and by failing to have my art be defined as an exercise in racial self-expression" (212). It seems hardly coincidental that this passage appears directly following the reproduced title page from the retitled book in question—indeed, I would read this moment as a kind of turning point in the novel, another, subtler text-within-a-text, the start of Monk's mental and social breakdown (or disappearance). From *My Pafology* to *Fuck*: the change in name seems to map precisely onto the title's shift from Van Go's perspective to Monk's, from a kind of misspelled (misspoken) and ironic, imagined articulation of the blackest excess to a horrified and frank reaction to the obscene realization that indeed, I as bourgeois subject am (still) implicated in that excess. In Patricia Williams's words, "I must assume, not just as history but as an ongoing psychological force, that irrationality, lack of control, and ugliness signify not just the whole slave personality, not just the whole black personality, but *me*."[26]

Here, then, I want to reconsider Monk's curious comment to the book agent early in the novel: "I told him that I was living a *black* life, far blacker than he could ever know, that I had lived one, that I would be living one" (2). What is this *black* life of Monk's? The audacious promise in these words is powerful, for Monk's *black* life is one that does not necessarily resemble the lives he has been told constitute that blackness which is "true, gritty real" (2), and yet he nonetheless stakes a compelling claim for its racial authenticity (arguably, its value—*pace* Lindon Barrett). *Was living, had lived, would be living*—black present, past, and future, which Monk claims for himself in the face of all of those who would dismiss such a possibility for a bourgeois figure such as he. There is something valuable there, the notion that Monk's blackness can contain his (class and other) difference, the nuance that, if others cannot always see it, *he* knows is there. This is the *interiority* that makes black *anteriority* possible, source of the imagining black self "that go[es] far, far beyond the limited expectations and definitions of what black is, isn't, or should be."[27]

But the flaw in Monk's specific claim to blackness—which sets his claim apart from Alexander's expansive theory of black creativity and forecloses the futurity that Campt's work suggests might emerge from it—seems to be that this blackness is derived not from his own choices but from others', choices specifically to (mis)read the black body he wears, the "house that was [his] disguise" (251). When Monk states—just a few lines after he asserts the existence of his own *black* life—that he doesn't believe in race, that his own racialization is merely a function of those who would "shoot me or hang me or cheat me and try to stop me because they do believe in race," specifically tying this belief to his "brown skin, curly hair, [and] wide nose" (2), he speaks precisely to Holland's notion of a black body marked for death, a black object—not subject—whose very existence "mires the body in a location it might not want to occupy."[28]

Thus Monk's efforts to free himself not only draw him further in but distort the possibilities for who and what a black subject might be, now or in the future, by erasing the creative possibility of the "black interior" that Alexander describes. In creating Stagg, a "black" body that is all surface and no substance, Monk casts himself as Stagg's (invisible) interior, and ironically erases the possibilities for black nuance, implied by his own "*black* life" and by, for instance, the life of the young woman with blue fingernails whom he misjudges (21). Again, *interiority* seems to be crucial here; the question of whether it matters (or more precisely, whether the only thing that matters) is the way that blackness is imposed upon us, the narrowness and outrage of that imposition, the sense that it misses so much of who we are. Does embracing that imposition, knowing what we do of our interior selves—that "internal difference, complexity, or syntax which [is] always and everywhere so apparent"—in fact expand the possibilities for what blackness can be?[29] And conversely, does casting it off, or seeking to, make that lie at the center of blackness, those "claims of blackness's atomic simplicity that have never been serious enough to refute," its only so-called truth?[30]

Certainly, *Erasure*'s final line of dialogue seems to suggest as much. Monk's dazed "Egads, I'm on television" (265), the repetition with a difference of the last words of *My Pafology/Fuck*'s comically abject protagonist, Van Go ("Hey, Baby Girl. Look at me. I on TV" [131]), traps Monk squarely under the camera's gaze, making him a (racial) spectacle, a "prisone[r] of the Real," in Alexander's words—where that Real is the vacant, "real (black) thing" he has created in Stagg.[31] Yet the book does not end here, and its final words make for a more powerful, if far more enigmatic, gesture toward the meaning of blackness for the black and bourgeois subject in a post-soul moment.

After a visual break from the previous scene, *Erasure* concludes with the three italicized words "*hypotheses non fingo,*" Latin for "I feign no hypotheses," referencing Sir Isaac Newton's words about gravity in the *Principia*:

> I have not been able to discover the cause of those properties of gravity from phenomena, and I feign no hypotheses [*hypotheses non fingo*]; for whatever is not deduced from the phenomena is to be called an hypothesis; and hypotheses, whether metaphysical or physical, whether of occult properties or mechanical, have no place in experimental philosophy.[32]

It should perhaps not surprise us that Monk's final words—recall that the text of *Erasure* is meant to be his private journal—reference Newton and his famous refusal to speculate upon the reasons behind the laws of gravity. If we replace "gravity" with "race" or "blackness" we get a sense of what kind of character work Monk's reference does—reminding us that he will not or cannot advance any theories, metaphysical or physical, spiritual or technical, about what race is, or why, despite the fact that he doesn't believe in its existence, it continues to constrain his life as it does.

Yet the remainder of the passage in Newton from which the words *hypotheses non fingo* are drawn moves us at least some distance beyond Monk's perspective, suggesting that it is the what, not the why, that matters. Newton goes on to write, "To us it is enough that gravity does really exist, and acts according to the laws which we have explained, and abundantly serves to account for all the motions of the celestial bodies, and of our sea."[33] Perhaps, when it comes to race, this embrace of its existence, of the manner in which it accounts for the motions of our diverse bodies—this fact of blackness (with necessary apologies to Fanon) can be *enough* precisely because it defies explanation. Like a work of art, blackness is open to interpretation, even—and especially in the case of the living art that is the post-soul black subject—interpretation from within, shaped by an interior that is formidable precisely in its imaginative reach.[34]

Ultimately, then, *Erasure*'s ending suggests that the contrary positions within the black bourgeois may be irresolvable, and points to the difficulty, and the unintended consequences, of striving to move beyond the racialized body and its attendant histories. As Margo Crawford reminds us, "Every attempt to move beyond blackness should remind us that blackness has always been *beyond*."[35] Monk's mistake is that he imagines blackness as *only* an imposition from without. As such, he cannot envision, nor create, a black future for himself that allows him to be both black and whatever or whomever else he might imagine. His rage, before penning *My Pafology,* about Juanita Mae Jenkins's success and his own relative lack of success is nothing if not an inability to "imagine beyond current fact."[36] As such, *My Pafology/Fuck* is, for Monk, a foreclosure of genuine (black) possibility even as the sale of the work as both a book and a film vastly expands his economic options. Stagg, who is blackness as only surface—literally, the embodiment of "the limited expectations and definitions of what black is, isn't, or should be"—erases Monk and whatever possibilities for interiority Monk might possess, and thereby also erases the potentiality of a black future, or, ultimately, even a coherent black present.[37] In the next and final chapter of *Black Bourgeois,* I turn from the question of futurity to the related question of "progress" to consider how the black bourgeois subject's privilege has been conscripted into a narrative of racial progress that proves, ultimately, to be false.

5 Flesh, Agency, Possibility

Social Death and the Limits of Progress in *John Henry Days* and *Man Gone Down*

> In a sense, Afro-Pessimism is not an intervention so much as it is a reading, or meta-commentary, on what we seem to do with, or how we relate to, what black creative intellectuals continue to generate without being able to bring fully into account. It is a reading of what is gained and lost in the attempt—the *impulse*—to delineate the spatial and temporal borders of anti-blackness, to delimit the "bad news" of black life, to fix its precise scope and scale, to find an edge beyond or before which true living unfolds.
>
> —Jared Sexton, "Afro-Pessimism: The Unclear Word"

Kevin Willmott's 2004 feature-length mockumentary, *C.S.A.: The Confederate States of America,* tells an alternative history of the United States—the version of this nation that would have ensued if the South had won the Civil War. The film resonates with present-day America in multiple ways, perhaps most strikingly in a spoof commercial for a CSA television program called *Runaway,* which depicts contemporary paddy-rollers pursuing and capturing escaped slaves in a close-to-home parody of the long-running U.S. reality show *Cops.* In a 2008 interview, Willmott goes so far as to argue that the Confederacy "did win," noting that the century following Lincoln's assassination was "slavery lite (Jim Crow segregation, chain gangs, peonage, lynching)," with the Civil Rights movement and its aftermath the first moment in which this nation might actually be understood as the United (rather than the Confederate) States of

America. In his words, "We have been struggling ever since as to what country we really want to be—the CSA or the USA."[1]

We might well read Willmott's film as an example of an Afro-pessimist work, in line with the current school of thought arguing that slavery defines the condition of black life in the modern world and theorizing blackness "as [a] condition—or relation—of ontological death."[2] Yet in positing the *historical* continuation of slavery (even "slavery lite"), as well as its presumable end in the 1960s, Willmott himself actually side-steps the *ontological* concerns raised by Afro-pessimism regarding the totalizing nature of slavery, what Jared Sexton calls "a strange and maddening itinerary that would circumnavigate the entire coastline or maritime borders of the Atlantic world, enabling the fabrication and conquest of every interior—bodily, territorial, and conceptual."[3] Indeed, the epigraph above suggests precisely that Willmott's revised historical timeline—even as we might understand his particular creative rereading of American history to be a fairly radical one—qualifies as an example of an attempt to "delineate the spatial and temporal borders of anti-blackness," to find an "edge" beyond which *real* black *life* ("true living") begins.[4]

Notes Sexton in another context, "The question of the possibility of racial slavery is, we might say, the question of the possibility of global modernity itself, including the development of historical capitalism and the advent of European imperialism and its colonial devolutions."[5] If slavery is, as Afro-pessimists assert, not a historical event that has ended but the foundational logic and an ongoing condition of Western modernity, then the "C.S.A." is not only local but global, not merely a governing civic structure but an ideology and a mode of thought—a manner of comprehending the world. And, for Sexton, to speak to this totalizing structure "is to speak the name of race *in the first place,* to speak its first word."[6] In light of our project in this book—to examine how contemporary texts represent what I am calling the black and bourgeois dilemma—we might well ask, taking Afro-pessimism seriously, how such a totalizing structure, in which *blackness* is so freighted, can even produce a "black and bourgeois" subject. To what extent can a middle-class, "privileged" status obtain for such a subject when the totalizing ontology of blackness would seem to obfuscate, if not erase, such distinctions?

Although I will shortly turn to two early-twenty-first-century novels that I think speak in especially profound ways to these questions, it might be worth considering the intellectual concerns they pose first in the abstract. In a recent special issue of the online journal *Rhizomes* that he edited on the topic, Dalton Anthony Jones describes Afro-pessimist thought as "the effort to make an honest accounting of the question, 'where does my body stand in relation to my flesh and how can they both, one without sacrificing the other, find a stable place to stand in this world or, in the meantime, how can I at least find a way to speak the contradiction and violence of that displacement?'"[7] In light of Jones's binary language here, not to mention our shared affinity for Spillers's conceptualization of body/flesh, I would argue for reading this definition of Afro-pessimism as of a piece with the pattern of dualistic thinking that I identified in this book's introduction as a recurrent preoccupation of black (American) thought, tracing back at least to Du Boisian double consciousness—despite the fact that Afro-pessimism is rarely understood within such a tradition. Yet the duality is, at minimum, implicit in Jones's language: "body" and "flesh" here evince a sense of the self as simultaneously, on the one hand, marked, violated, and excluded, and on the other, *existing within* this exclusion, this (social) death, acknowledging it and yet continuing to move, to persist, through it, if never beyond it.

This implicit sense of duality is obscured in some ways by the rhetorical *starkness* of the terms that many Afro-pessimist thinkers use to define blackness, to understand it as fundamentally a state of *non-being*. As Frank Wilderson notes:

> This violence which turns a body into flesh, ripped apart literally and imaginatively, destroys the possibility of ontology because it positions the black in an infinite and indeterminately horrifying and open vulnerability, an object made available (which is to say fungible) for any subject.[8]

For Wilderson, here also invoking body and flesh, blackness, which is "always already positioned as Slave," is therefore socially and ontologically dead—and indeed this "ontology of slavery" forms the condition of possibility for white (Human) life in the modern world.[9] As Sabine Broeck summarizes, "human life . . . is predicated on the usability and disposability of Black life."[10] For Sexton, the work of Afro-pessimism is the work of dwelling within the knowledge of this circumstance and condition, what Wilderson calls "the ontological and epistemological time of modernity itself."[11] Sexton writes: "A simple enough term for withstanding the ugliness of the world—and learning from it—might be *suffering* and Afro-Pessimism is, among other things, an attempt to formulate an account of such suffering, to establish the rules of its grammar."[12] Sexton emphasizes, however, that this attempt takes place without recourse to, in Bryan Wagner's words, "the consolation of transcendence."[13] In other words, blackness is suffering—or more precisely, a rigorous thinking of black-being-in-modernity is a catalog of suffering—but it is a kind of unrelieved suffering, a suffering that cannot be escaped or sidestepped, a suffering that is limitless not only in terms of scope but also in terms of duration, such that there is no "edge beyond or before which true living unfolds" for those who move through the world as black. As Sexton goes on to note, for many of Afro-pessimism's critics, the consolation of transcendence exerts "special force" upon the project of "thinking, no less of speaking and writing, about those whose transcendence is foreclosed in and for the modern world," such that to give a genuine hearing to the Afro-pessimist school of thought becomes both offensive and unbearable.[14]

And yet. Even some of those whose work we might understand as deeply Afro-pessimist in approach offer a kind of loophole—perhaps a "loophole of retreat"—to this unrelieved suffering of blackness.[15] Christina Sharpe, for instance, in her poetically and thoughtfully rendered analysis of living "in the wake," a wake "produced and determined, though not absolutely, by the afterlives of slavery," nonetheless insists upon something more than—parallel to, or perhaps simultaneous with—black suffering.[16] This is evident not only in the inclusion of "though not absolutely" in the sentence above but also in statements like this one: "And while the wake produces Black death and trauma . . . we, Black people everywhere and anywhere we are, still produce in, into, and through the wake an insistence on existing: we insist Black being into the wake."[17] Or, in the words that conclude *In the Wake,* which are drawn from an earlier publication of Sharpe's as well as repeated elsewhere in her monograph: "While *we are constituted through and by continued vulnerability to this overwhelming force, we are not only known to ourselves and to each other by that force.*"[18] Or, as part of a personal anecdote about her own family, "Even as we experienced, recognized, and lived subjection, we did not *simply* or *only* live *in* subjection and *as* the subjected."[19] For Sharpe, "wake work" is the practice, "in the midst of so much death and the fact of Black life as proximate to death," of attending to "the largeness that is Black life, Black life insisted from death"—a practice that is founded upon and operates through *care* and that again returns us to a kind of implied duality, a simultaneity, of black death and black life.[20]

Another contributor to the *Rhizomes* special issue on Afro-pessimism, cinema scholar Rizvana Bradley, expresses something similar when she distinguishes between race and blackness, understanding them not as mutually exclusive but rather complementary and, in part, dialectical: "I think of blackness as fluid and coextensive with a history of collective resistance to the colonial idea and imperial concept of race, and I critically consider the transformative, resistive potential of blackness to the violent conception of the raced body."[21] In other words, for Bradley, while race is "a world historical idea and a cultural fiction, engineered and deployed in the interest of imperialism, colonialism, [and] New World slavery," blackness operates as both coeval with and distinct from, or resistant to, the (gratuitous, cf. Wilderson) violence that brings "the raced body" into being.[22] While Bradley is particularly attentive to the ways that "black femininity becomes the bearer of the burden of the racial mark, and of blackness," I am more interested in how and why we might, again, think about the simultaneity and opposition of race (violently deployed fiction) and blackness (resistive potential to that fiction) she outlines, precisely because this thinking brings a kind of implicit Afro-pessimist duality into view. Like Sharpe's vision of "Black life insisted from death," or even Jones's sense of a black body standing "in relation to" black flesh, "one without sacrificing the other," Bradley's conception of blackness as *potentiality,* coexistent with and in opposition to race, speaks to something more than—or simultaneous with—black suffering.

For me, then, the black and bourgeois dilemma, while it does not mark precisely the same sort of duality or doubleness, nonetheless also emerges from, or perhaps steps into, the gap between black "body" and "flesh," that space of simultaneity where blackness both is, and is in excess of, the violence that racializes. In part this simultaneity answers my earlier question of how an *ontologically* black subject might possibly be bourgeois. Sexton avers that "racial blackness operates as an asymptotic approximation of that which disturbs every claim or formation of identity and difference as such," while Sharpe argues, similarly, that blackness must be understood as *anagrammatical,* "as a/temporal, in and out of place and time putting pressure on meaning and that against which meaning is made."[23] I take these points as legitimate ones, but I wonder whether we might also consider how this very disturbance and pressure continues to obtain when we think blackness in relation to privilege. Just as Sharpe suggests that "*girl* doesn't mean 'girl' but, for example, 'prostitute' or 'felon,' *boy* doesn't mean 'boy' but 'Hulk Hogan' or 'gunman,' 'thug' or 'urban youth'"—for black subjects, *privileged* can never simply mean "privileged" but is transformed into, say, "uppity" or "ungrateful," or disappeared from legibility entirely.[24] The black and bourgeois dilemma is a dilemma or paradox *as such* precisely because its terms refuse to cohere.

And yet. On the one hand, the preceding explains the impossible simultaneity of privilege and "racial blackness"; on the other, there remains that corollary simultaneity, of "black life insisted from death." As several of the texts I examine in this volume make clear, even for "privileged" black subjects, blackness remains both an inevitable imposition and a desired, if confounding, object of pursuit—a position many if not most characters *seek* to occupy. As Erica Edwards notes in another context, "race is not a fact, not a given, but a fiction that we *want.*"[25] Thus I also conceive of the black and bourgeois dilemma, in part, in a kind of slant relation to Afropessimism, growing out of what Terrion Williamson has so eloquently articulated as *black social life*:

> Black social life is, fundamentally, the register of black experience that is not reducible to the terror that calls it into existence but is the rich remainder, the multifaceted artifact of black communal resistance and resilience that is expressed in black idioms, cultural forms, traditions, and ways of being.[26]

Williamson attends to blackness as it is understood from within, as it exists "wholly within the parameters of what Hortense Spillers has called . . . the 'intramural,' what Elizabeth Alexander refers to . . . as the 'black interior,' and what Toni Morrison calls 'interior life.'"[27] This is blackness as lived on the ground, so to speak, defined not by what Sexton calls the "modern world system" but by black people who "inhabit and rupture this episteme with their, with our, knowable lives."[28] This is the other piece of the black and bourgeois dilemma, the paradox taken in reverse, a perspective that "originates in the view of the American galaxy taken from a dark and essential planet."[29] How does black flesh speak back, defiantly, to a "modern world system" that insists upon defining privilege through and against our black bodies? How might we think about the contradictory simultaneity of the black and bourgeois as both a comment upon how blackness disrupts and incoheres privilege and as a means of reflecting upon the potentiality of black refusal?

In this chapter I want to put two twenty-first-century black novels—Colson Whitehead's *John Henry Days* (2001) and Michael Thomas's *Man Gone Down* (2007)—in conversation with these questions. These novels come the closest to representing, in this book, a post-post-soul aesthetic and temporal sensibility, in that both of them anticipate the precarious position of the black bourgeois subject in the second decade of the twenty-first century.[30] In both novels, bodily vulnerability informs the black and middle-class status of the protagonists and ultimately shapes each figure's relationship to labor, a preoccupation and structuring metaphor in both texts. Yet Whitehead's and Thomas's novels differ as well, not only in how each novel navigates history but also in how each narrates its characters' relationship to life and (social) death.

Thomas's narrative repeatedly raises, but ultimately undercuts and resists, a teleological understanding of African American history and the unnamed narrator's place within it; Whitehead, by contrast, highlights the parallels between and even the contiguous nature of protagonist J.'s and John Henry's stories, even though they take place more than a century apart—a conjoining that reframes the sweep of "American history" as a catalog of black death. In different ways, these novels challenge cherished notions of African American (economic and social) progress, highlighting instead the still-open question of black agency. Together, they present two parallel refusals. Thomas's narrator in *Man Gone Down* refuses to accept the death he knows is inevitable, a refusal that is temporary; J. in Whitehead's *John Henry Days* instead refuses to resist death's inevitability, a refusal that both permeates the entire narrative and, paradoxically, creates the space for belief—however vexed—in another kind of black possibility.

"Put Off Death for a While and Dream"

Thomas's *Man Gone Down,* like Whitehead's *John Henry Days,* has at its center a deeply vulnerable man, a man trying and failing to shore up his own black privilege—though if, as we will see, Whitehead represents his protagonist's vulnerability as structural, a function of his relationship to the shifting winds of capitalism and to his own inadvertent stumble down the historical path of racial martyrdom, Thomas writes his unnamed narrator as what seems like an isolated individual, fallen *out* of his history. An unemployed, unpublished writer, "broke" and in immediate need of some $12,000 to pay his sons' private school tuition and rent the family a new Brooklyn apartment—money that would, in other words, allow his family to maintain their precarious middle-class status—his fiscal vulnerability is easily apparent.[31] But this economic precarity is buttressed by other, more visceral sorts of vulnerabilities, tied to the protagonist's race and gender and to the wounds and weaknesses of his abject black body.

Abjection is, for this character, much more than an abstraction—the first chapter of the novel reveals that the narrator was brutally raped as a seven-year-old boy in the bathroom of the Brighton Boys Club, an assault that leaves him convinced, or at least concerned, that he is "too damaged" (9). This phrase and phrasing—"I wonder if I'm too damaged"—recurs, mantra-like, throughout the novel, not only as the narrator tries and frequently fails to connect, sexually and romantically, with women—including the white, Boston Brahmin woman who becomes his wife—but also at each moment that the narrator weighs the value and meaning of his life as a twenty-first-century multiracial black man. And, indeed, the "damage" inflicted upon him by this past sexual violence is linked, in the text, directly to his racial subjectivity, imagined as "collateral damage of the diaspora" (9).

The protagonist's various vulnerabilities—fiscal and material, corporeal and sexual, racial—work in concert in Thomas's text to comment upon the positioning of the black and bourgeois subject in the (post-) post-soul moment, a transitional period between the post-soul and our more *immediate* present, what I am calling the Black Lives Matter (BLM) moment. This notion of the *post-soul*—which, as I noted in this book's introduction, was coined by Nelson George and subsequently used by scholars like Bertram Ashe and Mark Anthony Neal to situate black cultural production in the decades following the end of the Civil Rights and Black Power movements—briefly gave way, after Barack Obama's election in 2008, to the notion of the "post-racial," which carried with it a sense that race no longer mattered, or no longer should matter, that the presence of a black man in the White House made racism an ugly anachronism. Yet by 2012 the subsequent racial backlash had led us to a new moment, the Black Lives Matter moment (and what some are calling the New Nadir). As I write, in 2018, it has become increasingly clear that the United States is in no way post-, or past, racial stratification or (especially) anti-black racism. The unwieldy language of the "post-post-soul" thus becomes particularly useful to situate Thomas's and Whitehead's novels, which in their fatalism anticipate our cultural transition not to the Obama era but to the BLM moment. "Post-post-soul" signals a temporal shift—the end of the post-soul moment—without insisting, as does the terminology of "post-racial," that this ending necessarily indicates a kind of forward progress.

Both Thomas's and Whitehead's narratives are, at best, wary of the idea of such progress. Indeed, one of the things I posit in this chapter is that Thomas's novel (despite the fact that it was published just prior to Obama's historic election and the subsequent rise to prominence of the very term "post-racial") expresses a stalwart skepticism toward the notion of racial transcendence, even as it looks somewhat askance at the ostensible terms of black racial belonging. The narrator's multiple sites of susceptibility, the risks and weaknesses of his social position, define this ambivalent viewpoint toward race and racial belonging—vulnerability, in other words, is the fulcrum on which his sense of himself as a racialized subject precariously, but also productively, balances.

Let me return then, first, to the narrator's fiscal vulnerability. *Black Bourgeois* is about the embodied conundrum of black and bourgeois subjectivity, the sense that black and middle-class subjects live within and thus must navigate the contradiction between material privilege's concealment of the body and blackness's reliance upon an exposed, hypervisible, racially marked body. Thomas's text may seem a curious one to read through this larger lens because of the economic precarity of its protagonist, which would seem to obviate his status as "bourgeois"—but this vulnerability is precisely why *Man Gone Down* functions so appropriately as a post-post-soul narrative, one that despite its 2007 publication date speaks particularly well to the vicissitudes of the coming BLM era. In a sense, the struggles of Thomas's narrator to stay afloat, financially, uncannily anticipate the struggles that many other putatively "bourgeois" black subjects would experience in the wake of 2008's economic crisis and subsequent recession, fueled by a housing market collapse that disproportionately affected black homeowners, as well as a "jobless recovery" during which black rates of unemployment have remained twice as high as those of whites.[32] These real-world circumstances highlight the always-already precariousness of middle-class status for black people, and so the struggles of Thomas's narrator solidify rather than destabilize his (racialized) class positioning. This is particularly true if we consider what scholars such as Kevin Kelly Gaines and Michele Mitchell have pointed out—that middle- and upper-class status for African Americans has historically been at least partly aspirational, a matter of ideology and self-perception "in a society that relentlessly denied black Americans both the material and ideological markers of bourgeois status."[33]

This is not to suggest that we can read class statically across time nor to argue that either Thomas's narrator or real-world blacks in the first two decades of the twenty-first century face the same socioeconomic and political landscape that blacks did a century ago. It is, however, to acknowledge that the gross disparities in black and white wealth that emerge from this nation's particular racial history persist in the present and often have material consequences even for those black Americans who have amassed significant educational and cultural capital.[34] After all, Thomas's struggling narrator is nonetheless a Harvard dropout, with a Hunter College BA and several years of doctoral study under his belt (his unfinished dissertation is titled "Eliot, Modernism, and Metaphysics"); one of the many "odd jobs" he has worked is as an adjunct lecturer of English literature.

Indeed, despite his current financial straits and undeniably working-class economic origins, it is difficult to read the narrator as anything but *bourgeois,* part and parcel of precisely the sort of gentrifying hordes that he claims to despise but to which he has been, until recently, in the position of reluctant insider:

> "They" had always considered Claire as one of their own, and perhaps, after I became a father, they considered me that too. Somehow they let us in—they let me in. And although I don't think that I changed a bit, we became part of the "us," that seemingly abstract and arbitrary grouping that is able to specifically manifest itself: the right school, the right playground, the right stores and eateries, the right strollers, the right books and movies, the right politics, and the right jobs to bankroll all the rightness and distance them from asking whether it was perhaps all wrong. And yes, there were subdivisions of the us, but the only relevant divide was those who could afford to pay and those who could not—an us and a them. (122)

The narrator doesn't think he's "changed a bit," yet he fits right in. While we might read this as delusion, it also suggests that those racialized markers of class aspiration in the narrator's history (e.g., his pharmacist paternal grandfather's origins among free, formerly landed blacks in North Carolina [56]) complicate even his sense of himself as a working-class boy, such that while his current troubles reposition him on the outside of the class-conscious "us" of his pricey Brooklyn neighborhood, the very terms of the narrator's struggle mark him as a particular kind of bourgeois figure. In his search for a new apartment, for instance, Thomas's protagonist (called "high-minded" and an "aesthete" by others, in not entirely complimentary ways) never entertains the idea of leaving his pricey Cobble Hill neighborhood and never seriously considers enrolling his children in public school. The story he tells—to the headmistress of his children's school, as he pleads for leniency on the tuition bill—of his own mother lying about their address in order to get him into a better school, in "a nearby suburb that had an excellent reputation for education" (239), again speaks to a kind of class aspiration in his history. It echoes and informs his own black and bourgeois insistence on achievement for his children, particularly his "brown boy," Cecil, who, the narrator insists, must "sit up straight, chew with his mouth closed, and display a certain amount of dignity" (153) because of the racialized judgment that awaits him.

Of course, *Man Gone Down*'s narrator constantly feels vulnerable to this judgment himself, a vulnerability that returns us to the question of his body. As his fiscal desperation increases, with the deadline for procuring or producing this $12,000 ever more quickly approaching, his body is increasingly *at stake* in his progress. His initial efforts to raise funds find him accepting a series of carpentry jobs as a day laborer, jobs that reduce him to his body, first as a "big man" (129) methodically pulverizing a concrete slab for hours at a stretch, even goaded, on a dare, into lifting a chest-sized rock over his head for the princely sum of $10 (141), and then on to another job where the finely detailed work he is assigned—sanding the grit from window trim—nonetheless culminates in a fistfight when the boss's business partner calls him a "big nig" (280). Thus ends that precarious source of income, but the narrator's corporeal performance is further tied to his economic fate when the lawyer acquaintance whose home he is staying in (while his wife and children spend the summer in Massachusetts with his wealthy mother-in-law) invites him to play in a high-stakes golf game with a couple of colleagues.

The narrator's athletic performance on the golf course is fraught with risk—it has the potential to win him the money he needs but also to take everything he has. His first swing, which he believes, "if it is bad, will be [his] last" (366), hits true, and the ball "is like a supersonic missile, ripping the air," again putting his body, his *black* body, on the line; as he notes: "My people were on that ball" (367).[35] But the text doesn't allow for either a simple or a simply triumphant physical victory, in part because he is more than his body's brute power. Considering the irony of his competitor's physical weakness compared to his strength, he thinks, "I outweigh him by fifty pounds—so whose failing is it that I'm tyrannized by his credit cards and his titles? . . . Somebody, some martyr wannabe, raised me right, or wrong, and I'm stuck with my gut and my own head rebelling, in chorus, the refrain: Broke-ass chump" (370). Thomas offers us pointed irony here, given the narrator's own expressed disdain for "*black entrepreneurship*" (109)—his musing, early on in the text, that "If you and yours have been exploited for capital, then why, in turn, would you covet that capital. . . . As though freedom had a price that could be expressed monetarily" (109–10). Perhaps *freedom* does not, but in the "broke-ass chump" moment on the golf course, the narrator seems to acknowledge the ways that financial and social capital—in this case, the "credit cards and . . . titles" that "tyrannize" him—nonetheless operate as markers for status and respect. His belief, however reluctant, in the legitimacy of this link between capital and status is what obviates the possibility of his body outweighing, or literally *outclassing,* his competitor.

The text also undercuts a simple bodily triumph because the very body that might lead the protagonist to victory contains within it such abjection, that "damage" that he has ruminated on for much of the novel and that is finally narrated to us, in detail, on the golf course. I want to consider just a portion of that scene, which spans a couple of pages in the novel—specifically, the passage in which Thomas's narrator links his sexual violation to racial abjection, not coincidentally in the moment when he believes he's lost the game, lost the bet, the moment before his precarious redemption, a redemption that is itself based in deception and (therefore) risk:

> Everything you ever were will gush from you through a breach, and everything you would have been will be gone. The tear in your anus a symbol denoting the eternal, fathomless gap. No one has ever reached that. I know no one ever will. The scarred brow, stigmata to remind you and them that you will never be whole. And I know it's so feeble, but I wish it would all go away—but it is me: the line of Ham, the line of Brown, the crooked soul finger, the jagged keloid scar that everyone eventually points to. I wish I would go away, but I shoot through everything—the tree, the dappling on the log, the voices that seem

> to rise up out of the bay. Everything begs for meaning, for origin, for redemption, and I can't do it. I know that I'm too damaged. I've seen signs and confirmations—evil, chaos. Never good. Never a sign of pure, lasting, invulnerable good. (375)

I want to read this moment, in this scene, against two other moments near the end of the novel. The first is the protagonist's final conversation with his mentor, his insistence that despite "their" best efforts, no one could ever make him assimilate, "civilize" him (399). For him, "that is the heart of resistance—holding out for the good: That is what I always thought it was to be black, other, or any different title I can paste on myself" (399). There is a tension here, almost an opposition, between the racial abject who believes his "damaged" body and spirit exclude him from "pure, lasting, invulnerable good" and the racial subject who insists upon "holding out for the good," who sees his ability to resist the imposition of a "civilizing" social hierarchy as the very site of his blackness, his Otherness—the site of his own power.

Yet there is also a sense in this passage that the goal of those "civilizing" forces may be precisely to reach into black abjection and subdue it, to smooth over and conceal, if certainly not to heal, the "eternal, fathomless gap." The fact, then, that "no one has ever reached that" and that "no one ever will" speaks to an unassimilable power at the center of the protagonist's (abject) black body, an unassimilable power at the figurative center of blackness, what Darieck Scott calls "blackness in what we could think of as a fundamental or ontological or existential mode."[36] Scott writes, further:

> Though sexuality is used against us, and sexual(ized) domination is in part what makes us black, though sexuality is a mode of conquest and often cannot avoid being deployed in a field of representation . . . as an introjection of historical defeat, it is in and through that very domination and defeat also a mapping of political potential, an access to freedom.[37]

If, as Scott's words here suggest, there is a black power in abjection, then that power lies not in a "pure" or "invulnerable" good but in the sort of good that comes from insistence upon and acceptance of the impure, the "crooked" and "jagged" markings on and maneuverings of the body, a body that is supremely vulnerable and "will never be whole" (Thomas 375).

The narrator of the novel seems not to believe in this power, however. Indeed, in concert with the refrain of "too damaged" throughout the novel, another recurrent motif is the notion of his thwarted call to lead "his people," a call that is repeatedly framed as dependent upon not just his intellect but his *bodily* wholeness: "I was born a poor black boy of above-average intelligence and without physical deformity, and therefore I should lead my people. It didn't work out that way" (199). This language sardonically points to how low the bar might actually be set for self-appointed black male leadership—"above-average" intelligence and simple lack of "deformity" read as perhaps the bare minimum of qualifications for such a role, in contradistinction to the far more elusive and esoteric quality of "charisma" (*pace* Erica Edwards) that we might expect. It is also worth noting that the *poverty* ("a poor black boy") of the charismatic male leader is built into this description by the narrator, again gesturing toward the idea that a bourgeois black person is distanced from racial authenticity by class privilege. The narrator, then, fails in his attempts to meet these requirements on multiple levels—as I note, his relationship to poverty is contested throughout the novel (he describes his adolescent self as a "newly suburbanized black boy" [158]) and especially once he has married a white woman from a wealthy family and joined the Brooklyn elite. Perhaps most important, however, this failure—particularly in the narrator's eyes—relates to the ways his own racialized abjection, which centers on his violated body, seems to undercut his call to leadership precisely because it replaces the absent physical deformity with a much more profound existential wound.

The second moment I want to consider in concert with the scene of the narrator's violation returns us to the so-called post-racial. In the final pages of the novel, as he dozes on a dark Greyhound bus on the way to his family, *Man Gone Down*'s protagonist dreams of an exchange he had with his father as an adolescent—his father asks him whether he has a girlfriend, and expresses concern when he says, "the girls at school are rich and white, Dad . . . [and] I'm not" (421). His father "tried to show me something by slowly gesturing in front of his face with his hands: the size and shape of his idea. . . . 'I believe . . . in a wider society . . . not *whiter,* a *wider* one'" (422). This is perhaps the novel's conception of, or concession to, the notion of a post-racial world. Yet this "wider society," in the narrative, is a social possibility that stands in deliberate opposition to a fantasy of race-neutral color blindness—"not whiter, [but] wider." It points, instead, to a kind of social *expansiveness,* enabling the vulnerable blackness that "shoot[s] through everything" to coexist with, indeed to produce, something more, a "larger hope and love, waiting to be reborn," an "imagined" illumination that is "real, consuming, sacred" and that, as Thomas's protagonist notes, "leads me to other things I can really touch: my few friends, here and gone, my children, and my wife" (425). This emphasis on the materiality of human connection may resist "the burn of shame" (425), but it also reveals the impossibility of any "pure, lasting, invulnerable good," because that good seems to depend upon the narrator's physical presence, his ability to "really touch" these links to a *wider* world—and his presence is one that the text has already outlined as precarious and temporary.

Thus the narrator's resistance is not, or not merely, to "civilizing" forces but to the death that he knows awaits him as a black subject. Yet if this novel rejects the teleology of racial progress by undercutting the notion of the narrator as leader "of [his] people," it also undercuts the efficient cruelty of black death, and its inevitability, simply via the narrator's *refusal.* The narrator well understands his socially ordained fate—"I'd already considered my experience and already understood on some basic level that things weren't going to work out, that I was, in every sense of the phrase, *born to lose,* that the day when people like me, whatever and whomever they may be, win wouldn't be a good day for others" (208–9)—and this passage, in particular, foreshadows his ill-gotten victory on the golf course, a victory he reaches only by cheating and deceiving his competitors. Yet the text has already made clear that the narrator is "born to lose" precisely *because* of the same social forces (namely, race and class) that enable certain others always to win at his expense; the narrative thus seems to suggest, through the narrator, a means of maneuvering past this fate, however temporarily.

Describing a conversation with his wife in which the two consider alternatives to their current dilemma ("private or public, New York or elsewhere, and can we afford to live in a town that has good public schools" [68]), the narrator notes:

> And then I tell her something about my past, that there weren't any ski trips or beaches or whatever people do to luxuriate and that the only thing I came out of those years with intact was the dim notion that I wasn't quite ready to resign myself to any fate prescribed for me because of melanin or money—that I'd put off death for a while and dream. (68–9)

Lacking the privilege to "luxuriate," the narrator's only souvenir from his childhood is his "intact" spirit of refusal, his ability to "put off death" and imagine something other than his prescribed fate. The question of *choice* looms large here, both in relation to the narrator's racialized destiny and his imagined potential as a racialized subject.

The narrator's position within the arc of (black) progress, his sense of himself "as a future leader of [his] people" (201), brings with it a breathtaking burden of scrutiny and responsibility, not to mention competing alliances:

> I was born a poor black boy of above-average intelligence, and therefore as a future leader of my people I was given the light for me to keep—not to let shine but to hold on to in the darkness like a star shrouded by night's sky cloak until I was ready to reveal it. But it's a strange thing to go through life as a social experiment: promethean metaphors; this school and that school; this test and that test; Moses and Jesus and Martin and Malcolm; Socrates to Baldwin; Shakespeare to Dylan; Jeremiah and the community; community centers; marches, church basements, and city hall stairs; and the good white schools with the good white people. (201)

The narrator, comparing himself as potential leader to everyone from Jesus to Malcolm X, and pointing out the complementary (or contradictory) social training of the cultural mulatto that would yield knowledge spanning from "Socrates to Baldwin," emphasizes that his status as "social experiment" is at least as much about his begrudging acceptance in white spaces as it is about his link to the black community. Yet after a group of white boys taunt him because his mother is "*funny looking*" (199), the narrator's "choice" to react violently, to channel his longtime "rage held in waiting . . . via [his] fist into that little pink face" (200), means that "all promises and contracts were cancelled" (201). His access to the "good white schools [and] good white people" is immediately revoked, revealing the precarity—indeed, the preordained defeat—built into the position he ultimately loses.

It is perhaps not surprising that the novel narrates this first explosion, and expulsion, in such close detail and then glosses over a similar but arguably much more serious incident, the confrontation that gets the narrator kicked out of Harvard (150). The narrator is assaulted by a police officer and dares to resist; while the dean who decides his fate focuses on the fact that he "hit a police officer" (149), the narrator's revelation that his own arm is in a sling and that his "collarbone was broken" (149) suggests a much different explanation for the confrontation, one rooted in the police officer's violence, a violence seemingly invisible to "Dean Ray, the white-haired jowl beast" who refuses to help the narrator. Instead, "the old world had regarded the promise of the new—he looked at me like he had won. One more dumb nigger down" (150). Here, with another reference to the narrator's racialized "promise," the narrator's expulsion from Harvard returns us to that first expulsion, the one triggered when his angry childhood self punches a taunting white boy in the face.

What most interests me about both of these moments is the refusal contained in even the narrator's seemingly involuntary reaction, a refusal, in this case, to do the socially acceptable thing and swallow his rage. This rage is depicted in the text as an internal "locomotive," the violence of which must always be borne by its occupant, no matter how much it makes him suffer. The narrator tells us:

> Most people don't understand, or have never experienced rage. It isn't singular, random, episodic. It's cumulative, with a narrative thrust like a black-iron locomotive. It's always there or on its way, started initially by some unseen engineer, some fireman wraith endlessly shoveling endless coal into the fire. Hot locomotive rage. Inexorable. And you

> can keep switching that train, switching it, keep it on the long runs of rail through your wastelands until one day when that rage is closing in, you don't switch. You let it run. (200)

In its description of the narrator's black interior as his "wastelands," this passage tells us something about the embodied costs of blackness, the way a lifetime of exclusion and mistreatment take their toll. And the repeated internalization of the consequences of such experiences breaks the individual who bears it—the rage circulating "through your wastelands" suggesting a kind of internal destruction of the subject, the self sacrificed on the altar of keeping the peace, protecting those "good white people" from facing the consequences of their innocence.

We might also think of this description, however, of the "inexorable" locomotive, as an equally useful metaphor for black death and its inevitability. If death, too, is a train "always there or on its way," then the best one can do, in the narrator's estimation, seems to be to put off the inevitable, to seize, however briefly, what is always a contingent and provisional reprieve. Later in the novel the narrator recalls the words of his only black friend, Donavan, a playwright and former basketball star who had had a schizophrenic break and now "roam[ed] the streets of Lower Manhattan and south Brooklyn" (28), his body ravaged by psychotropic medication. In the voice of his unnamed narrator, Thomas writes: "Donovan once said that our action is our choice, our fate made by our own hands. I choose not to be me. I choose not to be afflicted, not to bear witness" (275–56). This is a choice that seems impossible, not only because the narrator seems irrevocably tied to himself, making "I choose not to be me" a declaration absurd on its face. The choice is also impossible because it rejects both the promise and the curse of black subjectivity—it rejects the narrator's sense of himself as a future leader of his people as well as the failure and death that accompanies that racial positioning. In the face of such an articulation, which seems to grant the narrator as bourgeois individual the power to defy collective circumstance, it is perhaps not surprising other analyses of this text dismiss Thomas's narrator as no different from his white class counterparts.[38] Another way to understand this refusal, however, is to acknowledge it, like the narrator's win on the golf course and the accompanying financial windfall, as precisely a *temporary* pause in a larger, inexorable path toward his fate.

Indeed, if we are tempted to read the conclusion of Thomas's novel optimistically, a variation on the message that the "little, changing face of love" (428) conquers all, our knowledge, as readers, of the continuing precarity of the narrator's circumstances makes such a reading difficult. The narrator is still unemployed, still broke; he has spent his last $50 on a bus ticket north, to reunite with his family. The apartment he has secured is theirs only for another month, until the next rent check comes due; his sons' private school tuition paid only for the first semester. He has managed to "switc[h] that train" to another track for now, but what happens when it comes around again, and again? For another, albeit no more satisfactory answer to this question, we might now turn to Colson Whitehead's early-twenty-first-century novel, *John Henry Days,* which also tackles these questions of choice and inevitability, and in ways that similarly suggest the impossibility of a reprieve from the "inexorable" fate of black death.

"As If Choices Are Possible"

The protagonist of *John Henry Days,* J. Sutter (his first name is never spelled out), is a freelance journalist—a press "junketeer," in industry parlance—who racks up sponsor freebies and makes his living one travel reimbursement at a time. He is on "The List," an ever-changing stable of freelancers who are invited, seemingly with no effort on their part, to various promotional events; the writers on the List don't always file stories on the promoted object or place or person, but they do so often enough to maintain "the ultimate percentage . . . the unconquerable ratio of events covered to events not covered."[39] In the novel, the List is portrayed as not only an immutable force of nature—"The List had been pushed from the earth by tectonic forces" (55)—but also a preternaturally (self-)aware entity, with near-mystical knowledge of writers' movements and their compliance, or noncompliance, with expectations:

> The men and women on the List were astonished to find themselves contacted by email, having only just signed up for an email account a

> few days before and not having given their new email address to many people. They did not complain. It was convenient. If they wondered about the mechanism of the List, they kept their concern to themselves, or voiced it in low tones. They feared expulsion. (54)

Of course, what this description of the List highlights are the panoptical surveillance and extended disciplinary reach of the early-twenty-first-century labor market—even for freelance workers like J., who presumably do not owe allegiance to any particular employer. J. may be an "inveigler of invites and slayer of crudités, [a] drink ticket fondler and slim tipper, open bar opportunist, master of vouchers, queue-jumping wrangler of receipts" (56), but he is also a contract laborer, dependent upon the List, and the access it provides, for both the freebies he accrues (which are not so much swag as alternative forms of payment) and the legitimate work he produces for publication and a paycheck. The precariousness of his economic position as a freelancer is emphasized from the moment his character is introduced. Idling in an airport on his way to his next gig, J. anxiously ponders how to swipe a discarded receipt from the floor of the terminal. This boon for him ("pure luck, a pristine receipt newly plucked from the great oak of consumption") is quite literally another traveler's trash: "He chides himself for waiting so long to pick it up. Why would anyone want it besides him? It is litter" (10).

J. is also "going for the record," or as he puts it, "on a jag," meaning he is attending a press event every day and has been for several months. J.'s trip to the small town of Talcott, West Virginia, ostensibly to cover the festival taking place there on the occasion of the unveiling of a John Henry postage stamp, is a part of this thus-far-unbroken "junket jag" (15). The "record," set by one Bobby Figgis, extends such behavior to a full year, with disastrous consequences ("He had been devoured by pop" [111]) that turn Figgis's name into a two-word cautionary tale. Figgis arrives at his pursuit of the "record" via an ill-advised, drunken bet with a colleague. J., by contrast, seems simply to find himself there:

> He tries to remember why he started. He sees himself kissing Monica the Publicist at the Barbie event. They were on the second floor of FAO Schwarz in a display of radio-controlled toys. His hand moved

> down the back of her black publicity dress and he heard a whirring sound. The toys were active, autonomous rambunction, tanks mostly, with a few hot rods from the future thrown in the mix. The robots collided with each other and spun off. They ran into the bottom of shelves and got caught there, unable to understand why they could not progress. They let out whines of frustration. She bit into his tongue and he tasted his blood. The next evening he went to a TNT event for their latest Civil War movie. . . . The day after that he went to the Palladium to see the hot new band from England and the next thing he knew he was going for the record. (41–42)

J. seems to stumble inadvertently down Figgis's path, yet the text's juxtaposition of J.'s body with the toy robots speaks obliquely to his possible motivation. J.s humanity, and particularly his body—mortal and vulnerable in a moment of semi-public intimacy with his occasional consort, Monica the Publicist, a vulnerability made especially clear to readers as she bites his tongue hard enough to draw blood[40]—is in ironic contrast with the radio-controlled toys, moving both autonomously and without conscious awareness, unable to navigate the obstacle of the shelves but still emitting lifelike "whines of frustration" when they cannot advance. The toys are only the first signal, in this novel, of the deadening, "robotic" nature of contemporary labor, a transformation that shapes J.'s working life as even enterprises like journalism, once viewed as straightforwardly middle class, have become the provenance of a proverbial army ("tanks, mostly") of contract laborers.

For J., then, going for the record is an act of defiance, or perhaps a defense of his own humanity in the face of ultimately dehumanizing working conditions—conditions that seek to turn him into a kind of machine even as his livelihood is threatened by new forms of technology. The novel, published in 2001 and set in 1996, reveals J.'s naively cavalier perspective about the internet as merely a new kind of employer:

> J. hasn't worked for the web before but knew it was only a matter of time: new media is welfare for the middle class. A year ago the web didn't exist, and now J. has several hitherto unemployable acquaintances who were now picking up steady paychecks because of it. Fewer

> people are home in the afternoons eager to discuss what transpires on talk shows and cartoons and this means people are working. It was only a matter of time before those errant corporate dollars blew his way. He attracts that kind of weather. (19)

As readers, however, particularly nearly two decades after the novel's publication, we are aware of how the expansion of the web has shrunken and transformed print journalism, leading to the shuttering of multiple publications and the disappearance of many jobs, a process that had already begun in 2001 as Whitehead, himself a former journalist, completed the novel. The looming threat of obsolescence thus hangs over J.'s pursuit of the record, the "competition between him and himself. Or him and the List. Depended on how you looked at it" (233) that he initiates by pursuing Bobby Figgis's feat—if not also his *fate,* a point to which I will return later.

In this J.'s efforts parallel the other central figure in the novel, John Henry himself, who in Whitehead's hands steps out of the realm of myth and becomes just another man (indeed, "nothing but a man" [101]),[41] born into slavery and working, post-Emancipation, for the railroad as a "driver"—meaning someone who hammers a drill bit into bare rock in order to create a hole large enough for dynamite, which then advances the train tunnel deeper into the mountain. John Henry in *John Henry Days* is an extraordinary laborer, one who earns the most pay because he works the hardest and fastest, even as his labor is understood to be part and parcel of an expendable post-Emancipation black workforce that exists to be exploited ("There was no shortage of niggers" [86]). J., too, is both exceptional in his ability to make a modest living from the "deep abstraction" of freelance journalism (135) and just another anonymous worker, fungible part of a larger system of exploitable labor—he and his publicist girlfriend "cog and flywheel" (221) in the machine of pop. And for both characters, J. and John Henry, the impending doom under which they work is more than figurative, as the question of their labor's obsolescence is accompanied by the imminent threat of injury and death.

In John Henry's case, the grueling nature of the work itself presents the threat; we are introduced to his character just as the thundering blow of his sledgehammer has shattered the hand of a young boy, an inexperienced kid who had been filling in for John Henry's usual "shaker," a kind of assistant to the driver who "had to twist the bit between blows to loosen the dust in the hole and keep the bit level for the next blow" (83). Yet the boy whose hand is destroyed ("not the first [John Henry] had maimed" [84]) is, more than mere casualty, a harbinger for the destructive fate that awaits John Henry himself, a death both signaled and momentarily forestalled by each death that precedes it:

> Yesterday a blast in the Western cut shook out a large section of the arching in the east heading, and a stone from the cave-in crushed the skull of one of the drill runners. . . . They buried him with the rest down the hill. No one knew if he had any family. [John Henry] saw the light swimming in the gloom and as he stepped out of the tunnel he felt like Jonah stepping from Leviathan's belly. He knew the mountain was going to get him but the Lord had decided it would not be this day. (85)

The mythology of John Henry suggests a man who is born knowing he would die as a result of his labor—labor that, despite his extraordinary strength, is infinitesimal in the face of the mountain's colossal size, and is also expendable, even ultimately obsolete, within the sphere of industrial capitalism.

While it may seem an exaggeration to parallel the dangerous circumstances under which a nineteenth-century steel driver and ex-slave worked with the relative comfort and ease of a late-twentieth-century junketeer, wrapped from head to toe in free clothing and consuming, gratis, "five proud slabs of prime rib" from the buffet table, Whitehead does exactly this, highlighting the physical perils of J.'s version of contract labor by juxtaposing the lyrics of the "Ballad of John Henry," sung by a local boy at the press dinner, with J.'s silent choking on an errant bite of beef, a "stern and vengeful plug of meat" (76). J.'s near-death experience at the banquet is presaged—albeit comically—by the experience of his junketeer colleague One Eye, who "had been blinded in a tragic ironic quotes accident a few years before":

> The bartender yelled out last call for the open bar, and One Eye jumped up on instinct, just as the freelancer [standing above him]

> punctuated his clever description by forming air quotations with the index and forefingers of his hands. . . . The force of the irony, coupled with One Eye's eager and frantic upward movement, drove the free-lancer's pincer fingers deep into the junketeer's eye socket. (52)

This scene, like many others in the novel, is openly humorous, yet One Eye's injury and subsequent disability are real and motivate One Eye's own symbolic attempt to "beat" the List, in his case by deleting his name (127).

J.'s choking incident is narrated with far more gravitas, however, as the italicized lyrics to the ballad detailing the John Henry myth frame and highlight J.'s imminent death:

> *John Henry was just a baby,*
> *When he fell on his mammy's knee;*
> *He picked up a hammer and a little piece of steel,*
> *Said, "This hammer will be the death of me, Lord, Lord,*
> *This hammer will be the death of me."* (75)

Whitehead's narrator suggests J.'s jaded indifference to both the poignancy of the song's content and the boy's gorgeous singing voice, which has given the rest of the banquet room pause. The other diners are "enraptured, all of them, openmouthed in beatitude and slack in delight at the nimble phrasings of the boy. Except for J. J. attacks the prime rib" (76). J.'s lusty consumption of the meat is fueled by his junketeer precarity—"he doesn't know what time he'll eat tomorrow and he needs the meat" (76)—and so this precarity leads directly to the far more urgent precarity of choking, as the "plug" of meat "catches in his throat. He can't breathe" (76).

As J. makes this realization the narrative shifts back to the John Henry ballad, further highlighting the laborer's futile competition with the steam drill and its foreordained mortal consequences: "*He said, 'I will beat that steam drill down / Or hammer my fool self to death*'" (76). The implication of this line—that John Henry's own choice to challenge the stream drill, no matter how constrained a "choice" it may have been, is the reason he will die—is paralleled directly with J.'s decision to pursue the record, a similarly constrained "choice" that has led him to what appears to be the moment of his own death: "What's this guy singing? He's choking on the stubborn plug of meat. John Henry, John Henry. He works on the C&O Railroad. He pushes puff, he is going for the record" (77). The slippage between the two "he"s in these lines suggests a continuity, if not contiguity, between John Henry's and J.'s stories, their mutual proximity to death uniting the two men across time, and in space.

Indeed, J.'s rapid-fire thoughts as his brain is denied oxygen return again and again to his death's inevitability, which he situates in his "Southern" location: "I'm a sophisticated black man from New York City and I'm going to die down here" (77), he notes, going on to rail, "This place will fucking kill him. He should have known better. A black man has no business here, there's too much rough shit, too much history gone down here. The Northern flight, right: we wanted to get the fuck out. That's what they want, they want us dead. It's like the song says" (78–79). J.'s abrupt invocation of the John Henry song here is another moment of the text paralleling John Henry's and J.'s narratives, as J. ascribes both his own and John Henry's bodily vulnerability to an undefined but presumably white, Southern "they" who "want us dead." In fact, the conclusion of this scene—just before J. is rescued by (white) stamp collector Alphonse Miggs, who has himself traveled to the John Henry Days festival, handgun in tow, to make a violent statement about his own social precarity—connects both J. and John Henry to a much larger history of black death at white hands:

> He jumps out of his seat. My eyes must be popping out my head like some coon cartoon. His hands point to his throat. Can't these people see what's going on? The boy keeps singing. The pain is in his throat, around his throat and he would like them to make it stop. All these crackers looking up at me, looking up at the tree. Nobody doing nothing, just staring. They know how to watch a nigger die. (79)

Invoking the act of lynching with references both to his throat and to "the tree," these lines simultaneously invoke the lynching photograph—which invariably documents white spectators in close proximity to a hanging black corpse, their faces calm, indifferent, or even gleeful at the intimate spectacle of black death.[42] And Whitehead alternates between third- and first-person narration in this passage in such a way that the final two lines of the chapter, and of this first section of the book—"Nobody doing nothing, just staring. They know how to watch a nigger die"—could be ascribed either to J. or to the disembodied voice of the narrator, giving the words a gravitas that exceeds J.'s individual desperation and bitterness as his own death approaches, and instead lends them an air of historical inevitability.

Black death may link J. and John Henry in this scene, but such death—indeed, black death as mere spectacle, emptied, in Sexton's words, of even its power *as* death—appears elsewhere in the novel as well, and in each instance the narrative similarly indicts white spectators for their callousness while emphasizing the wanton sacrifice of black flesh.[43] J.'s fellow junketeer, for instance, Dave Brown, describes being at the Rolling Stones's 1969 free concert at the Altamont Speedway outside San Francisco and witnessing the murder of a young black man who was in attendance. His narrative is clearly based on the real death of black concert attendee Meredith Hunter, who was beaten and stabbed to death by Hells Angel Alan Passaro, an incident inadvertently captured on film in footage for the documentary *Gimme Shelter.* Brown narrates this death as a "sacrifice":

> The Angels did what the people demanded, even if they didn't know they demanded it. . . . [O]nstage the Stones played "Under My Thumb," a song about getting over on your girlfriend, to hundreds of thousands while the Angels performed their sacrifice.
>
> "Sacrifice to what?"
>
> "To the culture. The kids had brought a new thing into the world, but they hadn't paid for it yet. It had to be paid for." . . .
>
> "So this guy is like the Crispus Attucks of the seventies." (99)

This theme of sacrifice threads throughout Whitehead's novel—notes Talcott local Josie, "Pain is a down payment on happiness. You pay for happiness with grief in this world" (363)—and each time someone's life must be sacrificed for a seismic cultural shift, the life lost is black. As Tavia Nyong'o notes of Crispus Attucks—a man of (at least partial) African descent who was the first person killed in the Boston Massacre in 1770 and who is widely understood to be the first American casualty of the

Revolutionary War—"Attucks's contested legacy to this day continues to touch upon issues that strike at the heart of American identity and its racial unconscious."[44] Through the reference to Attucks, Whitehead's text reiterates that black flesh and black death have symbolic meaning in the United States, that black bodies are those repeatedly "sacrificed" to what might be called national progress.

It is with this context in mind—of black death and black bodily sacrifice in the name of "progress"—that we must consider the ambiguous death that hangs over the novel, which suggests, although it never directly states, that J. does indeed lose his life on this particular press junket. Early in the novel we learn that the second day of the "John Henry Days" celebration has been marred by violence, initially and erroneously described by a distraught college intern as the work of a postal worker, who "opened fire Sunday afternoon on a crowd of people gathered for the unveiling of a new postage stamp, critically wounding three people before being shot and killed" (26). Although the text reveals much later that the shooter was actually the disaffected stamp collector Alphonse Miggs, who, rather than opening fire on the crowd shoots up into the air, and that those wounded or killed were shot by a police officer as he tried to subdue Miggs (367), one detail from this earliest scene is accurate. The intern sees one of the casualties for herself: "For a second, the men standing over the journalist part and she can see his bloody chest and slack mouth" (25). Later in the novel, a casual conversation between post office higher-ups reiterates that those shot were "members of the media" (370) and reveals that not one but two of them have died:

> POSTAL EMPLOYEE #1:
> . . . Two dead and one wounded, did you hear that? The second guy died today.
>
> POSTAL EMPLOYEE #2:
> Shame. They bringing the cop up on charges?
>
> POSTAL EMPLOYEE #1:
> Just doing his job, really. Taking out the homicidal madman. Sure he hits two bystanders but that's his job. Sucks that they're

> members of the media, for his sake, but he got the guy before he could hurt somebody. Preserving the peace.
>
> POSTAL EMPLOYEE #2:
> Gonna sue like crazy. The journalists' families. Cop kills two bystanders while trying to get one guy? Gonna sue the town like crazy. (370)

The question of whether one of these dead journalists is J. thus colors the entire text, and Whitehead gives us clues throughout that point both toward and away from this possibility. Not only does Josie, for instance, co-owner with her husband of the Talcott Motor Lodge, believe that J.'s room is haunted by a ghost, "attached to the mountain by its mountain death" (105), but she frets, before the event and tragedy take place, "This annual fair, the John Henry museum when they complete it. . . . It is a new beginning but by her sights, it hasn't been paid for yet. There's some blood to be paid" (363). As readers, we are forced to wonder whether J.'s blood—his death—is the so-called payment for this particular instance of "progress."

Indeed, J.'s near-demise at the banquet, death by prime rib, seems to foreshadow his ultimate fate: "He's going to die on a junket? This is some far-out shit, this is a fucking ironic way to go" (76). One Eye, preoccupied by his own desire to remove his name from the List, insists about the choking incident, "It was a sign, J." (124), and when One Eye goes on to attempt to recruit J. into a quasi-legal scheme to gain access to the List, J.'s skepticism takes the form of fatalistic, racialized pessimism:

> "First, we break into Lawrence's room."
>
> "What?"
>
> "To see if he has the List. We'll hit his copy, and then we'll hit Lucien's."
>
> "I'll be in jail and you'll get off scot-free," J. says, backing away. "White people can get away with that, not black people. Not down here. We get caught, if they don't string me up, I'll get railroaded for sassing the judge or something. You're laughing but I'm not joking. I'll be laying asphalt with the work gang."

> "This isn't Mississippi in the fifties, J.," One Eye says, cocking his head.
>
> "It's always Mississippi in the fifties," J. answers. (127)

Arguably, J.'s sense here that time—progress—moves differently for black people, that in some crucial way he and other blacks are always trapped in the most threatening and violent circuits of this nation's history, is ironic given his bourgeois upbringing.[45] He had been, the text tells us, "raised in a cocoon, programmed for achievement" (175), and "his parents were in on it, J. had come to realize, by their deep middle-class sin" (171). J. embodies the black and bourgeois dilemma that I have outlined, the tension between the hypervisible, hypervulnerable racialized body, for whom it is "always Mississippi in the fifties," and the covering protection (the "cocoon") of middle-class status.

This status, for J., spans at least two generations, as the text makes it clear that J.'s father, Andrew Sutter, grew up on Strivers Row in Harlem (270). The revelation of this fact—in a chapter that describes Andrew's sister, Jennifer, discovering the sheet music for the John Henry ballad in a corner store in the early 1950s, only to have it thrown away as "gutter music" by their status-conscious mother—makes J.'s ancestral relationship to privilege abundantly clear. Yet the text marks even his grandmother's bourgeois pretensions as the product of, and perhaps as an overzealous reaction to, histories of racial oppression:

> "When we walk to church on Sunday morning down Broadway," her mother said, cheeks red in her light brown skin, "you see the dirty men with their shirts all out their pants, drinking the devil's liquor and stinking to high heaven when good people are going to church. Do you know what they've been doing all night?"
>
> "No ma'am." . . .
>
> "Staying up all night drinking and listening to music like this!" her mother screeched. "Because they are good-for-nothing niggers who don't care about making a better life for themselves. They want to stay up all night and carry on and pretend that just because they don't have to pick cotton they have no more duties to attend to. We can't do anything about good-for-nothing niggers who don't want to take

> their place in America, but we can watch ourselves. This is Strivers Row. Do you know what striving means?"
>
> "It means that we will do our best," Jennifer recites.
>
> "It means that we will survive." (279–80)

The invocation of picking cotton so close on the heels of that American strivers' maxim, of "making a better life for" oneself, suggests that the history of slavery in the United States gives particular shape to *black* bourgeois notions of self-improvement and collective "duties." And Mrs. Sutter's final commentary on the meaning of "striving," asserting that to strive is not simply to "do our best" but in fact to "survive," suggests, too, that bourgeois striving is a matter of life and death—the moral and sartorial rectitude of the Sepia Ladies Club providing the thinnest but most essential of barricades between the Sutter family and the (social) death embodied by the black underclass.[46] That this boundary is *imagined,* and imaginary, the protections it offers illusory and insubstantial, should perhaps go without saying, but it certainly takes on the contours of a real thing within Mrs. Sutter's anxious and status-conscious rant.

This is the "cocoon" of privilege into which J. is born—a cocoon that is also a prison, as his desire to flee from it makes clear. He hopes to make his escape from his parents' world in order to "take his place" in the "unruly" machinery of the city (175). Yet his first foray into the working world exposes J. to the callousness of whites—even presumably progressive whites whom he admires—toward black bodies. A flashback to college-age J. depicts his awestruck, silent attendance at his first editorial meeting at the *Downtown News* (a thinly veiled *Village Voice*), where white journalists cavalierly wordplay with the name of Eleanor Bumpurs[47] in order to come up with a catchy title for their front-page story on her death at police hands:

> [J.] sat along the back wall, on the floor. . . . He did not intend to speak unless addressed. He listened to the old hands of the *Downtown News* to see how it worked.
>
> "Bumpurs—I'm trying to riff on that."
>
> "Cops and Bumpurs. Do the Bump. Bump me in the morning and didn't just walk away."

> "Bump, jump, lump, stump . . ."
> "The cops knock on the door and—"
> "Knockin' on Heaven's Door."
> "Maybe we should focus on the cops."
> "Knock knock. Who's there? Cop. Cop who? Cop come to kill ya." (176)

This flippant extemporizing on the part of the "old hands" continues, in the novel, for three excruciating pages, as Whitehead allows us, as readers, to experience the meeting's tone through J.'s silently observing eyes; throughout, the dialogue makes clear that Bumpurs herself barely registers as a human being to the writers and editors in the room, one of whom repeatedly asks his colleagues, mid-discussion, "Anyone see [popular 1980s sitcom] *Cheers* last night?" (177).

We come to understand that apart from J., everyone in the room is white, because when they begin casting about for "someone" to "write a sidebar over the weekend. To get the black angle" (178) their attention eventually turns to J. as the only apparently black face:

> "I don't know, what about our boy Malefi?"
> "He hasn't been returning my phone calls lately."
> "Why not?"
> "Too busy?"
> "What, busy changing his name again? What about the guy who wrote the graffiti piece two weeks ago. We put it on the cover. Is he . . ."
> "You mean is he . . ."
> "Yeah, is he black, Afro-American, what do you think I mean?"
> "No. He's a professor at NYU."
> Jimmy Banks looked over at J. J. had his arms drawn around his knees in a cannonball position. "You," Banks pointed. "What's your name?" (178)

The paper's usual native informant, Malefi, is unavailable; by placing the phrase "our boy" in the editor's mouth, Whitehead cleverly slips between the condescension implicit in white male appropriation of urban slang and a much older usage of "boy" that highlights whites' infantilization of and sense of ownership over black men. And the *News*'s other nearby "expert" on African American cultural production, in this case hip-hop/graffiti, turns out to be a "professor at NYU," a fact that is presented as prima facie evidence for why he, of course, is not black. This leaves J. as a possible alternative—but once he is revealed to be only an "intern," not a staff writer, the editors' interest in him and in "the black angle" vanishes, as it is suddenly "too late for a sidebar anyway" (179). J. may recede back into anonymity in this moment, but the lesson of the scene—whites' callousness toward black life—continues to circulate in the novel.

In addition to the notion of black fleshly sacrifice, *John Henry Days* is preoccupied with the question of choice and agency and the way choices are circumscribed by life circumstances—a notion that is understood very differently by J. and his white colleagues. This is evident in the junketeers' discussion of John Henry:

> "I'm all into the prophecy thing, you understand," Frenchie grunts, his arms splayed in a gesture of Gallic expansiveness. . . . ["]What I don't get is, if you read the horoscope and the experts tell you to be careful about financial transactions or look out for Tauruses, what do you do? You keep the purse strings tight and look out for those horns. John Henry has a premonition that Big Bend is going to be the death of him. So you avoid Big Bend Tunnel. Meet a guy named Benjamin Tounelle, he's a big guy, you avoid him too. He could have avoided the whole situation if he listened to his horoscope."
>
> "There goes Frenchie again, bringing the topic around to fate versus free will."
>
> "Everything's a think piece to this guy."
>
> "Think he had a choice?"
>
> "We all have choices. Look at that atrocious shirt you're wearing, J.—that's a choice." (351)

The suggestion from Frenchie that John Henry could have done things differently prompts a telling question from J.—"Think he had a choice?"—that is met with teasing derision, but Frenchie's response, "We all have choices," also indicates a fundamentally different perspective on "choice" than that expressed by any of the black characters in the novel. For those characters, including J., agency is, at best, heavily circumscribed by one's life chances, which are heavily circumscribed by race—and each "choice" available fits within a preordained journey that ends with, or perhaps is defined by, fleshly vulnerability and mortality.

In a chapter written from the perspective of a 1930s blues singer named Moses, for instance, recording a version of the John Henry ballad as a "race record," the question of both John Henry's and Moses's choices is linked to the racialized, sure knowledge of impending death:

> Goodman says, how about we start with that John Henry thing you did last night?
>
> You like that.
>
> It had a nice mood.
>
> Moses wouldn't call it nice. He'd call it something else. Most John Henry songs he's heard from people, they tend to talk about the race and the man's death. He sang a version like that a few times but it never sounded right to him. The words "nothing but a man" set him thinking on it: Moses felt the natural thing would be to sing about what the man felt waking up in his bed on the day of the race. Knowing what he had to do and knowing that it was his last sunrise. Last breakfast, last everything. Moses could relate to that, he figured most everyone could feel what that was like. Moses certainly understood: that little terror on waking, for half a second, am I going to die today. Am I already dead. (260)

Even though Moses goes on to ruminate that it was one thing to feel such fear momentarily and quite another "to know for sure, that today is your last day" (260), the power of his rendition of the John Henry ballad seems to lie in the way "most everyone" can access this feeling of being circumscribed, marked, and manipulated by a final inevitability: "What a dead man thinks" (260). This category, "most everyone," however, clearly does not extend to the white man paying Moses to record the side, whose bland description of the song, "It had a nice mood," signals his inability to share in the racialized identification with John Henry's lack of choice, his fearful proximity to death.

J., however, is deeply aware of this proximity—even as he is also aware of the ways that privilege both protects and diminishes him. When he enters the abandoned tunnel where legend suggests John Henry worked (before Amtrak built a newer, larger tunnel next to it), he is acutely aware of the ways that his version of labor quite literally pales in comparison to John Henry's. J. is in the tunnel with Pamela, a black woman from New York whose late father was a John Henry collector and zealot; she is in Talcott for the celebration both to decide whether to donate her father's collection to the John Henry museum and to bury his remains near his idol's. Pamela, who over the course of the weekend becomes a love interest for J., asks him, "What do you think it looked like to him . . . before he was an inch in, before he started. He had a big mountain in front of him" (320). This scene returns to and extends a moment nearly a hundred pages before, when J. wonders idly as he waits outside for his ride, "The mountain is in front of him. Maybe it is Big Bend. He thinks about what it must have been like before the road made it just another hill, to look at it and think, I'm going through this mountain. Then this line of thought evaporates and he half wishes he had a beer" (236–37). J.'s assessment of himself, in this scene, is as a sort of failure or disappointment: "Under the word heroic draw a line and list all the meanings. He doesn't have a single one in him" (237). An antihero in the most literal sense, he cannot imagine John Henry's perspective, cannot disentangle himself from the modern technology and distractions that make up his freelance life—represented in the chapter by a running, italicized litany of voice messages from the business offices of various publications, primarily quibbling over payment or small semantic choices in his copy ("*We're going with dimwit one word. One word dimwit. Call if there's a problem*" [237]).

In this later moment, however, perhaps because of Pamela's presence—her proximate black womanhood serving as, in Bradley's words, "the particularly vexed 'subaltern' figure through which we might think and conceptualize the epistemic injustice and violence that constitute and limit our thinking about both blackness and gender"—J. is able to delve more deeply into the question.[48] His thoughts as he stands in the tunnel with her immediately veer toward the mortal, corporeal dangers John Henry would have faced:

> He remembers the stories of accidents from the p.r. packet, where the miners were caught by cave-ins, crushed or trapped by rock and left to

> asphyxiate. He read about a train that got stuck in this tunnel during a cave-in or mechanical failure and people suffocated on the engine smoke. After last night he can imagine suffocating in here, choking on soot. This feeling seeps into him and resounds against his bones, where he can feel the angry tonnage of the mountain pressing down on his body, as if he has the mountain on his shoulders. Or he is in its fist, and it is squeezing. (320–21)

This passage is curious not only for the way J.'s awareness of the mountain as dangerous adversary is mediated through the canned narratives of the "p.r. packet" but also for how his perspective splits between that of the miner and that of the (bourgeois) passenger, both laborer and unlucky consumer "choking on soot" and left to die. The feeling of precarity that "resounds against" J.'s bones, then, that "press[es] down on his body," is a sense of vulnerability that cuts across the contradictory positioning of the black and bourgeois subject; the mountain is a force that pierces the imagined cocoon of bourgeois safety and brings it in line with the mortal exigencies of black flesh.

For J., the clarity of this vulnerability is, ultimately, seductive. He thinks to himself, later in the same scene, "That's how he feels now—small. Step in here and you leave it all behind, the bills, the hustle, the Record, all that is receipts bleaching back there under the sun" (321). Indeed, J.'s sense of the tunnel's power is intimately tied to the ways that the mountain, because it promises death, dwarfs and trivializes his life's petty concerns, simultaneously disabling the technologies that make his bourgeois comfort possible:

> What if this were your work? To best the mountain. Come to work every day, two, three years of work, into this death and murk, each day your progress measured by the extent to which you extend the darkness. How deep you dig your grave. He wins the contest. He defeats the Record. This place confounds devices, the steam drill and all that follows. This place defeats the frequencies that are the currency of his life. Email and pagers, cell phones, step in here and fall away from the information age, into the mountain, breathe in soot. Unsettling but calming, too. The daily battles that have lost meaning are clearly

> drawn again, the opponents and objectives named and understood. The true differences between you and them. And it. (321–22)

The final lines of this passage leave these "daily battles" unmarked, but one way to read them is as racialized conflict, which loses meaning precisely because J.'s class privilege obscures the stakes of each encounter. In this reading, the "you" and the "them" could be defined as a racial self and Other, black and white, whose "true differences" are both amplified and trivialized by the mountain ("it"). Of course, because these characteristics remain unspecified in the passage, it may also be the case that the "true differences" aren't about race at all but rather about one's relationship to labor and to the ways that the mountain diminishes all such efforts. The clarity the mountain provides would thus ultimately be about life and death, about surviving the daily journey into the tunnel and back out again. For J., moreover, this moment of recognition while inside the mountain includes a moment of recognizing that the task he has set for himself, to beat the record, may be, ultimately, meaningless. Musing on the "decades of healing and forgetting" that have created the smooth stone walls that surround him, he wonders, "How long does it take to forget a hole in your self. He wins the contest but then what?" (322). Rather than provide an answer to this question, the text immediately presents J. with a request, from Pamela, to help her bury her father's remains—a task to which J. agrees and which turns the book toward its ambiguously fatalistic conclusion.

The process of burying Pamela's father—although he has been cremated and his ashes are stored in an urn, she wants to bury him, urn and all, rather than scattering his remains—proves life-altering for J. The two of them walk up the mountain together, taking turns holding the box in which the urn is stored, and trade stories about their lives. Pamela speaks of John Henry, of her father's obsessive history with the John Henry mythology, his trips to Talcott and Hinton for nebulous research, in the process narrating his gradual estrangement from his wife and daughter: "She said her father had come down here three times. She and her mother were not invited along, nor did they wish to accompany him. . . . The third time he went she and her mother were gone" (370–71). In turn, J. tells Pamela about his efforts to go for the record, and about the List, as a prelude to describing his "strange" (371) dream of Bobby Figgis, who, in the dream, hails him on a cobblestone street, downtown, and directs him to "where he was supposed to go. His final destination of the night," a bar inside a "beat-up metal door, above which a red light glowed" (373). Upon entering, and being greeted like a regular, "he suddenly remembered that he had been there many times before, all the time in fact, every night, and for every night after" (373).

J.'s dream suggests that his pursuit of the record can only lead him to his death—and more specifically to an eternally looping afterlife (or perhaps a hellscape, signaled by the glowing red light), in which J. walks through a superficial and empty scene, "somewhere downtown and hip" (372), guided to his final destination by an unexpectedly hale and hearty "apparition of Bobby Figgis" (372). The imagery of the dream only reinforces the sense, in the text, that the path J. is currently on mirrors Figgis's, that J. is on track to be, like Figgis, "devoured by pop" (111). But his trip up the mountain with Pamela, where the two of them work together to dig a hole with their bare hands, suggests to him an alternative outcome, one in which his life might serve as reward instead of sacrifice, in which rather than repeat John Henry's martyrdom, or Bobby Figgis's, he might go on to live another day:

> She asked him if he had to die to bring this weekend into being. All his life he wanted something like this weekend, a celebration of John Henry. His collection would have been a star attraction, he could have made speeches. . . . She asked him, would this have still happened, the fair, the museum, if he was still alive. Or did he have to give up himself for this to happen. The price of progress. The way John Henry had to give himself up to bring something new into the world. (378)

This passage repeats the theme of blood sacrifice that circulates throughout the novel, yet it implies that the sacrifice may have already been made, potentially liberating J. from a similar fate. While there is a slippage in the first line, with the unattributed "he" suggesting both Pamela's father *and* J., as the passage continues and focuses more clearly on her father, there is a sense that his life, already over, was the payment for this weekend—and that J.'s does not have to be.

Thus J.'s odyssey up the mountain with Pamela has the potential to be lifesaving in a figurative and a literal sense. He comes to a new understanding of the possibilities of and for his life with a story that is unlike any other story he has written:

> She asked him on the way down if he got his story. J. Sutter said yes. He had a story but it is not the one he planned. . . . He had put on paper some of the things she had said the day before but now he thought what happened today was the real story. It is not the kind of thing he usually writes. It is not puff. It is not for the website. He does not know who would take it. The dirt had not given him any receipts to be reimbursed. He does not even know if it is a story. He only knows it is worth telling. (387)

In addition to this revelation, which holds the promise to change the trajectory of his professional life, J. also might have been absolved of the need to die for the weekend's festivities, to give his life to "pop"—but only if he is willing to walk away from his pursuit of the record, something that John Henry was unable to do. Thus we might ask not only whether J. is willing to resist John Henry's (and Bobby Figgis's) fate but also whether such resistance is possible. Pamela suggests that it is, that indeed resistance—refusal to die in a variation on the same struggles of one's ancestors—is precisely the point of those earlier deaths: "You could look at it and think the fight continued, that you could resist and fight the forces and you could win and it would not cost you your life because he had given his life for you. His sacrifice enables you to endure without having to give your life to your struggle, whatever name you gave to it" (378). Here Pamela's words echo a conventional progress narrative, in which subsequent generations are absolved from sacrifice by those sacrifices that came before.

The novel's ending, however, seems to undercut the redemptive optimism represented by Pamela's character. Indeed, not only does this novel express, via its lovingly detailed narratives of earlier players in the John Henry story, the sense that, in Ta-Nehisi Coates's words, our ancestors "were not bricks in [our] road, and their lives were not chapters in [our] redemptive history," but the metaphor of the mountain, and specifically the journey *up* the mountain, actually points us to a more recent historical martyr.[49] Martin Luther King Jr.'s final speech, on April 3, 1968, popularly known as his "I've Been to the Mountaintop" speech, was given in Memphis one day before King was shot and killed. King's penultimate lines use the analogy of the mountain (likely drawn from Moses's journey up Mount Nebo in Deuteronomy) to speak to the precarity of his own life and the sense that he might not survive to see the "Promised Land" of black progress, language that has subsequently been understood as prophetic:

> Like anybody, I would like to live—a long life; longevity has its place. But I'm not concerned about that now. I just want to do God's will. And He's allowed me to go up to the mountain. And I've looked over. And I've seen the Promised Land. I may not get there with you. But I want you to know tonight, that we, as a people, will get to the Promised Land.[50]

As readers we are thus left to wonder whether J.'s journey up the mountain in *John Henry Days* is, like King's, a way of presaging his death—allowing him a glimpse of a kind of progress, the possibility for another kind of life, while denying him the chance actually to live it. Musing, later, on "the darkness, the vastness outside the streetlight. The mountain and all that it meant," J. cannot sleep, and when he sleeps his dreams disturb him, such that "he lay in his bed and shook" (388). The narrator acknowledges, "It was only when they were walking up the road to the graveyard that his discomfort eased. In the graveyard, with his hands in the dirt" (388). And while these lines might seem to suggest that the journey up the mountain has the capacity to save him from "the great rock within" (388), the moment they describe, "in the graveyard, with his hands in the dirt," is also a moment of his body being in close proximity to—literally inside—a grave. Is it the dirt, then, the authenticity of physical labor, that "eases" him? Or is it literally the embodied confirmation, "his hands in the dirt," of the affective sense that he is already dead, a dead man walking, such that his physical presence "in the graveyard" is a kind of homecoming?

Pamela presents J. with a choice: to pursue the record and beat the List, or to leave the John Henry Days festival early before the ceremony where two journalists will be shot and killed:

> He had a decision to make in the parking lot. Pamela had stood before him and said to him, I'm leaving before the ceremony. When they reached the motel she said, I think I've done everything I needed to do. She looked into his face. The town can have it all and I'm going to take an earlier plane and go home, she said. You could leave, too, she said. (387)

What Pamela holds out to him here is more than the conventional romantic narrative resolution, a heterosexual coupling to foreclose death via the promise of reproductive futurity.[51] Instead, her offer seems intimately tied to the implications of the sentences "I think I've done everything I needed to do" and "You could leave, too." Pamela, carrying the financial and emotional burden of her father's obsession with John Henry, his collection which, after his death, she put in storage along with the urn containing his ashes, has finally released the sundry items in her possession, in the process releasing the weight of her father's life on her own. She holds out the choice she has made, to return to New York without this weight on her shoulders, to J. as an option that he, too, could exercise. And we wonder, along with J., whether he has also done everything he needed to do and whether his encounter with Pamela might lead him to another sort of to-do list other than "today's event, tomorrow's event and the ones after," the press junkets that extend his labor in pursuit of the record and that "loom over him" like John Henry's mountain (387). Could he perhaps—we wonder—turn away from this Sisyphean task, choose a trajectory for his life that doesn't lead him to an inevitable and untimely death?

When I last taught this novel, many of my graduate students surprised me with their persistent optimism about J.'s fate, their conviction that it must have been one of the other journalists who had died in the narrative, not J., and their willingness to believe, though the text never depicts as much, that after the novel's final page he would enter the taxi and leave with Pamela. Perhaps I shouldn't have been surprised—we all want to believe in the possibility of capital-p Progress, the possibility that contemporary black lives can and should be more than "people turned to fuel for the American machine."[52] It was with genuine contrition that

I reminded them of the lines we all had read, lines that are not so much ambiguous as ambivalent about the fate they make perfectly clear: "There is still time. It will not take him long to get his little things together. They will wait if he asks. He stands there with the sun on his face deciding, as if choices are possible" (389). The thesis of the novel, and its tragedy, is contained in those last five words, which refuse us the possibility that J. can *choose* his way out of the mortality fated to him.

That the story does not *end* with these words, however, returns us to Williamson's notion of black social life, "the way black people go about making themselves, both because of and regardless of the conditions of their making."[53] Referencing Sexton, Williamson positions her understanding of black social life not in opposition to Afro-pessimism but rather within its fissures, or what we might call its blind spot—its focus on blackness within "the modern world system" to the exclusion of considering "what [black] folks think about themselves."[54] Thus the final two lines of *John Henry Days* attend not to J.'s impending, seemingly inevitable death, even if that death has been signaled quite clearly a few lines before, but rather to the connection he has forged with Pamela on the mountain and a subsequent exchange between them:

> She asked one last thing when they came down the mountain. When they came down the mountain she asked, what's the J. stand for? He told her. (389)

These lines conceal as much as they reveal, emphasizing the depth of intimacy between J. and Pamela. We might guess, particularly given all of the parallels that the novel has set up between the two men, that the J. stands for "John," but the text ultimately denies us this knowledge, leaving us as readers on the outside of the conversation.[55] Indeed, the actual words of the exchange are not detailed here, only the fact that it occurred—she asked, and he told her. The near-chiasmic repetition of "she asked" and "when they came down the mountain" emphasizes not only the seriousness—rather than the idleness—of the question but also the importance of its timing, arriving as it does after the two have shared a moment of connection over Pamela's father's ashes, their "hands in the dirt" together.

Not only does their exchange undo J.'s typical position as journalist/laborer, in that J. is the subject of Pamela's curious (social rather than investigative) questioning, but the fact that he responds to her question also suggests a higher level of connection. We might assume that a character like J. is asked not infrequently what the solitary initial of his name "stands for" and also that—given that no one in the text seems to know his given name—he typically rebuffs such questions. But when Pamela asks, after their time together, he tells her. In this, the novel suggests, finally, that optimism or pessimism may not be the point and that black life is, indeed, "*lived* in social *death*."[56] Whitehead, like Sexton, would seem throughout the novel to emphasize both the lived and the death—but in these final lines he returns emphasis to the living and reminds us, ultimately, that J.'s life matters *while he lives it,* no matter how (and in service to what larger struggle) it might end.

Conclusion

Black and Bourgeois in the Era of #BlackLivesMatter

> The world is wrong. You can't put the past behind you. It's buried in you; it's turned your flesh into its own cupboard.
>
> —Claudia Rankine, *Citizen*

I began this book with an account of a racial assault on two middle-class black people in a coffee shop; it seems fitting that as I sit down to write these concluding pages, another location of the same national coffee chain is in the news, also because of a racial incident. On the surface, the circumstances differ in significant ways: in the earlier incident Dr. Bob Hughes and his colleague, paying customers, were assaulted and spit upon by another customer, a private citizen; in this more recent case, two men, described in initial accounts as "black real estate agents" waiting in a Rittenhouse Square Starbucks for a business meeting with a real estate developer they knew (before the simplifying apparatus of national media flattened the story to "two black men" who waited for "a friend"), allegedly were asked to leave by the location's manager because one of them asked to use the restroom before making a purchase. Upon their refusal to depart after being denied access, as they continued to wait for their anticipated meeting, this manager called the police, who subsequently arrested the two men for trespassing. They were detained for nine hours before being released, as not only did the Philadelphia district attorney find no evidence any crime had been committed but Starbucks declined to press charges.[1]

So yes, the circumstances differ; yet to watch the cell phone video of this incident, captured by a white female patron outraged by the events, is to recognize the corollary, or perhaps the underbelly, of Hughes's experience, two years before, in a Seattle Starbucks with his "professionally attire[d]" female colleague. The two young entrepreneurs in the Philadelphia video, while neatly and stylishly dressed, are not in formal professional clothing; one wears a black hoodie with white lettering, dark jeans, and Nike sneakers, while the other wears fitted sweatpants and a plain black top, with an olive green windbreaker and white sneakers. Notably, the white man they are meeting, who arrives as they are being walked out of the shop in handcuffs, is wearing a white button-down shirt, a light-blue down vest, blue jeans, and white sneakers—in other words, he is dressed in a similarly casual vein. His whiteness, however, confers an air of both professionalism and authority upon him despite his casual clothing, as evidenced by his ability to confront the police loudly, with incredulity and no legal repercussions, while his potential business partners are escorted out by multiple officers, handcuffed and in silence.

Similar to the expulsion of the group of black women from the California wine train in 2015, the presence of these black men's presumably "unprofessional" bodies in the raced and classed space of the upscale community café (located in Center City Philadelphia's "most expensive and exclusive neighborhood") is deemed by the white manager to be *trespassing* rather than simply waiting.[2] Would the outcome have been different if, like Hughes before them, the men had donned "professional" attire for their meeting? Experience, observation, and history suggest otherwise—suggest, in fact, that outcomes for black bodies "out of place," even if those bodies are privileged ones, are largely more subject to the whims of the whites (or their surrogates) they encounter than to their bodily performances.[3] Indeed, reading this incident in concert with Hughes and his colleague's experience suggests a "damned if you do, damned if you don't" situation for black folks in America: to appear in professional attire, clearly marked as materially privileged, is perhaps to trigger a punitive response designed to put one back "in place," while to appear in casual clothing is to risk being understood as impoverished and therefore allegedly dangerous, a fear-inspiring representative of purported black criminality.

Throughout this book I have argued that post-soul authors—writing in an era after the Civil Rights and Black Power politics of the 1960s and

1970s had waned but before the emergence of quintessential post-soul, bourgeois, and "post-racial" political figure, Barack Obama—narratively imagine black privilege as an existential and representational paradox. This paradox, the black and bourgeois dilemma, is that of a black subject simultaneously protected and caged by privilege, a middle-class subject whose black flesh is often a source of pride but always, as well, a target of violence. Here in the final pages of this project, I want to think, again, about how these ideas continue to circulate in our immediate present, what I am calling the Black Lives Matter (BLM) era. Via a closer look at work emerging from this immediate contemporary moment, we might again recognize the prescience of texts from the late twentieth and early twenty-first centuries, some of them published decades ago, which have nonetheless *anticipated* our immediate present in their emphasis upon bourgeois body and black flesh in opposition, on the recurrent paradox of a subject simultaneously black and middle-class. This emphasis is more than simply an assertion that racism continues to exist; it is a reminder of how that racism can create unlivable lives even for black people with every advantage, precisely because the black and bourgeois dilemma is one of existential impossibility.

As I conclude *Black Bourgeois,* I want to consider several contemporary works by black women that seem to be commenting upon this impossibility. I begin with Claudia Rankine's *Citizen,* and in fact employ Rankine's poetic reflection on the experience of the microaggressed as a kind of framework to understand the position of the black (bourgeois) subject in the BLM moment. Rankine's text—which, as she has noted in interviews, is a meditation upon how the racial microaggression contributes to and creates an environment in which black death becomes ubiquitous—is, like this book, preoccupied with the body, with flesh (as in the above epigraph) and the way that it carries memory, history, and racial assault within it.[4] Rankine as critical and theoretical frame allows me to think more expansively about how this question of black and bourgeois embodiment, this paradoxical viscerality, circulates in two other, visual texts from our present moment, Issa Rae's HBO comedy series, *Insecure* (2016–), and Ava DuVernay's OWN drama, *Queen Sugar* (2016–), based on a 2014 novel of the same name by Natalie Baszile. These popular works, both part of an emergent renaissance in black television, centralize class privilege as they grapple with what we might call the life-or-death emergency that is African American life in our immediate present. These works, particularly DuVernay's *Queen Sugar,* delve into a recurrent sense of racial crisis and precarity that circulates in the BLM era, even as they speak to nuances of black middle-class experience that would initially seem to distance their characters from blackness's most immediate dangers.

Early on in *Citizen,* Rankine's speaker turns her attention to tennis powerhouse Serena Williams and the way that countless bad calls—calls of foot faults and balls out of bounds, calls that seem unfair even to observing commentators, calls that cannot be proven to be but must, in truth, be motivated by racial bias—over the course of Williams's career have taken a physical and mental toll:

> Yes, and the body has memory. The physical carriage hauls
> more than its weight. The body is the threshold across which
> each objectionable call passes into consciousness—all
> the unintimidated, unblinking, and unflappable resilience
> does not erase the moments lived through, even as we
> are eternally stupid or everlastingly optimistic, so ready to
> be inside, among, a part of the games.[5]

Rankine's words here, and in particular her shift to the first-person-plural pronoun "we," push us as readers to consider, via our consideration of Williams, the limits of black "unintimidated, unblinking, and unflappable resilience." These words ask us, in fact, to understand Williams's bodily memory of racial insult, her frustrated optimism and hope for better, her rage at these continued moments of unfairness, as our own.

Rae's *Insecure* tells the story of central character Issa (played by Rae), who works for a nonprofit organization providing educational support to inner-city schools, and her best friend, Molly, a corporate lawyer. If their friendship is the cornerstone of the series, the two women's relationships with men have provided much of the attendant conflict over the first two seasons. The end of season one finds Issa cheating on her longtime boyfriend, Lawrence, also a recurrent character on the show, and the subsequent end of their relationship, punctuated by Lawrence's sexual liaison with an acquaintance, Tasha.[6] Season two picks up on this rebound relationship as it eventually fizzles out, and follows both Issa and Lawrence as they navigate dating and single life after years of living together.

Rae has stated in interviews that she sees *Insecure* as an Obama-era show, reflective of and perhaps enabled by the presence of Barack Obama and his family in the White House for eight years.[7] Yet by its second season, even this show—typically a gorgeously lit, richly decorated landscape of well-dressed, impeccably coiffed, smooth-skinned bourgeois black people at play—cannot escape direct reference to the troubling racial politics of Obama's second term (the beginning of the BLM era) and the precarity that surrounds black bodies in our immediate present. In season two, episode four of the series, one story line follows Lawrence as he rushes to buy alcohol at the grocery store in preparation for a major black social event across town—driving a Jaguar, a luxury car he can afford now that he has gotten a job in the tech sector.[8] Stuck in traffic, he follows several other cars in making an illegal U-turn and is quickly pulled over by an approaching police car, which hails him with both flashing lights and siren.

To us as viewers, the source of Lawrence's immediate panic is evident and only reinforced when the officer's partner calls sternly "Keep your hands where I can see them!" as Lawrence reaches into his pocket, after dropping his debit card to the floor in the confusion. *Yes, and the body has memory.* Black men and women who ended up losing their lives under similar circumstances—from Philando Castile to Sandra Bland, among many others—haunt the scene and shape the viscerality of his fear as Lawrence waits for the white officer to approach his window. Yet, true to genre, the interaction soon takes a swerve for the comedic. After questioning Lawrence on the basis of his paradoxical privilege ("Is this your car?") and chiding him for his U-turn, the officer says, "I'll let you off with a warning today, Hot Rod"—language that foreshadows later events in the episode—and then jokes, "I should write you a ticket just for being a Hoya." A stunned and still-fearful Lawrence takes a moment to

Lawrence (Jay Ellis) pulled over by police. "Hella LA" (television still), *Insecure,* HBO, August 13, 2017.

realize the officer is referring to his Georgetown University license plate, as the officer continues, "I'm a Villanova guy—we beat the shit out of you guys last year!" Lawrence's pretense of laughter as he dazedly agrees, "Yeah, you did—you beat us," signals the freighted double meaning of these words, the way that the officer's statement can be read as a comment upon how the "team" of law enforcement has engaged fatally with the "team" of black people over the previous year, which at the time of the episode's airing (mid-August 2017) would have included the deaths of Korryn Gaines, Keith Lamont Scott, Terence Crutcher, and Jordan Edwards, among others, at police hands.[9]

Lawrence's police encounter is thus only partially played for laughs, haunted as it is by the bodily strain of this history, and his awareness of it *(the body is the threshold across which each objectionable [death] passes into consciousness).* Yet his subsequent encounter with two white-presenting women at the grocery store seems to scar him just as profoundly.[10] Unable to pay for his beer because his debit card was misplaced during the police stop, he accepts the women's offer to buy it for him, and after some flirtation in the parking lot he finds himself at their apartment, anticipating a hookup. *Even as we are eternally stupid or everlastingly optimistic, so ready to be inside, among, a part of the games.* Yet the sexual encounter that ensues, a threesome with the two women, proves unsatisfying for all parties, as the women, disappointed that Lawrence has orgasmed before they wanted him to, complain, "We've been with a bunch of other black guys who could come and keep going." Lawrence's stunned reaction ("a *bunch*?") only intensifies as the two leave him on the bed and begin reminiscing out loud about previous encounters: "You know who could fuck? LaMarcus." Like the elusive, authentically black "Clevon" who serves as foil for Monk Ellison's bourgeois inauthenticity in *Erasure,* here "LaMarcus" suggests a blacker, more sexually powerful competitor, capable and willing participant in the women's dehumanizing fetishization of the black "Hot Rod."

In this moment, Lawrence's class privilege, performatively signaled via the difference between the names "Lawrence" and "LaMarcus," places his black habitus in jeopardy, as his cisgendered, masculine black body—and the assumed hypersexuality that supposedly should accompany that body—is appraised by these two women and found wanting, a racialized and sexualized violation that compounds the fear and pervasive sense of vulnerability he experienced in the police encounter. It is no wonder that Lawrence later transposes the terms of his friend Chad's exuberant reaction to what Chad imagines has been a sexual juggernaut of an experience; in reply to "You wore 'em out! My man 'Rence! Wearing that ass out!" Lawrence offers with little enthusiasm, "Yeah man. I am . . . pretty . . . worn out." Rather than confirming the evening as a success in cross-racial sexual experimentation, this response reveals, instead, Lawrence's grief and exhaustion. *The physical carriage hauls more than its weight.* Lawrence is "worn out" from the bodily toll of a day that has confronted him, in myriad ways, with his own racialized precarity and objectification.

When *Citizen* turns to the question of police brutality, the provocation and conundrum of black class privilege serves as its opening frame. An unnamed police officer's violence may—or may not—be a consequence of the black subject/suspect's ability to make his "home" in a neighborhood of means:

> Maybe because home was a hood the officer could not afford, not that a reason was needed, I was pulled out of my vehicle a block from my door, handcuffed and pushed into the police vehicle's backseat, the officer's knee pressing into my collarbone, the officer's warm breath vacating a face creased into the smile of its own private joke. (107)

In this passage, part of a section of *Citizen* titled "Stop-and-Frisk" (a "script for situation video" created in collaboration with John Lucas, a documentary photographer and Rankine's partner), an anonymous speaker describes the indignity of being pulled over by police—*pulled out of my vehicle . . . handcuffed and pushed into the police vehicle's backseat.* The scene in this passage widens out, over pages, to a sense of the ubiquity and similarity of such stops, their recursivity: "Each time it begins in the same way, it doesn't begin the same way, each time it begins it's the same" (107).

Rankine asks readers to recognize this recursivity, to see the ways that the repetition of this narrative—literally a script that plays out over and over on America's streets, country, city, and suburban—erases black humanity, flattens each black subject into that "one guy" who is always already guilty. The way this scene plays out might be a consequence of the affront of black privilege, or might simply be a function of the way that public blackness operates as a perpetual case of mistaken identity, for rich, middle class, and poor alike.

If Rae's *Insecure* lightens an initially terrifying police encounter only to return us to black fear and vulnerability via an unexpectedly troubling depiction of another, sexual, encounter that we might expect to be purely amusing or pleasurable, DuVernay's *Queen Sugar* uses the account of a similar police encounter to dwell both visually and affectively in black pain. The series, which tells the story of the Bordelon siblings, who inherit a sugarcane farm from their late father, includes significant attention to Charley Bordelon West, half sister to the other two Bordelon children, Nova and Ralph Angel. After her father's death, Charley, the estranged wife and manager of basketball star Davis West, moves to Louisiana with

Micah (Nicholas Ashe) being walked into the police station. "After the Winter" (television still), *Queen Sugar,* OWN, June 20, 2017.

her teenage son, Micah. Davis, disgraced after his involvement in a team sex scandal is revealed on video, eventually follows the pair and begins playing in Louisiana in order to repair his relationship with Micah; ironically, the police encounter in question is set in motion by Davis's extravagant birthday gift to Micah at the top of season two, a new luxury convertible.[11]

The first part of this encounter takes place in the second season's first episode. We see an older white police officer first pull Micah over and then pull his gun on the teen as Micah tries to follow instructions to retrieve the car's registration by leaning over to the glovebox. The next time Micah appears in this episode, it is as he is being walked into the police station by this officer—in handcuffs, and visibly shaken. When Charley, Nova, and Davis eventually walk out of the station with him, the camera pans down to reveal what only Nova notices as Charley and Davis bicker over Davis's willingness to perform a "Step'n Fetchit act" to gain special consideration from the officers—Micah was apparently so terrified by this experience that he at some point urinated on himself. *Yes, and the body has memory.* While this image alone provides a visual cue to the extent of Micah's distress, only much later in the season, in the eighth episode, do we learn the full extent of what Micah has suffered.[12]

Upon being confronted by Davis after yet another outburst in which Micah erupts in uncharacteristic rage and defiance—a recurring motif throughout season two, signaling Micah's unaddressed trauma from the police encounter—Micah responds to his father's "What happened to you?" by revealing a far deeper violation than the officer's pulling of his gun. Through tears, his eyes averted from his father and the viewer, he recounts:

> He put me in the back with cuffs on, right? He told me he was taking me in. He was being nice to me, sort of, you know, talking to me. I tried to tell him that I was your son but he didn't believe me. Then he drove past the police station. Said we were going for a ride. That's when he stopped being nice. Out of nowhere he said that he hated "fancy-talking niggers," you know that I sounded like I grew up with a silver spoon in my mouth. So . . . we pull up in an alley somewhere. And it's *dark.* And he gets out of the car and he says—he says "I'ma take that silver spoon out your mouth boy"—he kept saying that, I'm gonna take that spoon out your mouth boy, put something else in it. So then he gets out of the car. He opens the door, takes out his gun, he pushes me down, and he puts the gun in my mouth. And he pulled the trigger, Dad.

At this point the camera's focus shifts briefly to Davis, whose face reflects his own distress before he rushes to comfort Micah, sitting down and wrapping an arm around him, saying "It's alright"; the next words from Micah are muffled by their embrace: "He didn't have to do that." *Queen Sugar* highlights, in this scene, the particular challenge to state-sanctioned white racism presented by the upper-middle-class black body, driving a car the officer could never buy, living in a neighborhood where the officer cannot afford to reside. *Maybe because home was a hood the officer could not afford, not that a reason was needed.* Micah is one of this privileged number, these "fancy-talking niggers"—a phrase that gestures not only toward pricey educations and commensurate vocabularies but also toward particular kinds of accents and ways of speaking. It seems important to note not only that Micah attends an exclusive New Orleans private school but that he had been, until very recently, raised in California, and his speech bears the mark of that place and not the southern space where he now resides.

This officer, as does the officer in the recollection of *Citizen*'s speaker, *pushe[s]* Micah *into the police vehicle's backseat.* But the officer of Micah's retelling goes further than the violence of handcuffs, of *knee pressing into . . . collarbone.* The phallic and queer implications of the "silver spoon" the officer rhetorically places in the teenager's mouth, which he then replaces with, literally, the barrel of a gun, disrupt naturalized conceptions of black racial and gender identity. Micah as black and bourgeois young man is queered first by his imagined fellating of the silver spoon of material privilege and then by the actual gun barrel forced into his mouth, as this officer's *own private joke*—his interior resentment, rage, and desire—transform into a cruel and outwardly directed sexual violation. The pulling of the gun's trigger extends this raced and classed violation to a reminder, again, of black precarity regardless of class status; it serves as a visceral message to Micah as black "suspect" that police officers are endowed with the power of the state, and the will of the people, to kill black subjects with impunity.

Micah's muffled but outraged "He didn't have to do that" as he recounts this part of his experience points both to the fact that such prompting is unnecessary—in the episode's present moment, America in the year 2017, no black person over the age of ten or eleven would likely be unaware of this power held over our lives—and to the fact of its excess. The officer has already violated, humiliated, and *threatened* Micah by forcing the gun into his mouth, because of course the existence of the trigger, his knowledge that it could be pulled, is a reminder that he could die at any moment; actually to pull the trigger is to trick Micah into believing that the moment of his death has arrived. Indeed, this scene forces us to recall Micah's urine-soaked pants from episode one and to realize that *this* moment of terror, the moment he believed himself dead, and not simply the process of a routine police booking, is likely when he lost control of his bladder. Here, DuVernay creates narrative space to reimagine Micah's character as not simply a sheltered rich kid who can't handle, even briefly, what poor and working-class black people endure on a regular basis, but rather as a black child forced, like so many other black children, to confront far too soon the ubiquity and omnipresence of black death, and worse, to accept that this death is always already coming for him, in particular. It has reached and overtaken him. It is here.

Black Bourgeois, then, is in part a chronicle of how contemporary black cultural production interrogates and illuminates this dilemma: black flesh proudly worn yet targeted for death; privilege as imprisoning cocoon and as always insufficient hiding place; the familiar violence of these contradictions and how to inhabit their aftermath. I return to *Citizen*:

> How to care for the injured body,
>
> the kind of body that can't hold
> the content it is living?
>
> And where is the safest place when that place
> must be someplace other than in the body? (143)

For Rankine, here, the microaggression operates as bodily *injury,* the sort of abiding injury that makes safety impossible. For where is *that place,* the place of safety, that is *someplace other than in the body*? We bring our bodies with us; they are the vehicles in which we travel. As the old saw reminds us, wherever you go, there you are. When the body is injured in such a way—not (always) literally, but certainly metaphysically, and also perhaps physiologically, which is to say within its very systems, the internal structures that allow for the organism's healthy function—how to soldier on? How to hold what one's body *can't hold,* and live with *the content it is living* that is nonetheless unlivable?

Before I conclude my discussion, I want to step back, to think for a bit about why these cultural texts produced by black women turn to stories of police violence in their attention to the question of black vulnerability and precarity, and particularly to the ways that the privileged black body is subject to this everyday threat. There are many bourgeois black women characters throughout both series, and both series do attend to certain kinds of class- and corporeality-inflected dilemmas that these characters experience (I am thinking, for instance, of corporate lawyer Molly's attempts to break into the white and male "boys club" of the senior partners at her firm, or businesswoman Charley Bordelon's efforts to establish her sugar mill in the face of all manner of undermining opposition from the wealthy white family who currently monopolizes the business—not coincidentally, the same family that once owned Charley, Nova, and Ralph Angel's Bordelon ancestors as slaves). When Nova calls her sister a "bourgie bitch" in season one, she gives voice to what audience members have already come to recognize about Charley—at least on the surface, we are meant to understand her character as a version of the light-skinned (or "yalla," cf. Morrison's *Tar Baby*), haughty, and out-of-touch black career woman who believes she is better than those around her precisely because of both her financial and her skin-color capital. This role on *Insecure* is occupied by the series' only married friend, Tiffany DuBois (played by Amanda Seales), who wears her hair long and blonde, scrutinizes Issa's hipster clothing choices, and generally operates as the diva of the friend group. Of course, neither series leaves these characters in the realm of simple stereotype. We ultimately see cracks in Tiffany's facade of bourgeois perfection, as the show reveals her marriage had gone through major struggles offscreen, with her husband living in a hotel for months; Charley's character on *Queen Sugar* is revealed to be both more loyal to her family and more passionate about her racial identity than either her class or racial origins (Charley's mother is white and wealthy) would at first lead us to believe.

Nonetheless, to delve most fully into black and bourgeois precarity and the vulnerable paradox of black middle-class subjectivity, both series include extended narrative attention to the police encounter, specifically the encounter of a bourgeois black man with a (seemingly or actually) hostile law enforcement officer. While this might seem merely coincidental, or a concession to contemporary events, I would argue that these episodes of *Insecure* and *Queen Sugar* are doing something more—namely, visually framing black male vulnerability to police as a stand-in for the paradox of black and bourgeois subjectivity more broadly, so that we might read these black men's bodies as *surrogates* for a precarious and vulnerable blackness writ large. I say this not to diminish the specificity of black men's experiences with police—although the #SayHerName movement has emerged in part to call attention to the ways that black women are also victims of police and other state-sanctioned violence, and recent statistics show black women are the group most likely to be unarmed in police encounters, such that this specificity may be more a matter of whose experiences receive more attention than of substantive difference or of either gender having it "worse."[13]

Instead, I am interested in how these two small-screen narratives helmed by black women, narratives that repeatedly center black women in numerous ways, are so similar in their turn to black men when they want to speak to a particular kind of paradoxical black and bourgeois precarity. I want to suggest that this narrative turn, rather than reflecting a shared willingness to ignore or downplay black women's experiences—which seems highly unlikely from two show runners (Rae and DuVernay) who have demonstrated their commitment to telling black women's stories—is in fact about what police as a collective signify and how the violent confrontation between police officers and black bodies might be understood as archetypal, or as what Frank Wilderson would call an *antagonism,* "an irreconcilable struggle between entities, or positions, the resolution of which is not dialectical but entails the obliteration of one of the positions."[14] I am reminded here of a recent music video that does particularly powerful work to communicate this: Run the Jewels' and Zack De la Rocha's "Close Your Eyes (And Count to F**k)," which premiered in 2014. The video, which features *Atlanta*'s LaKeith Stanfield as a young black man ("Kid") being pursued by an officer ("Cop"), played by Shea Whigham, represents interaction between the men as far more than police/perp but rather as the tangle of two weary adversaries in an unwinnable war.[15] *Insecure* and *Queen Sugar* visually invoke this antagonism and suggest that Lawrence's and Micah's experiences speak in broader ways to how even materially privileged black subjects carry *the injured body,* the body made precarious and vulnerable to and by racist assault. Further,

Run the Jewels and Zack De la Rocha, "Close Your Eyes (And Count to F**k)," video still, dir. A. G. Rojas; Park Pictures, 2014.

as I will argue below, despite the way these particular scenes with Lawrence and Micah might be said to represent black men's experiences, black women are central to how both shows, but *Queen Sugar* especially, work in broader ways to conceptualize racial solidarity within and beyond social (class) conflict.

Perhaps it is too pat to read anything more than nostalgia and individualized longing into Lawrence's arrival, after his long day contending with racial stereotype and the precarity of his own black and bourgeois body, at Issa's apartment. The camera widens from its tight shot of Lawrence's face as he ends his conversation with Chad ("I am . . . pretty . . . worn out") to reveal that he is parked outside the Dunes complex where he and Issa once lived together and where she still, at that moment in the show's arc, resides. *And where is the safest place when that place must be someplace other than in the body?* Perhaps that place is "home," a home to which Lawrence now cannot actually return. If this suggests a kind of tragic estrangement for Lawrence's character, *Insecure* does offer other intimations of the sorts of contingent and fugitive home spaces that are possible for its characters, largely through the lens of female friendships. In *Queen Sugar,* by contrast, black women play a formidable role in Micah's healing, not just via his participation in his aunt Nova's anti-police-brutality activism but via an altered relationship to *looking,* seeing and being seen, that is facilitated by black women and girls.

In the same episode as Micah's breakdown and confession to his father of his experience at the hands of the police officer, there is an earlier scene in which Micah, his girlfriend Keke (Tanyell Waivers), and her friend LaTisha (Trina LaFargue) emerge from an open wrought-iron gateway into a fenced-in courtyard, lush with foliage. Micah is dressed in his private school uniform, while Keke and LaTisha, both adolescent black girls, are in casual but fashionable clothes—a sun dress, a T-shirt and colorful shorts, high-top sneakers. These cues suggest that the school day has just ended and that the girls, who do not attend Micah's school, have come to meet him at his campus. Their conversation immediately raises the question of black privilege and racial belonging, as Micah, professing his interest in the French novel *The Three Musketeers,* says of its author, Alexandre Dumas, "Besides, Dumas was kind of a . . . undercover brother." LaTisha expresses immediate skepticism with a sharp "What?" while Keke scoffs, affably, "Ain't no such thing as a sort of a black dude. Either you are or you aren't, and it ain't hard to tell." At this moment, while the camera is still focused on the three friends, we hear a police siren, and the attention of all three is drawn, along with the camera's eye, beyond the fence to an unfolding scene of a white officer detaining two black male adolescents who are seated on the curb, handcuffed and looking at the ground, as the officer stands behind them speaking into his radio.

Whether Micah was planning to agree with or to protest the notion that there "ain't no such thing as a sort of a black dude"—on the basis of skin color, material privilege, or ability to pass for white—the sound of the siren forecloses this conversation and seemingly obviates the need for such debate, as it immediately places all three, as black subjects, on high alert. LaTisha asks, "Y'all should we stay? Make sure that goes down okay?" And without waiting for Micah's agreement, Keke responds, "Yeah, girl. Just in case," at which point LaTisha raises her tablet to begin filming the encounter. Here Keke and LaTisha, with Micah's tacit approval, enact what Simone Browne calls *dark sousveillance,* which she conceptualizes as not just a particular action but "an imaginative place from which to mobilize a critique of racializing surveillance," critique which might then include "antisurveillance, countersurveillance, and other freedom practices."[16] Keke and LaTisha's recognition of the potential for this police encounter not to "go down okay" is a part of the girls' critique of the police as state actors empowered to discipline and bring under control black bodies by any means at their disposal, up to and including lethal force; their decision to hang around the area and film the encounter "just in case" thus might be understood as both precautionary or protective, and condemnatory. It also, of course, brings Micah's arrest back into narrative view. Although at this point in episode eight's story arc the extent of his violation by the officer has not been revealed, even the start of the arrest as depicted in episode one of the season is memorable for its isolation (Micah is pulled over on a deserted road), for the lack of *sous*veilling eyes to stay and watch, and wait to see, just in case.

Notably, there is also a moment, while Micah, Keke, and LaTisha are behind the fence, watching the adjoining scene unfold, that a handful of Micah's white classmates (all also in school uniform) approach. One, "Christian," hails Micah and walks up to him, and once he has been introduced to Keke and LaTisha the group engages in some playful banter, as Christian assures Keke that "[Micah] talks about you *all* the time." None of the white teens appear to have noticed the police activity at all, and Christian goes so far as to invite Micah and friends to the movies. We see Micah look over at the scene beyond the fence again, concerned, before declining and promising to see Christian at school tomorrow. The scene ends with LaTisha returning to filming and Keke and Micah, now arm in arm, again watching the police encounter.

I find this conclusion—and this scene as a whole—telling in multiple ways. First, while the scene opens by positing, aurally, that "ain't no such thing as a sort of a black dude," the visuals of the scene almost simultaneously contradict this claim and reinvoke divisions of class, depicting Micah and Keke on the opposite side of the fence's bars from the two poor black kids in police custody. The class privilege of those on Micah's side of the fence is obvious—that privilege is marked not only by Micah's prep school uniform but via such visual and even embodied details as Keke's glowing skin and subtle jewelry, or her and LaTisha's impeccably done hair and bright, fashionable clothes. While the handcuffed young men on the other side lack the same look of well-cared-for vitality, costumed in faded colors that suggest wear, their skin closer to ashen than glowing, what most clearly positions them, materially, is the barrier of the fence itself—shot through iron bars that recall the bars of a jail cell, the imagery of the scene suggests the two youths are (always) already imprisoned. Thus while the sounds of the scene—not only the cheerful claim that "ain't no such thing as a sort of a black dude" but the interpolating and terror-inducing call of the police siren, which enfolds all of the black characters in the frame—insist upon one meaning, the scene's visuals suggest another. Micah, Keke, and LaTisha view the handcuffed boys through a fence that not only figuratively marks the boys as "criminal" but operates as a form of class and caste discipline, presumably protecting those on the inside and excluding those on the outside. And even as we as viewers *know* that this disciplining barrier might at any point be turned against class "insiders" like Micah precisely because of their blackness, we also *know*—are made to know both by the visuals of this scene and by our recollection of Micah's turn as the young black boy in handcuffs—that being on one side of the fence versus the other, even in a contingent or temporary way, has meaning and, often, tangible consequences.

Queen Sugar asks us to hold both of these truths together as we watch: Keke and Micah's material privilege over the boys via their temporary positioning within the confines of the fence, *and* their shared vulnerability with them as black subjects *all* always within reach of the police. In this moment of contradiction the series captures, all too clearly, the black and bourgeois dilemma, the ambivalent paradox of a subject protected (and confined) by privilege while also and always vulnerable to racism because, in the words of Reginald McKnight's Bertrand Milworth, "black is black."[17]

Most important, perhaps, the scene offers a lesson in racial—rather than class—solidarity, in the power of the teens' choice to remain at the site of the police encounter as witnesses. Micah, Keke, and LaTisha could have accepted the invitation from Christian (whose name signifies at best his symbolic status as the white American Everyman, at worst his figurative alignment with white evangelical Christian racism) to go the movies. In so doing, they would have abandoned the kids beyond the fence—black people who look like them but who exist in a very different relationship to the bars between them—to whatever "just in case" catastrophe might await at the hands of the state.

They do not.

This act—of tarrying, of bearing witness—is a choice. It neither resolves nor dissolves the black and bourgeois dilemma. But it offers an action to take, one that makes clear, to us and to them, where their loyalties lie. What exists beyond that single action remains murky, but a final turn to Rankine's *Citizen* might point toward a possibility:

> The rain this morning pours from the gutters and every-
> where else it is lost in the trees. . . .
> . . . The trees, their bark,
> their leaves, even the dead ones, are more vibrant wet.
> Yes, and it's raining. Each moment is like this—before
> it can be known, categorized as similar to another thing
> and dismissed, it has to be experienced, it has to be seen.
> What did he just say? Did she really just say that? . . .
> . . . The moment stinks. Still
> you want to stop looking at the trees. You want to walk out
> and stand among them. And as light as the rain seems, it
> still rains down on you. (9)

I return to *Citizen* here because of what this passage suggests about both the power of witness and its limits. There is a moment, as Micah, Keke, and LaTisha *sous*veil the boys' encounter with law enforcement, that one of the handcuffed boys looks up from the ground, at his surroundings; while it is unclear what exactly he sees, we are never shown eye contact between him and Micah. A mutual looking, a kind of cross-class understanding, is what we as viewers might wish or hope for from the scene, but the episode remains focused on what Micah sees, on the view from the inside of the fence. That view is only one angle of vision, however, and if *it's raining* then we are, all of us, subject to that water, shower or deluge.

What *rains down* beyond the fence touches down inside its boundaries as well—they are permeable, and we are, anyway, never fully inside. And while *it has to be seen,* we might also honor the desire *to stop looking*—not to turn away, but *to walk out and stand among them.* There is joy in that *vibrant* splendor of *wet* leaves, rain-darkened flesh. The only shelter is the communion we find there.

Acknowledgments

This book, in this incarnation, has been in progress for a decade; in the years since I began thinking and writing about these works, I've given birth twice, changed institutions once, and gone through innumerable second-guesses and false starts—and in that time I've accumulated a long list of people to thank.

Most recently, a faculty fellowship award from the National Endowment for the Humanities made it possible for me to spend the spring and summer of 2018 focused solely on the final revisions to the manuscript. I am grateful for the honor, and the time. Thank you to Maria Gillombardo and my history colleague Craig Koslofsky for their patient work with me, under the auspices of the Office of the Vice Chancellor for Research here at the University of Illinois, on my proposal for the fellowship—work that also helped me immensely to sharpen and clarify my vision for the project.

I also want to acknowledge, with immense gratitude, the authors, filmmakers, and performers whose work I engage in these pages—Andrea Lee, Spike Lee, Trey Ellis, Rebecca Walker, Danzy Senna, Shay Youngblood, Reginald McKnight, Percival Everett, Kevin Willmott, Colson Whitehead, Michael Thomas (the most philosophical and hilarious of colleagues), Claudia Rankine, Issa Rae, Ava DuVernay, and the greatest to ever do it, Toni Morrison—thank you for telling these stories and shining a light on the complexity of African American life.

The thirteen years I spent at Hunter College were always generative and fulfilling; I am grateful for the thoughtful community of colleagues I found there, both within the English department and beyond it, including Cristina Alfar, Barbara Webb, Jeremy Glick, Kelvin Black, Michael Thomas, Harriet Luria, Leigh Jones, Janet Neary, Angie Reyes, Jackie Brown, and Anthony Browne. I am also grateful to a bevy of Hunter students for the excellent conversation in my undergraduate and MA seminars on "Black Post-Soul Narratives" and "African American Literature and the Politics of Color," and to Melissa Clairjeune, Ian Green, Rasheed Hinds, Makeba Lavan, Jenny LeRoy, Esther Ohito, and Elise Song—my students in the very first "Bourgeois in the Flesh" doctoral seminar, at the CUNY Graduate Center, in spring 2014. Thank you for sharing your voices and engaging so enthusiastically with this project's ideas.

At the University of Illinois, my thanks go to two supportive department heads, Ron Bailey and Vicki Mahaffey, as well as to many delightful colleagues in English and African American studies. Special thanks to my aces Christopher Freeburg and Irvin Hunt, to Derrick Spires and Nafissa Thompson-Spires, and to other colleagues who make this an enjoyable place to work, including Janice Harrington, Siobhan Somerville, Trish Loughran, Susan Koshy, Jamie Jones, Bob Parker, Curtis Perry, Rob Barrett, Merle Bowen, Gabriel Solis, Ruth Nicole Brown, Erik McDuffie, Faye Harrison, Stacey Robinson, and Karen Flynn. Special thanks go to Desiree McMillion for her camaraderie and hard work helping me to navigate tricky institutional waters while also making the most of my fellowship leave. Thanks, also, to David Wright and the rest of the Kirkpatrick Symposium committee for inviting me to share an excerpt of the project with our colleagues in spring 2016, and to Andrea Stevens for her thoughtful questions about the work. To the graduate students who enrolled in the updated "Bourgeois in the Flesh" doctoral seminar here at Illinois—Aaron Burstein, Chekwube Danladi, Ben DeVries, Hilary Gross, Andrew Kaplan, Sabrina Lee, Katie O'Toole, and Jarvis Young—my thanks to each you for your insights and your contributions to our many, and lively, conversations.

Thank you to faculty and graduate students at both Tufts University and the State University of New York at Buffalo—especially Graham Hammill and Christina Sharpe—who welcomed me for talks and offered productive feedback and suggestions on the project. The Rutgers University "Theorizing Black Literature Now" symposium was a vibrant, intellectually rich setting in which to share a more recent excerpt from the book. Thank you to everyone who contributed to the community in that space: Dennis Childs, Margo Crawford, Erica Edwards, Phil Harper, Keith Leonard, Shirley Moody-Turner, Aldon Nielsen, Miriam Thaggert, and Brent Hayes Edwards; I'm grateful to Carter Mathes and to my longtime partner-in-crime Evie Shockley for the invitation to participate.

Thank you to Laurie Rubel and Adria Imada for keeping me accountable to my writing during a crucial phase, and to the Faculty Success Program and the National Center for Faculty Development and Diversity for an amazing support system that has kept me focused and feeling empowered to get my work done. My thanks, as well, to Vershawn Ashanti Young and Bridget Tsemo for including a very early version of one of my chapters in the *From Bourgeois to Boojie* anthology. Special thanks to you both, as well as to scholar and playwright extraordinaire Lisa B. Thompson, for opening, with your work, a long-overdue conversation in literary and cultural studies about the black middle class in the twenty-first century.

Although this is not a "dissertation book," it still bears the marks of those who raised me as a scholar—I will always be grateful to, especially, Karla F. C. Holloway and Maurice Wallace for their continued support and mentorship over the years. My thanks, too, to the many black women role models I encountered at Spelman College who helped to set me on this academic path: Kimberly Wallace-Sanders, Judy Gebre-Hiwet, Gloria Wade Gayles, Cynthia Spence, Donna Akiba Sullivan Harper, Beverly Guy-Sheftall, and of course, Sister President Johnnetta Cole.

For their championing of my work behind the scenes, I am grateful to Valerie Smith, Dwight McBride, Cheryl Wall, and Robert Reid-Pharr—Robert merits special thanks not only for years of friendship but for all he has done to mentor and advise me on academic matters large and small. Thank you to those I have had the privilege of mentoring, including Aneeka Henderson, Imani Kai Johnson, Irvin Hunt, and Marquita Smith. I've learned so much from each of you. Thanks, too, to Brandon Callender and Kelly Giles—two former students who have become friends—your brilliance continues to inspire me, and I look forward to everything that's next for you.

I am especially grateful to colleagues and friends who have taken the time to read various pieces of this manuscript in draft form over the past decade, including Monica Miller, Evie Shockley, Michael Ralph, Irvin Hunt, Chris Freeburg, and Shanna Greene Benjamin, who deserves special thanks for stepping into the breach whenever I've needed a fresh pair of eyes on a very rough version of something, which is more times than I can count. Thank you to Eve Dunbar for reading a late and major revision with such swiftness and good cheer. Many thanks, again, to the wonderful Margo Crawford and to the other anonymous reader for the University of Minnesota Press—your frank responses to the manuscript and suggestions for improvement have made this a better book.

Thank you to all of those friends, old and new, who have been cheerleaders and supporters over the years—Mendi and Keith Obadike, Libya Doman, Kiini Salaam, Zenobia Connor, Nia Tuckson, Ian McLachlan, Monica Miller, Evie Shockley, Stephane Robolin, Chera Reid and Brian Tutt, Charles McKinney, Casey Greenfield, Tildy Lewis Davidson, Kacey Farrell, Sol Kim-Bentley, Mary Milstead, Nadya Mason, Jeffrey McCune, Denise Burgher, Brian and Kym Gaffney, Ibrahim and Nancy Ouedraogo, Gail and Oliver Ferguson, Trina and Travis Dixon, and, especially, my BFF Stefanie Dunning, the other half of my brain, who keeps me sane and makes me a better thinker and person every day.

I am, always, grateful for everyone in my extended family, especially Cicely and Ben Alexander, and Pam, Larry, and Dana Huley, who always manage to send their love and prayers for my success across any distance. Heartfelt, ongoing thanks to my mother, Betty D. Jenkins, who continues to find new ways to support me and lift me up, whatever twists and turns life takes. August and Asa, my hearts, thank you for reminding me why I do this. I love you. Kamau, there really aren't words for what you mean to me. The best word is *everything.* Thank you for who you are, for what you do, and for walking this forever ever road by my side.

Notes

Preface

1. See Damon Young, "I Have Post-Brokeness Stress Disorder," *New York Times,* June 9, 2018; Brittany Allen, "'Old' Money: Who Gets to Have It, and Who Gets to Be It?" *Shondaland.com,* June 14, 2018, www.shondaland.com/live/family/a21349872/old-money/.

2. See Gillian B. White, "How Black Middle-Class Kids Become Poor Adults," *Atlantic,* January 19, 2015, www.theatlantic.com/business/archive/2015/01/how-black-middle-class-kids-become-black-lower-class-adults/384613/; see also Emily Badger, Claire Cain Miller, Adam Pearce, and Kevin Quealy, "Extensive Data Shows Punishing Reach of Racism for Black Boys," *New York Times,* March 19, 2018, www.nytimes.com/interactive/2018/03/19/upshot/race-class-white-and-black-men.html. The latter piece, despite its misleading focus on only black boys/men, and attention largely to income and not wealth, nonetheless illustrates the racial disparity I speak of.

3. As andré carrington has noted, "The Andre Walker system is a quasi-scientific method for categorizing texture according to the shape, appearance, and structure of individual strands and full heads of hair, including the hair's resistance to normative beautification practices." See carrington, "Spectacular Intimacies: Texture, Ethnicity, and a Touch of Black Cultural Politics," *Souls* 19, no. 2 (2017): 189. See also Andre Walker, *Andre Talks Hair* (New York: Simon and Schuster, 1997).

4. No, really. My entire adolescence we watched TV on a little black-and-white tabletop set in the kitchen. U.S. retailers stopped selling black-and-white TV sets in the early 1990s, around the time I graduated from high school.

5. Megan Zahneis, "Women of Color in Academe Make 67 Cents for Every Dollar Paid to White Men," *Chronicle of Higher Education,* June 11, 2018.

6. Patricia J. Williams, *Open House: Of Family, Friends, Food, Piano Lessons, and the Search for a Room of My Own* (New York: Farrar, Straus, and Giroux, 2004), 90.

Introduction

1. Bob Hughes, "Are We in a Post-racial World? In a Word, NO! Make That, Hell No!" May 2, 2016, http://deanbobhughes.blogspot.com/2016/05/are-we-in-post-racial-world-in-word-no.html. The black woman colleague, Yoshiko Harden, goes unnamed in Hughes's original blog post but was eventually named in follow-up reporting about the incident. See Isolde Raftery, "9 Heartbreaking Responses to 'A Man Shouts Racial Slurs at a Seattle Starbucks,'" KUOW.org. June 9, 2016, https://kuow.org/stories/9-heartbreaking-responses-man-shouts-racial-slurs-seattle-starbucks/

2. The notion of black privilege itself as provocation is certainly relevant to an anecdote like this one, but similar incidents also remind us that *blackness* can often blind non-black observers even to the presence of privilege. Writer and comedian W. Kamau Bell's story of being violently shooed away from a Bay Area coffee shop in 2015 by a waitress who assumed he was "selling something" (i.e., soliciting legitimate white patrons) is just one of many examples of blacks of means being mistaken for, and treated as, outsiders and Others to a scene of privilege. This is especially acute in Bell's narrative, because he contrasts his treatment by the restaurant staff with the treatment of a dreadlocked, possibly homeless white man who panhandled freely in front of the restaurant that same day, wearing similar casual clothes (a hoodie). With significant sarcasm, Bell notes of this man, who was never similarly approached by café staff, "I guess in his hoodie he had a more Mark Zuckerberg type of feeling than me." See Bell, "Happy Birthday! Have Some Racism from Elmwood Cafe!" January 28, 2015, http://www.wkamaubell.com/blog/2015/01/happy-birthday-have-some-racism-from-elmwood-cafe.

3. As Simone Browne has recently pointed out, following Sylvia Wynter, the chapter of Fanon's *Black Skin, White Masks* originally translated from the French as "The Fact of Blackness" was in later editions shifted to "The Lived Experience of the Black." As Browne notes, "The 'Blackness' in the former could be taken to mean, as Wynter has put it, '*Blackness* as an objective fact'

while 'The Lived Experience of the Black' speaks to a focus on the imposition of race in black life, where one's being is experienced through others." It is this latter sense that Hughes's narrative of being seen not as two college administrators but as two black people seems to invoke. Browne, *Dark Matters: On the Surveillance of Blackness* (Durham: Duke University Press, 2015), 7.

4. Lisa B. Thompson, *Beyond the Black Lady: Sexuality and the New African American Middle Class* (Urbana: University of Illinois Press, 2009), 3.

5. The "social positions" quotation is from Sherry Ortner, "Identities: The Hidden Life of Class," *Journal of Anthropological Research* 54, no. 1 (Spring 1998): 7; the "class culture" quotation is from Julie Bettie, *Women without Class: Girls, Race, and Identity* (2003; Oakland: University of California Press, 2014), 42.

6. Ortner, "Identities," 8–9.

7. My use of "performativity" is meant to suggest Diana Taylor's *The Archive and the Repertoire: Performing Cultural Memory in the Americas* (Durham: Duke University Press, 2003). For a foundational text on identity (specifically, gender) and performance, see also Judith Butler, *Gender Trouble: Feminism and the Subversion of Identity* (New York: Routledge, 1990). Devon Carbado and Mitu Gulati call this social performance "working identity" and define it, fittingly, as "a range of racially associated ways of being" and a "set of racial criteria people can employ to ascertain not simply whether a person is black in terms of how she looks but whether that person is black in terms of how she is perceived to act." See Carbado and Gulati, *Acting White? Rethinking Race in "Post-Racial" America* (2013; Oxford: Oxford University Press, 2015), 1. Perhaps because of their disciplinary training and approach (both Carbado and Gulati are law professors), their analysis of these performances is limited to legally protected categories of "race" and "gender," with almost no attention to how the social or cultural labor of "Working Identity" might be informed by class status. Indeed, class as a discrete or intersectional identity category is so far from Carbado and Gulati's analysis that the words "class," "economy/economics," "labor," "money," "privilege," "wealth," or "work" do not even appear in the book's index. The phrase "types of work" does appear as a sub-term under the index category "Workplace" but leads to a discussion of "advancement tasks" versus "citizenship tasks" (54) in professional workplaces, specifically "law school faculties and law firms" (55).

8. Stuart Hall, Chas Critcher, Tony Jefferson, John Clarke, and Brian Roberts, *Policing the Crisis: Mugging, the State, and Law and Order* (1978; New York: Macmillan, 2013), 340, 341.

9. Bettie, *Women without Class,* 42, 41.

10. Ortner, "Identities," 6.

11. See Madhu Dubey's *Signs and Cities: Black Literary Postmodernism* (Chicago: University of Chicago Press, 2003) for an excellent breakdown of how these shifting economic structures and social circumstances have shaped black experience in the postmodern era. For a sociological text that addresses some of these concerns specifically for black communities, see Benjamin P. Bowser's *The Black Middle Class: Social Mobility—and Vulnerability* (Boulder: Lynne Rienner, 2006). See also new research on the widening black-white wealth gap: Chuck Collins, Dedrick Asante-Muhammed, Emanuel Nieves, Josh Hoxie, *Report: The Road to Zero Wealth: How the Racial Wealth Divide Is Hollowing Out America's Middle Class* (Institute for Policy Studies, September 11, 2017).

12. Lisa Henderson, *Love and Money: Queers, Class, and Cultural Production* (New York: New York University Press, 2013), 5. As Henderson notes, "cultural criticism" is particularly well suited to address this variation that exists between liberal and Marxist understandings of class, better allowing us to understand how "class categories work in vernacular and analytic ways to mark a cultural universe" (5).

13. Rita Felski, "Nothing to Declare: Identity, Shame, and the Lower Middle Class," *PMLA* 115, no. 1 (2000): 34.

14. Ortner, "Identities," 8.

15. Ortner, "Identities," 10.

16. For more on the ways that "bourgeois" status is and historically has been as much a cultural as a structural position for black Americans collectively and systematically denied access to economic resources, see Karyn Lacy, *Blue Chip Black: Race, Class, and Status in the New Black Middle Class* (Berkeley: University of California Press, 2007); Michele Mitchell, *Righteous Propagation: African Americans and the Politics of Racial Destiny after Reconstruction* (Chapel Hill: University of North Carolina Press, 2004); and Kevin Kelly Gaines, *Uplifting the Race: Black Leadership, Politics, and Culture in the Twentieth Century* (Chapel Hill: University of North Carolina Press, 1996).

17. See Abby Goodnough, "Harvard Professor Jailed; Officer Is Accused of Bias," *New York Times,* July 20, 2009, A13; Robin Givhan, "Oprah and the View from Outside Hermes' Paris Door," *Washington Post,* June 24, 2005, http://www.washingtonpost.com/wp-dyn/content/article/2005/06/23/AR2005062302086.html.

18. Harvey Young, *Embodying Black Experience: Stillness, Critical Memory, and the Black Body* (Ann Arbor: University of Michigan Press, 2010), 10, 13.

19. Jared Sexton, "Unbearable Blackness," *Cultural Critique* 90 (Spring 2015): 168. For the Spillers reference, see Hortense Spillers, "Mama's Baby, Papa's Maybe: An American Grammar Book," *Diacritics* 17, no. 2 (Summer 1987): 68; hereafter cited parenthetically in the text.

20. Sexton, "Unbearable Blackness," 159.

21. Lindon Barrett, *Blackness and Value: Seeing Double* (New York: Cambridge University Press, 1999), 27. See also Michelle Alexander's *The New Jim Crow: Mass Incarceration in the Age of Colorblindness* (New York: New Press, 2012).

22. See Henry Louis Gates Jr., "Did Black People Own Slaves?" *The Root,* March 4, 2013, https://www.theroot.com/did-black-people-own-slaves-1790895436; and Thomas J. Pressly, "'The Known World' of Free Black Slaveholders: A Research Note on the Scholarship of Carter G. Woodson," *Journal of African American History* 91, no. 1 (Winter 2006): 81–87.

23. Cedric Robinson, *Black Marxism: The Making of the Black Radical Tradition* (Chapel Hill: University of North Carolina Press, 2000); Stephen M. Best, *The Fugitive's Properties: Law and the Poetics of Possession* (Chicago: University of Chicago Press, 2004), 2. Robinson uses the phrase "racial capitalism" to highlight the ways that capitalism expanded upon—rather than jettisoned—the racialism of feudal Europe (28). He also, however, points out the evident links between "slave labor, the slave trade, and the weaving of . . . early capitalist economies" (116).

24. See Frank B. Wilderson III, *Red, White and Black: Cinema and the Structure of U.S. Antagonisms* (Durham: Duke University Press, 2010).

25. Alexander Weheliye, *Habeas Viscus: Racializing Assemblages, Biopolitics, and Black Feminist Theories of the Human* (Durham: Duke University Press, 2014), 44.

26. For more on black fungibility as the "ontological state of Blackness," see Tiffany King, "Labor's Aphasia: Toward Antiblackness as Constitutive to Settler Colonialism," *Decolonization: Indigeneity, Education and Society,* blog post, June 10, 2014, https://decolonization.wordpress.com/2014/06/10/labors-aphasia-toward-antiblackness-as-constitutive-to-settler-colonialism/. The foundational text for this line of argument about blackness is, of course, Saidiya Hartman, *Scenes of Subjection: Terror, Slavery, and Self-Making in Nineteenth-Century America* (New York: Oxford University Press, 1997).

27. Greg Thomas, "PROUD FLESH: Editorial Statement," *PROUD FLESH: A New Afrikan Journal of Culture* 1 (2002): 1.

28. Young, *Embodying Black Experience,* 20.

29. Young, *Embodying Black Experience,* 20.

30. Young, *Embodying Black Experience,* 20.

31. Pierre Bourdieu, *Distinction: A Social Critique of the Judgment of Taste,* trans. Richard Nice (1979; Cambridge: Harvard University Press, 1984), 102.

32. Bourdieu, *Distinction,* 466.

33. Bourdieu, *Distinction,* 466.

34. Bourdieu, *Distinction,* 466.

35. Nicole Fleetwood brilliantly addresses this notion of black women's (visual) excess, which she describes using the phrase "excess flesh," in her book *Troubling Vision: Performance, Visuality, and Blackness* (Chicago: University of Chicago Press, 2011); see esp. 105–46.

36. The company later admitted that these claims of verbal and physical abuse were false and formally apologized to the book club's members. The women's $11 million lawsuit against the company was settled in 2016. See Katie Rogers, "#LaughingWhileBlack Wine Train Lawsuit Is Settled," *New York Times,* April 20, 2016, https://www.nytimes.com/2016/04/21/us/women-settle-11-million-lawsuit-with-napa-valley-wine-train.html.

37. Young, *Embodying Black Experience,* 11; Sexton, "Unbearable Blackness," 162.

38. Zandria Robinson, *This Ain't Chicago: Race, Class, and Regional Identity in the Post-Soul South* (Chapel Hill: University of North Carolina Press, 2014): 36.

39. Patricia J. Williams, *Open House: Of Family, Friends, Food, Piano Lessons, and the Search for a Room of My Own* (New York: Farrar, Straus, and Giroux, 2004), 109.

40. Issa Rae, *The Misadventures of Awkward Black Girl,* season 2, episode 8, http://www.awkwardblackgirl.com/season-2/episode-8.

41. Given the way that "coloured" or mixed-race peoples in South Africa under apartheid were both legally and socially stratified from black Africans, Rae likely makes this character not just light-skinned but South African in order to emphasize the ambiguity of his racial identity—throughout their interaction J seems confused and unable to read precisely what Ty is claiming, racially—and to signal to viewers the particular irony of Ty's exclusion of J from "blackness."

42. P. Williams, *Open House,* 109.

43. P. Williams, *Open House,* 109. I discuss this implicit link in chapter 4 of my first book, *Private Lives, Proper Relations: Regulating Black Intimacy* (Minneapolis: University of Minnesota P, 2007); see esp. 119–23.

44. Lawrence Otis Graham, *Our Kind of People: Inside America's Black Upper Class* (New York: HarperCollins, 1999), 4.

45. See Joni Hersch, "Profiling the New Immigrant Worker: The Effects of Skin Color and Height," *Journal of Labor Economics* 26, no. 2 (2008): 345–86. A *New York Times* article about this study recounts the distinct economic advantage of light skin for ethnic immigrants to the United States. Quoting Hersch, the article notes, "On average being one shade lighter has about the same effect [on income] as having an additional year of education." Indeed, advantages based on skin color seemed to transcend racial categories: "Dr. Hersch took into consideration other factors that could affect wages, like English-language proficiency, education, occupation, race or country of origin, and found that skin tone still seemed to make a difference in earnings. That meant that if two similar immigrants from Bangladesh, for example, came to the United States at the same time, with the same occupation and ability to speak English, the lighter-skinned one would make more money on average." Hersch's analysis found that despite the existence of global colorism, this "skin-color advantage was not based on preferential treatment for light-skinned people in their country of origin. The bias . . . occurs in the United States." Associated Press, "Study of Immigrants Links Lighter Skin and Higher Income," *New York Times,* January 28, 2007, http://www.nytimes.com/2007/01/28/us/28immig.html?mcubz=3.

For a foundational scholarly text on black colorism, see Kathy Russell, Midge Wilson, and Ronald Hall, *The Color Complex (Revised): The Politics of Skin Color in a New Millennium* (1992; New York: Anchor Books, 2013); see also Kimberly Jade Norwood, ed., *Color Matters: Skin Tone Bias and the Myth of a Postracial America* (New York: Routledge, 2014). Fiction and memoir that have tackled intraracial colorism include Wallace Thurman's *The Blacker the Berry* (1929), Ernest Gaines's *Catherine Carmier* (1964), and Marita Golden's *Don't Play in the Sun* (2005).

46. Linda Chavers, "Cops Ignore Me Because I Have Light Skin: That Just Reaffirms Their Racism," *The Guardian,* August 13, 2015, https://www.theguardian.com/commentisfree/2015/aug/13/cops-racial-profiling-light-skinned-black-woman.

47. Lance Hannon, "White Colorism," *Social Currents* 2, no.1 (March

2015): 13–21. See also Avi Ben-Zeev, Tara C. Dennehy, Robin I. Goodrich, Branden S. Kolarik, and Mark W. Geisler, "When an 'Educated' Black Man Becomes Lighter in the Mind's Eye: Evidence for a Skin Tone Memory Bias," *SAGE Open* 4, no. 1 (January 9, 2014): 1–9.

48. Bourdieu, *Distinction,* 70. Notably, despite whites' clear preference for lighter skin and the resultant pervasiveness of colorism both inter- and intraracially, most blacks do not see light skin color as a disqualifier from blackness. See Jennifer L. Hochschild and Vesla Weaver, "The Skin Color Paradox and the American Racial Order," *Social Forces* 86, no. 2 (2007): 643–70. For a brilliant analysis of the racialized meaning of "beauty" in the United States, see Tressie McMillan Cottom, "In the Name of Beauty," *Thick: And Other Essays* (New York: New Press, 2018), 33–72.

49. Wallace Thurman, *The Blacker the Berry* (New York: Macaulay, 1929); Charles W. Chesnutt, *The Wife of His Youth and Other Stories of the Color Line* (Boston: Houghton Mifflin, 1899). We might think, as well, of the dynamics surrounding the Creole title character of Ernest Gaines's novel *Catherine Carmier* (New York: Atheneum, 1964), or, for a more recent, nonfiction example, Toi Derricotte's poignant memoir, *The Black Notebooks* (New York: Norton, 1997).

50. Cottom, "In the Name of Beauty," 56, 45.

51. Bourdieu, *Distinction,* 71–72.

52. See Margo Jefferson's memoir and social history of the black bourgeoisie, *Negroland* (New York: Pantheon, 2015). See also Graham, *Our Kind of People.*

53. Jared Sexton, *Amalgamation Schemes: Antiblackness and the Critique of Multiracialism* (Minneapolis: University of Minnesota Press, 2008), 84.

54. The example of James Blake, a light-skinned biracial former tennis pro who was tackled and arrested by a New York Police Department officer in September 2015 as he stood in front of his upscale midtown hotel, suggests, however, that whatever privilege light skin affords is incomplete and insufficient "protection." See Benjamin Mueller, Al Baker, and Liz Robbins, "Swift Apologies in Harsh Arrest of a Tennis Star," *New York Times,* September 10, 2015, A1.

55. *The Norton Anthology of African American Literature,* for instance, situates "The Contemporary Period" just after the "The Black Arts Era, 1960–1975," suggesting rather than stating outright that "contemporary" African American literature spans from 1975 to the present. While we need not take the *Norton* as the sole authority on African American literary history, it shares this delineation of the "contemporary" with the *Wiley Blackwell Anthology*

of African American Literature as well as the *Concise Oxford Companion to African American Literature,* the appendix of which outlines black literature's historical trajectory, describing work from the 1970s onward as "contemporary." These correspondences suggest, then, some professional consensus, at least on the approximate beginning of the "contemporary" era.

56. Kenneth W. Warren, *What Was African American Literature?* (Cambridge: Harvard University Press, 2011).

57. See Nelson George, *Buppies, B-Boys, Baps and Bohos: Notes on Post-Soul Black Culture* (New York: HarperCollins, 1992).

58. Mark Anthony Neal, *Soul Babies: Black Popular Culture and the Post-Soul Aesthetic* (New York: Routledge, 2002), 3, emphasis added. Neal has since shifted his own terminology from "post-soul" to both "postblack" and "NewBlack," but neither of these terms is as compelling for me, in part because each suggests a moving *beyond* blackness that I see as an impossibility. For more on "soul" as an analogue for Black Power–era blackness, see Monique Guillory and Richard Green, *Soul: Black Power, Politics, and Pleasure* (New York: New York University Press, 1998), esp. 1–2.

59. Andrea Lee was born in 1953, Percival Everett and Reginald McKnight in 1956, Spike Lee in 1957, and Shay Youngblood in 1959. Trey Ellis was born in 1962, Michael Thomas in 1967, Rebecca Walker and Colson Whitehead both in 1969, and Danzy Senna in 1970. Toni Morrison was born in 1931.

60. Bertram D. Ashe, "Theorizing the Post-Soul Aesthetic: An Introduction," *African American Review* 41, no. 4 (2007): 611.

61. Neal, *Soul Babies,* 103. While this point is persuasive, I might resist the way that Neal opposes "objectivity" to "nostalgia," largely because it is less clear to me that the anti-nostalgia motivating some post-soul critique is entirely "objective"—the very notion of nostalgia, which implies a certain kind of pleasure in and fetishization of memory, also suggests, for instance, the possibility of anger, confusion, or resentment on the part of those who cannot credibly participate in this pleasure. We might recall Elizabeth Alexander's observation of some middle-class black male characters from the late 1980s and early 1990s, that their "narrative ennui," a self-distancing from "stereotypical black-pride," actually reveals "a deeper and more fundamental rage at both received Civil Rights rhetoric and attendant narratives of patriarchal black manhood, which, in some fundamental way, have left them feeling both constrained and at sea." Alexander, *The Black Interior* (St. Paul, Minn.: Graywolf Press, 2004), 148–49.

62. Jenkins, *Private Lives, Proper Relations,* 23.

63. Michelle M. Wright, *The Physics of Blackness: Beyond the Middle Passage Epistemology* (Minneapolis: University of Minnesota Press, 2015), 34.

64. Raymond Williams, *Marxism and Literature* (1977; Oxford: Oxford University Press, 2009), 133–34.

65. Berlant, *Cruel Optimism,* 7.

66. R. Williams, *Marxism and Literature* 133.

67. Darieck Scott, *Extravagant Abjection: Blackness, Power, and Sexuality in the African American Literary Imagination* (New York: New York University Press, 2010), 10, emphasis added.

68. Berlant, *Cruel Optimism,* 54.

69. Margo Natalie Crawford, *Black Post-Blackness: The Black Arts Movement and Twenty-First-Century Aesthetics* (Urbana: University of Illinois Press, 2017), 223. I use the significantly outdated term "late capitalism" (Jameson) in concert with the currently more popular but also contested terminology of "neoliberalism" here to call attention, again, to the evolving and emergent nature of the "present" and the ways that such large-scale theoretical frameworks of our economic and social world themselves fragment and shift over time, in ways neither orderly nor absolute. From my vantage point in 2018, I might also note the numerous pronouncements of the End of Neoliberalism that have accompanied Donald Trump's election to the U.S. presidency.

70. Sexton, "Unbearable Blackness," 168.

71. Roland Murray, "The Time of Breach: Class Division and the Contemporary African American Novel," *Novel: A Forum on Fiction* 43, no. 1 (2010): 16.

72. Murray, "The Time of Breach," 13.

73. Hortense Spillers, "*Crisis of the Negro Intellectual:* A Post-Date," *Black, White, and In Color: Essays on American Literature and Culture* (Chicago: University of Chicago Press, 2003), 459.

74. Jessica Marie Johnson, "Black Love Post-Death," *Medium,* September 23, 2015, https://medium.com/focus-series/black-love-post-death-cef524ac3132.

75. See Bertram D. Ashe, "'Under the Umbrella of Black Civilization': A Conversation with Reginald McKnight," *African American Review* 35, no. 3 (Fall 2001): 427–37.

76. C. Riley Snorton, *Black on Both Sides: A Racial History of Trans Identity* (Minneapolis: University of Minnesota Press, 2017), 8.

77. Andrea Lee, *Sarah Phillips,* foreword by Valerie Smith (1984; Bos-

ton: Northeastern University Press, 1993), 4. Hereafter cited parenthetically in the text.

78. Adrienne McCormick, "Is This Resistance? African American Postmodernism in *Sarah Phillips*," *Callaloo* 27, no. 3 (2004): 817.

79. McCormick, "Is This Resistance?" 814.

80. Saidiya Hartman, "Venus in Two Acts," *Small Axe* 12, no. 2 (June 2008): 3.

81. Bourdieu, *Distinction,* 207.

82. Ta-Nehisi Coates, *Between the World and Me* (New York: Spiegel and Grau, 2015), 19.

83. McCormick, "Is This Resistance?" 823.

84. Coates, *Between the World and Me,* 107.

1. New Bourgeoisie, Old Bodies

1. Lawrence Otis Graham, *Our Kind of People: Inside America's Black Upper Class* (New York: HarperCollins, 1999), 17.

2. Graham, *Our Kind of People,* 17.

3. Graham, *Our Kind of People,* 4.

4. See F. James Davis, *Who Is Black? One Nation's Definition* (1991; University Park: Penn State University Press, 2001), esp. 4–6 and 13–16.

5. Harryette Mullen, "Optic White," *diacritics* 24 (Summer–Fall 1994): 81.

6. The quotation marks around "natural" mark the point that the body cannot be understood as a "raw" or originary source existing prior to the intervention of culture; the work of Hortense Spillers, Elizabeth Alexander, Maude Hines, and others suggests that the (black, female) body is culturally marked and interpreted even at its most "raw." I use the phrase "raw text," then, only to suggest a given body's phenotypical characteristics prior to deliberate manipulation—those one is born with, so to speak. See Spillers, "Mama's Baby, Papa's Maybe: An American Grammar Book," in *African American Literary Theory: A Reader,* ed. Winston Napier (New York: New York University Press, 2002), 257–79; Alexander, *The Black Interior* (New York: Graywolf Press, 2004); and Hines, "Body Language: Corporeal Semiotics, Literary Resistance," in *Body Politics and the Fictional Double,* ed. Debra Walker King (Bloomington: Indiana University Press, 2000), 38–55.

7. Karyn R. Lacy, *Blue-Chip Black: Race, Class, and Status in the New Black Middle Class* (Berkeley: University of California Press, 2007), 26.

8. Lacy, *Blue-Chip Black,* 29.

9. Lacy, *Blue-Chip Black,* 29.

10. The body of literature on this topic across sociology (let alone psychology and anthropology) is more extensive than can be reasonably summarized here, but for representative work about education and social class formation, stratification, and mobility, see, e.g., Aaron Pallas, "The Effects of Schooling on Individual Lives," in *Handbook of the Sociology of Education,* ed. Maureen T. Hallinan (New York: Springer, 2000), 499–525; Paul W. Kingston, Ryan Hubbard, Brent Lapp, Paul Schroeder, and Julia Wilson, "Why Education Matters," *Sociology of Education* 76, no. 1 (2003): 53–70; Hiroshi Ishida, Walter Muller, and John M. Ridge, "Class Origin, Class Destination, and Education: A Cross-National Study of Ten Industrial Nations," *American Journal of Sociology* 101, no. 1 (1995): 145–93; Joan M. Osgrove, "Belonging and Wanting: Meanings of Social Class Background for Women's Constructions of their College Experiences," *Journal of Social Issues* 59, no. 4 (2003): 771–84; and Elizabeth Aries and Maynard Seider, "The Interactive Relationship between Class Identity and the College Experience: The Case of Lower Income Students," *Qualitative Sociology* 28, no. 4 (2005): 419–43. It is also worth noting recent research that disputes received knowledge about education as a major factor in social mobility, though even this work suggests that higher education plays a stronger role than primary and secondary schools. See Jesse Rothstein, UC Berkeley and National Bureau of Economic Research, "Inequality of Educational Opportunity? Schools as Mediators of the Intergenerational Transmission of Income" (Cambridge, Mass.: National Bureau of Economic Research, 2018), 1–35.

11. Elizabeth R. Cole and Safiya R. Omari, "Race, Class and the Dilemmas of Upward Mobility for African Americans," *Journal of Social Issues* 59, no. 4 (2003): 799.

12. Tressie McMillan Cottom, *Lower Ed: The Troubling Rise of For-Profit Colleges in the New Economy* (New York and London: New Press, 2017), 21.

13. Graham, *Our Kind of People,* 17.

14. Sidonie Smith and Julia Watson, *Reading Autobiography: A Guide for Interpreting Life Narratives,* 2nd ed. (2001; Minneapolis: University of Minnesota Press, 2010), 13.

15. See Adolph Reed, "Black Particularity Reconsidered," *Telos* 39 (Spring 1979): 71–93; and Cornel West, "The Paradox of the African American Rebellion," in *Is It Nation Time? Contemporary Essays on Black Power and Black*

Nationalism, ed. Eddie S. Glaude Jr. (Chicago: University of Chicago Press, 2002), 22–38. See also Lacy, *Blue-Chip Black,* 30.

16. Here I should also note that the *Loving v. Virginia Supreme Court* case, which ruled laws against interracial marriage unconstitutional, was decided in 1967. Although it is beyond the scope of this chapter to address mixed-race history—for a thorough discussion of this history see Naomi Pabst, "Blackness/Mixedness: Contestations over Crossing Signs," *Cultural Critique* 54 (Spring 2003): 178–212—it certainly might be useful to keep in mind that the metaphoric *value* of the miscegenated-appearing black body also would have shifted as interracial unions and their offspring gained legal sanction. My thanks to Stefanie Dunning for reminding me of this point.

17. Although my use of the word *symbolic* evokes Lacan's symbolic order, I am less interested in a straightforwardly psychoanalytic interpretation of the penetrated-by-whiteness trope of black class privilege, although this approach has provided a rich field of inquiry for other critics. Margo Natalie Crawford's work, for instance, while not concerned specifically with class, analyzes skin color in American fiction through the Freudian concept of the fetish and the Lacanian phallus. See Crawford, *Dilution Anxiety and the Black Phallus* (Columbus: Ohio State University Press, 2008). See also Jacques Lacan, *Écrits: A Selection* (1953; New York: Norton, 1977).

18. See Peter Stallybrass and Allon White, *The Politics and Poetics of Transgression* (Ithaca: Cornell University Press, 1986).

19. Nicole R. Fleetwood, *Troubling Vision: Performance, Visuality and Blackness* (Chicago: University of Chicago Press, 2011), 109. While Fleetwood coins the term "excess flesh" to reference, specifically, the "too much"-ness of black women's bodies in the visual field, the notion of black embodiment as a kind of social and political surfeit has a broader history. Moira Gatens suggests, for instance, that "At different times, different kinds of beings have been excluded from the pact [of the modern body politic], often simply by virtue of their corporeal specificity. Slaves, foreigners, women, the conquered, children, the working classes, have all been excluded from political participation, at one time or another, by their bodily specificity." Gatens, "Corporeal Representation and the Body Politic," in *Writing on the Body: Female Embodiment and Feminist Theory,* ed. Katie Conboy, Nadia Medina, and Sarah Stanbury (New York: Columbia University Press, 1997), 83.

20. Stallybrass and White, *Politics and Poetics,* 23.

21. See William Muraskin, *Middle Class Blacks in a White Society: Prince Hall Freemasonry in America* (Berkeley: University of California Press,

1975), 12. See also Derrick E. White, "'Blacks Who Had Not Themselves Personally Suffered Illegal Discrimination': The Symbolic Incorporation of the Black Middle Class," in *Race and the Foundations of Knowledge: Cultural Amnesia in the Academy,* ed. Joseph Young and Jana Evans Braziel (Urbana: University of Illinois Press, 2006), 197–98. For more on social class and black aspiration see Michele Mitchell, *Righteous Propagation: African Americans and the Politics of Racial Destiny after Reconstruction* (Chapel Hill: University of North Carolina Press, 2004); and Kevin Kelly Gaines, *Uplifting the Race: Black Leadership, Politics, and Culture in the Twentieth Century* (Chapel Hill: University of North Carolina Press, 1996).

22. andré m. carrington, "Spectacular Intimacies: Texture, Ethnicity, and a Touch of Black Cultural Politics," *Souls* 19, no. 2 (2017): 179.

23. Diana Taylor, *The Archive and the Repertoire: Performing Cultural Memory in the Americas* (Durham: Duke University Press, 2003), 3; Valerie Smith, *Not Just Race, Not Just Gender: Black Feminist Readings* (New York: Routledge, 1998), xvii.

24. Eve Allegra Raimon, *The "Tragic Mulatta" Revisited: Race and Nationalism in Nineteenth Century Antislavery Fiction* (New Brunswick: Rutgers University Press, 2004), 4.

25. Raimon, *The "Tragic Mulatta" Revisited,* 5. As numerous scholars have pointed out regarding Harriet Jacobs's narrative, however, too much emphasis on this sexual vulnerability and attendant violation by white men had the potential to alienate white female readers, so Jacobs was careful to omit details of her own ordeal. See Jacobs's *Incidents in the Life of a Slave Girl* (1861; Mineola, N.Y.: Dover, 2001).

26. For more on intraracial colorism, see Jennifer Hochschild and Vesla Weaver, "The Skin Color Paradox and the Racial Order," *Social Forces* 86, no. 2 (December 2007): 643–70. See also Kathy Russell, Midge Wilson, and Ronald Hall, eds., *The Color Complex* (1992; New York: Anchor, 1993); and Cedric Herring, Verna M. Keith, and Hayward Derrick Horton, eds., *Skin Deep: How Race and Complexion Matter in the "Color-Blind" Era* (Chicago: University of Chicago Press, 2004). For an example of intraracial resentment of lighter women by darker women, see also Marita Golden, *Don't Play in the Sun* (New York: Anchor, 2004).

27. While Pabst justifiably critiques "the dismissive ways that 'light-skinned elites' are treated and conflated with black/white interracial subjects" ("Blackness/Mixedness," 197) in black literature and criticism, she also acknowledges the "overinvoked" and "ubiquitous" (195) nature of the tragic

mulatto trope. Rather than asserting a genuine equivalence between "light-skinned elites" and *actual* mixed-race subjects, I am interested in noting the way that light-skinned bodies often evoke the long-standing trope of the "tragic mulatto" no matter what their parentage.

28. Toi Derricotte, *The Black Notebooks: An Interior Journey* (1997; New York: Norton, 1999), 68, 77.

29. Perhaps due to renewed interest in issues of class, race, and postmodern identity—all of which are addressed in *Tar Baby*—numerous critics have turned to Morrison's text in the past fifteen to twenty years (beginning nearly two decades *after* its publication). Representative examples include Dorothea Drummond Mbalia, "*Tar Baby*: A Reflection of Morrison's Developed Class Consciousness," in *Toni Morrison,* ed. Linden Peach (New York: St. Martin's Press, 1997), 89–102; Julia Emberley, "A Historical Transposition: Toni Morrison's *Tar Baby* and Frantz Fanon's Post-Enlightenment Phantasms," *MFS: Modern Fiction Studies* 45, no. 2 (Summer 1999): 403–31; Letitia Moffitt, "Finding the Door: Vision/Revision and Stereotype in Toni Morrison's Tar Baby," *Critique: Studies in Contemporary Fiction* 46, no. 1 (Fall 2004): 12–26; and Yogita Goyal, "The Gender of Diaspora in Toni Morrison's Tar Baby," *MFS: Modern Fiction Studies* 52, no. 2 (Summer 2006): 393–414. See also chapter 4 in Crawford's *Dilution Anxiety,* esp. 95–111.

30. Toni Morrison, *Tar Baby* (1981; New York: Plume, 1982), 74, 48. Hereafter cited parenthetically in the text.

31. One irony of this description is that "natural" sponges are typically bleached from their original, light brown to a pale golden color before sale. In a kind of echoing reversal of Gideon's assertion that Jadine's moderately tan skin tone is only the result of weeks spent sunbathing, the text here reminds us of the artificiality and manipulability of the "natural." This is particularly true given that the sponge shares the edge of the bathtub with "a bottle of Neutrogena Rainbath Gel"; the intrusion of this branded product name into the narrative is a reminder of the way that cultural understandings of "natural" and "artificial" are informed by capitalist consumption, products of market and value.

32. See, e.g., characterizations of Jadine in Sandra Pouchet Paquet, "The Ancestor as Foundation in *Their Eyes Were Watching God* and *Tar Baby,*" in *Toni Morrison's Fiction: Contemporary Criticism,* ed. David L. Middleton (New York: Garland, 1997), 183–206, Eleanor Traylor, "The Fabulous World of Toni Morrison: *Tar Baby,*" in *Critical Essays on Toni Morrison,* ed. Nellie Y. McKay (Boston: G. K. Hall, 1988), 146; and James Coleman,

"The Quest for Wholeness in Toni Morrison's *Tar Baby*," *Black American Literature Forum* 20, nos. 1–2 (Spring–Summer 1986): 63–73. See also Mbalia, "*Tar Baby*."

33. Trudier Harris, *Fiction and Folklore: The Novels of Toni Morrison* (Knoxville: University of Tennessee Press, 1993), 128.

34. See Goyal, "The Gender of Diaspora," 396; Emberley, "A Historical Transposition," 406; and Moffitt, "Finding the Door," 24.

35. Judylyn S. Ryan, "Contested Visions/Double-Vision in *Tar Baby*," *MFS: Modern Fiction Studies* 39, nos. 3–4 (Fall/Winter 1993): 599.

36. See Paquet, "The Ancestor as Foundation," 201. See also Paul Mahaffey, "Rethinking Biracial Female Sexuality in Toni Morrison's *Tar Baby*," *Proteus: A Journal of Ideas* 21, no. 2 (Fall 2004): 38–42; Mahaffey repeatedly refers to Jadine as "biracial."

37. Granted, this reading sidesteps the more complex real-world racial and ethnic configurations that might contribute, in the post–Civil Rights era, to a "black" body's "miscegenated" appearance—not only the hybridity that historically has operated throughout and often signaled diaspora but also the inherent multiraciality of the postmodern global scene. These real-world circumstances mean that any number of racial and ethnic encounters might produce a putatively "black" body with uncharacteristic (as in, not characteristically African) features—a point of which Morrison herself seems well aware.

38. See Nella Larsen, *Passing* (1929; New York: Penguin, 2003); and Zora Neale Hurston, *Their Eyes Were Watching God* (1937; New York: HarperCollins, 1999).

39. As Spillers notes, "under conditions of captivity, the offspring of the female does not 'belong' to the Mother, nor is s/he 'related' to the 'owner,' though the latter 'possesses' it, and in the African-American instance, often fathered it, and, as often, without whatever benefit of patrimony" ("Mama's Baby, Papa's Maybe," 269).

40. Of course, this "penetration" extends to her sexual behavior; it is no coincidence that Jadine arrives on Isle des Chevaliers straight from the arms of not one but three white European suitors (44).

41. See Lacy, *Blue-Chip Black*, 24–26.

42. See, e.g., Mbalia, "*Tar Baby*," and Coleman, "The Quest for Wholeness."

43. Wahneema Lubiano, "But Compared to What? Reading Realism,

Representation, and Essentialism in *School Daze, Do the Right Thing,* and the Spike Lee Discourse," *Black American Literature Forum* 25, no. 2 (Summer 1991): 275.

44. Lubiano, "But Compared to What?" 276.

45. See, e.g., Paul Gilroy's "Spiking the Argument: Spike Lee and the Limits of Racial Community," in *Small Acts: Thoughts on the Politics of Black Cultures* (New York: Serpent's Tail, 1993), 183–91, in which Gilroy argues that "Lee's world is animated by a campaign against difficulty, complexity and anything else that does not fit the historic binary codes of American racial thought to which he subscribes and on which his allegories now rely: Straight and Nappy, Jiggaboos and Wannabees, . . . black and white" (186). For similar sentiments see Amiri Baraka, "Spike Lee at the Movies," and Houston A. Baker Jr., "Spike Lee and the Commerce of Culture," both in *Black American Cinema,* ed. Manthia Diawara (New York: Routledge, 1993), 145–53, 154–76; Tera Hunter, "It's a Man's, Man's, Man's World: Specters of the Old Re-newed in Afro-American Culture and Criticism," *Callaloo* 38 (Winter 1989): 247–49; and Eric Lott, "Response to Trey Ellis's 'The New Black Aesthetic,'" *Callaloo* 38 (Winter 1989): 245.

46. Toni Cade Bambara, "Programming with School Daze," in *The Spike Lee Reader,* ed. Paula J. Massood (Philadelphia: Temple University Press, 2008), 11.

47. Taylor, *The Archive and the Repertoire,* 6.

48. Bambara, "Programming with School Daze," 17.

49. See Patricia Hill Collins, *Black Sexual Politics: African Americans, Gender, and the New Racism* (New York: Routledge, 2004), 176–77; and E. Franklin Frazier, *Black Bourgeoisie* (1957; New York: Free Press, 1997), 220–21. See also Crawford, *Dilution Anxiety,* esp. 62–89.

50. Given how Lee portrays such queer undertones of fraternity culture, it should perhaps not surprise us that Dap and the Fellas openly deride the Gamma Phi Gammas as "fags" elsewhere in the film.

51. Cornel West, "The Paradox of the African American Rebellion," reprinted in *Is It Nation Time? Contemporary Essays on Black Power and Black Nationalism,* ed. Eddie S. Glaude (Chicago: University of Chicago Press, 2002), 25.

52. Lacy, *Blue-Chip Black,* 26.

53. *School Daze,* dir. Spike Lee (Columbia Pictures, 1988).

54. Lubiano, "But Compared to What?" 275.

55. In Ondine's words, "A daughter is a woman that cares about where she come from and takes care of them that took care of her" (282). While it might be argued that Jadine is seeking something else entirely from blackness or whiteness—and the book's final image of her depicts her on an airplane—this reading overlooks the fact that Jadine's final journey, in the text, takes her back to Paris. The cosmopolitan escape from constraint that Jadine seeks seems to be, perhaps necessarily, located in Europe, far away not just from Son but also from any semblance of African American community.

56. See, e.g., Andrea Lee's *Sarah Phillips* (1984; Boston: Northeastern University Press, 1993), which depicts a black bourgeois heroine who determinedly flees blackness; see also Trey Ellis's *Platitudes* (1988; Boston: Northeastern University Press, 2003), in which the seductions of material privilege are self-evident for both of the black teenage protagonists, while blackness remains a burden to be endured or escaped.

57. See Spike Lee with Lisa Jones, *Uplift the Race: The Construction of School Daze* (New York: Simon and Schuster, 1988), on brown-skinned actress Tyra Ferrell, deliberately cast as "the darkest Gamma Ray" (85).

58. Lee and Jones, *Uplift the Race,* 220.

59. Derricotte, *The Black Notebooks,* 183.

60. "Local Yokels" scene, *School Daze.*

61. Imani Perry, *Prophets of the Hood: Politics and Poetics in Hip Hop* (Durham: Duke University Press, 2004), 142. See also Robin D. G. Kelley, "Kickin' Reality, Kickin' Ballistics: Gangsta Rap and Post-Industrial Los Angeles," in *Race Rebels: Culture, Politics, and the Black Working Class* (New York: Free Press, 1996), esp. 209–11.

62. See Margaret Thomas, "Linguistic Variation in Spike Lee's *School Daze,*" *College English* 56, no. 8 (1994): 911–27, esp. 917–23.

63. See Saidiya Hartman's *Lose Your Mother: A Journey along the Atlantic Slave Route* (New York: Farrar, Straus, and Giroux, 2007), 205–10.

64. Lubiano, "But Compared to What?" 275. In "Spectacular Intimacies," andré carrington points out that "not all modes of self-fashioning that alter the embodied experience of identity are violent" (191) and even persuasively reads "hair straightening as a disidentificatory practice" (182). See also Kobena Mercer, who makes a similar point in 1994's *Welcome to the Jungle*—yet the opposition between chemically altered and "natural" hair remains a clear class trope in both Lee's and Morrison's narratives. Mercer, "Black Hair/Style Politics," in *Welcome to the Jungle: New Positions in Black Cultural Studies* (New York: Routledge, 1994), 97–130.

65. For an intriguing reading of these visual contrasts as examples of Morrison's use of surrealism, see Crawford, *Dilution Anxiety,* 101–4.

66. Lee and Jones, *Uplift the Race,* 156.

67. The "politically correct" quotation is in Hunter, "It's a Man's, Man's, Man's World," 248. The "sublimated public body" is a reference to Stallybrass and White, *Politics and Poetics,* 93.

68. Moffitt, "Finding the Door," 24.

2. "Half of Everything and Certain of Nothing"

1. Trey Ellis, "The New Black Aesthetic," *Callaloo* 38 (Winter 1989): 234, 238.

2. See Tera Hunter "It's a Man's, Man's, Man's World," *Callaloo* 38 (Winter 1989): 247–49; and Eric Lott, "Response to Trey Ellis's 'The New Black Aesthetic,'" *Callaloo* 38 (Winter 1989): 244–46. See also Madhu Dubey, "Postmodernism as Post-Nationalism? Racial Representation in US Black Cultural Studies," *New Formations* 45 (Winter 2001–2): 150–68, esp. 156–58.

3. Lott, "Response," 246.

4. Saidiya Hartman, "Venus in Two Acts," *Small Axe* 12, no. 2 (June 2008): 13.

5. Cheryl I. Harris, "Whiteness as Property," *Harvard Law Review* 106, no. 8 (June 1993): 1734.

6. Audrey Elisa Kerr, "The Paper Bag Principle: Of the Myth and the Motion of Colorism," *Journal of American Folklore* 118, no. 469 (2005): 273.

7. Note that I do not, here, intend to reinforce the stereotype that all mixed-race subjects are "light-skinned" (see Naomi Pabst, "Blackness/Mixedness: Contestations over Crossing Signs," *Cultural Critique* 54 [Spring 2003]: 194); at the same time, I find Pabst's claims around this point inconsistent. Simply to acknowledge, as she does, that some mixed-race individuals are not light-skinned, or to assert that some light-skinned elites "are offended when mistaken for having racially distinct parentage," is not to disprove a general truth that, in her own words, "light-skinnedness and tangible black/white mixedness do often occur simultaneously and are thus overlapping categories" (194).

8. Hartman, "Venus in Two Acts," 13.

9. Hartman, "Venus in Two Acts," 14.

10. Ellis, "The New Black Aesthetic," 235.

11. Ellis, "The New Black Aesthetic," 235.

12. Habiba Ibrahim, *Troubling the Family: The Promise of Personhood and the Rise of Multiracialism* (Minneapolis: University of Minnesota Press, 2012), viii.

13. For more on this see my discussion in chapter 4 of *Private Lives, Proper Relations: Regulating Black Intimacy* (Minneapolis: University of Minnesota Press, 2007), esp. 119–21.

14. Rebecca Walker, *Black, White, and Jewish: Autobiography of a Shifting Self* (New York: Riverhead, 2001), 5. Hereafter cited parenthetically in the text.

15. For a useful and pointed analysis of these sorts of narratives of interracial promise and the way that they desexualize and disappear the "interracial sexual relationship," see Jared Sexton's *Amalgamation Schemes: Antiblackness and the Critique of Multiracialism* (Minneapolis: University of Minnesota Press, 2008).

16. This passage in Walker's text resonates, perhaps deliberately, with Jadine's anxious response to the woman in yellow in Toni Morrison's *Tar Baby,* a woman with "skin like tar" who "made [Jadine] feel lonely in a way. Lonely and inauthentic." Morrison, *Tar Baby* (1981; New York: Plume, 1982), 45, 48.

17. Lori Harrison-Kahan, "Passing for White, Passing for Jewish: Mixed Race Identity in Danzy Senna and Rebecca Walker," *MELUS* 30, no. 1 (2005): 37.

18. It may be worth noting, here, that Walker directly and almost completely contradicts this point about blood ties in her subsequent memoir, *Baby Love,* which details her experience of (biological) motherhood.

19. Danzy Senna, *Where Did You Sleep Last Night? A Personal History* (New York: Picador, 2009), 13. Hereafter cited parenthetically in the text.

20. See, e.g., Brenda Boudreau, "Letting the Body Speak: 'Becoming' White in *Caucasia,*" *Modern Language Studies* 32, no. 1 (2002): 64; and chapter 3 of Michele Elam's *The Souls of Mixed Folk: Race, Politics, and Aesthetics in the New Millennium* (Stanford: Stanford University Press, 2011).

21. Elam, *The Souls of Mixed Folk,* 113.

22. Andrew P. Killick, "Music as Ethnic Marker in Film: The 'Jewish' Case," in *Soundtrack Available: Essays on Film and Popular Music,* ed. Pamela Robertson Wojcik and Arthur Knight (Durham: Duke University Press, 2001), 186.

23. Sherry Ortner, "Identities: The Hidden Life of Class," *Journal of Anthropological Research* 54, no. 1 (Spring 1998): 13.

24. Boudreau, "Letting the Body Speak," 67.

25. Ralina L. Joseph, *Transcending Blackness: From the New Millennium Mulatta to the Exceptional Multiracial* (Durham: Duke University Press, 2013), 74.

26. Ta-Nehisi Coates, *Between the World and Me* (New York: Spiegel and Grau, 2015), 20–21.

27. Senna quoted in Boudreau, "Letting the Body Speak," 59.

28. Simone Browne, *Dark Matters: On the Surveillance of Blackness* (Durham: Duke University Press, 2015), 7.

29. Harris, "Whiteness as Property," 1736, 1730, 1737.

30. Joseph, *Transcending Blackness,* 83.

31. Darieck Scott, *Extravagant Abjection: Blackness, Power, and Sexuality in the African American Literary Imagination* (New York: New York University Press, 2010), 259; Coates, *Between the World and Me,* 107.

32. For a vivid representation of the contrast between the island of Jamaica's centrality as a tourist destination for Westerners and its exploitation by Western economic and political organizations such as the IMF, see the 2001 documentary *Life and Debt,* dir. Stephanie Black (New Yorker Films, 2003).

33. This "punks" and "thugs" discourse, of course, returns us to Jim's thinly veiled racism. As Charles F. Coleman Jr. notes, the word "thug," always racially inflected, has in recent years become a regular euphemism for "nigger." See Coleman, "'Thug' Is the New N-Word," *Ebony,* 27 May 2015, https://www.ebony.com/news/thug-is-the-new-n-word-504/.

34. Boudreau, "Letting the Body Speak," 62.

35. See Pabst, "Blackness/Mixedness," 180.

36. Of course, strictly speaking, Harris's legal argument about whiteness as property does not apply to Birdie, as one whose "blood was tainted" and "could not legally be white" ("Whiteness as Property" 1739). I still find Harris's argument compelling as a way to think through the race and class implications of Birdie's position.

37. Patricia J. Williams, *Open House: Of Family, Friends, Food, Piano Lessons, and the Search for a Room of My Own* (New York: Farrar, Straus, and Giroux, 2004), 196.

3. Mapping Class

1. W. E. B. Du Bois, *The Souls of Black Folk* (1903; Chicago: McClurg, 1908), 3.

2. Katherine McKittrick, *Demonic Grounds: Black Women and the Cartographies of Struggle* (Minneapolis: University of Minnesota Press, 2006), xiii.

3. Bianca C. Williams, *The Pursuit of Happiness: Black Women, Diaspora Dreams, and the Politics of Emotional Transnationalism* (Durham: Duke University Press, 2018), 9.

4. Eve Dunbar, *Black Regions of the Imagination: African American Writers Between the Nation and the World* (Philadelphia: Temple University Press, 2013), 4. Dunbar's sense of blackness as a *region* is a persuasive geographical metaphor capturing the "third narrative space" (7) that midcentury writers such as Hurston and Wright used to "documen[t] and reimagin[e] a set of 'homegrown' experiences within a more worldly framework" (7).

5. In "No One Knows the Mysteries at the Bottom of the Ocean," their introduction to their edited volume *Black Geographies and the Politics of Place* (Boston: South End Press, 2007), McKittrick and Woods write: "The dilemmas that arise when we think about space and race often take three very separate approaches (bodily, economic/historical materialist, metaphoric) that result in reducing black geographies to either geographic determinism (black bodies inherently occupying black places), *the flesh (the body as the only relevant black geographic scale),* or the imagination (metaphoric/creative spaces, which are not represented as concrete, everyday, or lived). Consequently race, or blackness, is not understood as socially produced and shifting but is instead conceptualized as transhistorical, essentially corporeal, or allegorical or symbolic. In this process, which might be called bio-geographic determinism, black geographies disappear—to the margins or to the realm of the unknowable" (7, emphasis added).

6. McKittrick and Woods, *Black Geographies,* 7.

7. McKittrick, *Demonic Grounds,* 4.

8. McKittrick, *Demonic Grounds,* 4.

9. Shay Youngblood, *Black Girl in Paris* (New York: Riverhead Books, 2000), 7; Reginald McKnight, *He Sleeps* (New York: Picador, 2001), 1. Hereafter, each will be cited parenthetically in the text.

10. See Cornel West, "The Paradox of the African American Rebellion," in *Is It Nation Time? Contemporary Essays on Black Power and Black Nationalism,* ed. Eddie S. Glaude Jr. (Chicago: University of Chicago Press, 2002), 22–38.

11. Charisse Burden-Stelly, "Cold War Culturalism and African Diaspora Theory: Some Theoretical Sketches," *Souls* 19, no. 2 (2017): 214. See

also Brent Hayes Edwards, "The Uses of Diaspora," *Social Text* 19, no. 1 (Spring 2001): 45–73.

12. For more on the complex history and politics of respectability in African American culture, see, e.g., Hazel V. Carby, *Reconstructing Womanhood: The Emergence of the Afro-American Woman Novelist* (New York: Oxford University Press, 1987); Michele Mitchell, *Righteous Propagation: African Americans and the Politics of Racial Destiny after Reconstruction* (Chapel Hill: University of North Carolina Press, 2004); Darlene Clark Hine, "Rape and the Inner Lives of Black Women in the Middle West," *Signs* 14, no. 4 (1989): 912–20; Kevin Kelly Gaines, *Uplifting the Race: Black Leadership, Politics, and Culture in the Twentieth Century* (Chapel Hill: University of North Carolina Press, 1996); Evelynn Hammonds, "Towards a Genealogy of Black Female Sexuality: The Problematic of Silence," in *Feminist Genealogies, Colonial Legacies, Democratic Futures,* ed. J. Alexander and C. T. Mohanty (New York: Routledge, 1997): 93–104; or my own book, *Private Lives, Proper Relations: Regulating Black Intimacy* (Minneapolis: University of Minnesota Press, 2007). For an astute analysis of how black women's intellectual thought has been both constrained and enabled in productive ways by respectability discourse, see Brittney C. Cooper, *Beyond Respectability: The Intellectual Thought of Race Women* (Urbana: University of Illinois Press, 2017).

13. For more on Pentecostal worship and the resistant power of black flesh, see Ashon Crawley, *Black Pentecostal Breath: The Aesthetics of Possibility* (New York: Fordham University Press, 2016).

14. Eden herself points to Langston Hughes, Josephine Baker, James Baldwin, and Richard Wright as examples of this phenomenon. Popular narratives of Europe as an environment more welcoming to blacks persist even now; see, e.g., Eleanor Beardsley, "Paris Has Been a Haven for African Americans Escaping Racism," *Morning Edition,* National Public Radio, September 2, 2013, Paris.

15. Andrea Lee, *Sarah Phillips* (1984; Boston: Northeastern University Press, 1993), 15.

16. For more on the carceral aspects of urban geography, specifically Chicago, see Rashad Shabazz, *Spatializing Blackness: Architectures of Confinement and Black Masculinity in Chicago* (Urbana: University of Illinois Press, 2015).

17. Michelle Ann Stephens, *Black Empire: The Masculine Global Imaginary of Caribbean Intellectuals in the United States, 1914–1962* (Durham: Duke University Press, 2005), 12.

18. B. C. Williams, *The Pursuit of Happiness,* 92.

19. Saidiya Hartman, *Lose Your Mother: A Journey along the Atlantic Slave Route* (New York: Farrar, Straus, and Giroux, 2007), 84, 85, 88, 89.

20. Paul Smith, "Eastwood Bound," in *Constructing Masculinity,* ed. Maurice Berger, Brian Wallis, and Simon Watson (New York: Routledge, 1995), 77; Mark Anthony Neal, *New Black Man* (New York: Routledge, 2005), 21.

21. E. Frances White, "Africa on My Mind: Gender, Counterdiscourse, and African American Nationalism," in *Words of Fire: An Anthology of African American Feminist Thought,* ed. Beverly Guy-Sheftall (New York: New Press, 1995), 504.

22. Arguably, this hierarchy is built into the very foundations of the discipline of anthropology; as Ruth Behar suggests, traditional anthropology was "born of the European colonial impulse to know others in order to lambast them, better manage them, or exalt them." Behar, *The Vulnerable Observer: Anthropology That Breaks Your Heart* (Boston: Beacon Press, 1996), 4. See also Kwame Anthony Appiah, who writes that anthropology "has a professional bias toward difference." Appiah, "Cosmopolitan Reading," in *Cosmopolitan Geographies: New Locations in Literature and Culture,* ed. Vinay Dharwadke (New York: Routledge, 2001), 222.

23. John L. Jackson Jr., *Real Black: Adventures in Racial Sincerity* (Chicago: University of Chicago Press, 2005), 156.

24. Hartman, *Lose Your Mother,* 90.

25. Hartman, *Lose Your Mother,* 88.

26. Of course, this stripping of middle-class protections and the need to accept work requiring unskilled labor—e.g., work as a driver, care work, farm or factory work—is commonplace for educated immigrants to the United States, especially those from non-white countries whose credentials are not always recognized in the United States.

27. LaShawn Harris, *Sex Workers, Psychics, and Numbers Runners: Black Women in New York City's Underground Economy* (Champaign: University of Illinois Press, 2016), 6.

28. Lee, *Sarah Phillips,* 6–7.

29. Deborah Willis, ed., *Black Venus 2010: They Called Her "Hottentot"* (Philadelphia: Temple University Press, 2010), 4.

30. T. Denean Sharpley-Whiting, *Black Venus: Sexualized Savages, Primal Fears, and Primitive Narratives in French* (Durham: Duke University Press, 1999), 4.

31. Jennifer D. Williams, "Black American Girls in Paris: Sex, Race, and Cosmopolitanism in Andrea Lee's *Sarah Phillips* and Shay Youngblood's *Black Girl in Paris*," *Contemporary Women's Writing* 9, no. 2 (2014): 247.

32. For more on the history of, in particular, black women's labor in the United States, see Jacqueline Jones, *Labor of Love, Labor of Sorrow: Black Women, Work, and the Family from Slavery to the Present* (New York: Basic Books, 1985).

33. Harris, *Sex Workers,* 32.

34. As Jones notes, black women who worked in white American households as domestics were considered the "special prey" of the husbands and sons of the household (*Labor of Love,* 113). See also Paula Giddings, *When and Where I Enter* (1984; New York: Quill/William Morrow, 1996), 101.

35. McKittrick, *Demonic Grounds,* 4.

36. Z. Z. Packer, "Geese," *Drinking Coffee Elsewhere* (New York: Riverhead, 2003), 189–210.

37. McKittrick, *Demonic Grounds,* xix.

4. Interiority, Anteriority, and the Art of Blackness

1. Frantz Fanon, *Black Skin, White Masks,* trans. Charles Lam Markmann (1952; New York: Grove Press, 1967), 231. Hereafter cited parenthetically in the text.

2. Sharon Holland, *The Erotic Life of Racism* (Durham: Duke University Press, 2012), 4.

3. I am thinking here not only of Tina Campt's *Listening to Images* (Durham: Duke University Press, 2017), quoted above as an epigraph, or Sharon Holland's *The Erotic Life of Racism,* but also works like Kara Keeling's "Looking for M—: Queer Temporality, Black Political Possibility, and Poetry from the Future," *GLQ: A Journal of Lesbian and Gay Studies* 15, no. 4 (2009): 565–82, which also begins with Fanon's *Black Skin, White Masks* and his invocation of Marx's notion of "poetry from the future" to mark the possibility for "social revolution" (565); as well as C. Riley Snorton's *Black on Both Sides: A Racial History of Trans Identity* (Minneapolis: University of Minnesota Press, 2017), which also opens with a quotation from Fanon on the "problem of time" (vii). Of course, this brief list of texts concerned with black futurity and temporality deliberately sidesteps a much more vast creative and critical project collected under the rubric of Afrofuturism, a cultural aesthetic that incorporates science fiction and fantasy, magical

realism, and non-Western belief systems to challenge the racial homogeneity of conventional genre fiction and explore questions of black identity and subjectivity in futuristic contexts. For critical analysis of Afrofuturism and black speculative fiction, see foundational works by Ytasha Womack, Sheree R. Thomas, andré carrington, and Reynaldo Anderson and Charles E. Jones, among others. See also Alexis Pauline Gumbs's "Speculative Poetics: Audre Lorde as Prologue for Queer Black Futurism" in *The Black Imagination: Science Fiction, Futurism and the Speculative,* ed. Sandra Jackson and Julie E. Moody-Freeman (New York: Peter Lang, 2011), 130–45. Gumbs's analysis of the black lesbian as vampire offers a fascinating bridge between black queer and black speculative approaches to black futurity.

4. For this argument, especially, see Paul Gilroy's *Against Race: Imagining Political Culture beyond the Color Line* (Cambridge: Belknap Press, 2000). See also Debra Dickerson's *The End of Blackness: Returning the Souls of Black Folk to Their Rightful Owners* (New York: Pantheon, 2004).

5. "Not yet here" is meant to invoke José Esteban Muñoz's *Cruising Utopia: The Then and There of Queer Futurity* (New York: New York University Press, 2009), which begins with the words "Queerness is not yet here" (1); the "black future looks like" quotation is from Keeling, "Looking for M—," 578. Both Muñoz and Keeling are responding to an earlier, well-known reading of queerness as *against* (reproductive) futurity, Lee Edelman's *No Future: Queer Theory and the Death Drive* (Durham: Duke University Press, 2004), which famously makes an argument opposing (white and male) queerness to the future, represented in the figure of the child.

6. Campt, *Listening to Images,* 15 and 107.

7. Campt, *Listening to Images,* 107.

8. Campt, *Listening to Images,* 17.

9. Campt, *Listening to Images,* 17.

10. Elizabeth Alexander, *The Black Interior* (St. Paul, Minn.: Graywolf Press, 2004), 5.

11. Campt, *Listening to Images,* 17; Alexander, *The Black Interior,* 5.

12. Alexander, *The Black Interior,* 5.

13. Campt, *Listening to Images,* 17.

14. Percival Everett, *Erasure* (New York: Hyperion, 2001), 28, 2.

15. Colson Whitehead, *Sag Harbor* (New York: Bantam Doubleday/Anchor Press, 2009).

16. For a much longer analysis of Bertrand's sexualized, racial shame in *He Sleeps,* see Candice M. Jenkins, "'A Kind of End to Blackness': Reginald

McKnight's *He Sleeps* and the Body Politics of Race and Class," in *From Bourgeois to Boojie: Black Middle-Class Performances,* ed. Vershawn Ashanti Young and Bridget Harris Tsemo (Detroit: Wayne State University Press, 2011), 261–86.

17. For a sociological discussion of the ways being "cool" circulates in black male contexts, see Richard Majors and Janet Mancini Billson's foundational text, *Cool Pose: The Dilemmas of Black Manhood in America* (1992; New York: Touchstone, 1993).

18. Imani Perry, *More Beautiful and More Terrible: The Embrace and Transcendence of Racial Inequality in the United States* (New York: New York University Press, 2011), 128.

19. Perry, *More Beautiful and More Terrible,* 137, 147.

20. Holland, *The Erotic Life of Racism,* 8.

21. Holland, *The Erotic Life of Racism,* 26.

22. Roland Murray, "Not Being and Blackness: Percival Everett and the Uncanny Forms of Racial Incorporation," *American Literary History* 29, no. 4 (December 2017): 728, 733.

23. Murray, "Not Being and Blackness," 734.

24. I want to thank my former MA student at Hunter College, Helen Leshinsky, for pointing out this reading of Rinehart's name.

25. Uri McMillan, *Embodied Avatars: Genealogies of Black Feminist Art and Performance* (New York: New York University Press, 2015), 7, 9.

26. Patricia Williams, *The Alchemy of Race and Rights: Diary of a Law Professor* (Cambridge: Harvard University Press, 1992), 221, emphasis added.

27. Alexander, *The Black Interior,* 5.

28. Holland, *The Erotic Life of Racism,* 26.

29. Stefano Harney and Fred Moten, *The Undercommons: Fugitive Planning and Black Study* (New York: Minor Compositions, 2013), 48.

30. Harney and Moten, *The Undercommons,* 48.

31. Alexander, *The Black Interior,* 7.

32. Isaac Newton, *The Mathematical Principles of Natural Philosophy,* trans Andrew Motte and N. W. Chittenden (1687; New York: Putnam, 1850), 506–7.

33. Newton, *The Mathematical Principles,* 507.

34. Recently, in a different context, Marcus Anthony Hunter also turns to gravity as a metaphor for racial identity, though his focus is largely on racial gravity as constraint. He writes: "The history, acts and agitation between the

oppressor and the oppressed since the colonial period has [*sic*] participated in making race function much in the way that Einstein characterizes gravity. Much like how gravity affects matter in the natural world, in the social world race in varying degrees draws people apart and together, binds people to sidewalks, neighbourhoods and institutions of civil society" (2). Hunter, "Racial Physics or a Theory for Everything That Happened," *Ethnic and Racial Studies* 40, no. 8 (2017): 1174.

35. Margo Natalie Crawford, *Black Post-Blackness: The Black Arts Movement and Twenty-First-Century Aesthetics* (Urbana: University of Illinois Press, 2017), 227.

36. Campt, *Listening to Images,* 17.

37. The quotation is from Alexander, *The Black Interior,* 5.

5. Flesh, Agency, Possibility

1. Kevin Willmott and Marleen S. Barr, "Black 'Science Faction': An Interview with Kevin Willmott, Director and Writer of *CSA: The Confederate States of America,*" in *Afro-Future Females: Black Writers Chart Science Fiction's Newest New-Wave Trajectory,* ed. Barr (Columbus: Ohio State University Press, 2008), 239, 237.

2. Frank Wilderson, "Civil Rights," Incognegro.org (2008), retrieved from http://www.incognegro.org/afro_pessimism.html. See also Orlando Patterson, *Slavery and Social Death: A Comparative Study* (Cambridge: Harvard University Press, 1982).

3. Jared Sexton, "The Social Life of Social Death: On Afro-Pessimism and Black Optimism," In*Tensions* 5 (Fall/Winter 2011): 30.

4. Jared Sexton, "Afro-Pessimism: The Unclear Word," Special Issue: "Black Holes: Afro-Pessimism, Blackness, and the Discourses of Modernity," *Rhizomes* 29, no. 1 (2016): paragraph 16, https://doi.org/10.20415/rhiz/029.e02.

5. Jared Sexton, "Unbearable Blackness," *Cultural Critique* 90 (Spring 2015): 166.

6. Sexton, "Social Life of Social Death," 30.

7. Dalton Anthony Jones, "Northern Hieroglyphics: Nomadic Blackness and Spatial Literacy," Special Issue: "Black Holes: Afro-Pessimism, Blackness, and the Discourses of Modernity" *Rhizomes* 29, no. 1 (2016): paragraph 21, https://doi.org/10.20415/rhiz/029.e01.

8. Frank B. Wilderson III, *Red, White and Black: Cinema and the Structure of U.S. Antagonisms* (Durham: Duke University Press, 2010), 38.

9. Wilderson, *Red, White and Black,* 7, 18.

10. Sabine Broeck, "Inequality or (Social) Death," Special Issue: "Black Holes: Afro-Pessimism, Blackness and the Discourses of Modernity," *Rhizomes* 29, no. 1 (2016): paragraph 15, https://doi.org/10.20415/rhiz/029.e11.

11. Wilderson, *Red, White and Black,* 340.

12. Sexton, "Afro-Pessimism," paragraph 8.

13. Sexton, "Afro-Pessimism," paragraph 8. The quotation from Wagner is from *Disturbing the Peace: Black Culture and the Police Power after Slavery* (Cambridge: Harvard University Press, 2009), 2.

14. Sexton, "Afro-Pessimism," paragraph 8.

15. My reference here is to Harriet Jacobs's hiding place, a garret under the roof of her grandmother's house, which she described as a "loophole of retreat." For a fascinating reading of this space as an exemplary instance of black women's geography, see Katherine McKittrick, *Demonic Grounds: Black Women and the Cartographies of Struggle* (Minneapolis: University of Minnesota Press, 2006), ch. 2, esp. 37–44 and 59–63.

16. Christina Sharpe, *In the Wake: On Blackness and Being* (Durham: Duke University Press, 2016), 8.

17. Sharpe, *In the Wake,* 11.

18. Sharpe, *In the Wake,* 134 (see also 16); and Christina Sharpe, "Blackness, Sexuality, and Entertainment," *American Literary History* 24, no. 4 (2012): 828.

19. Sharpe, *In the Wake,* 4.

20. Sharpe, *In the Wake,* 17.

21. Rizvana Bradley, "Living in the Absence of a Body: The (Sus)Stain of Black Female (W)holeness," Special Issue: "Black Holes: Afro-Pessimism, Blackness and the Discourses of Modernity," *Rhizomes* 29, no. 1 (2016): paragraph 2, https://doi.org/10.20415/rhiz/029.e13.

22. Bradley, "Living," paragraph 2.

23. Sexton, "Afro-Pessimism," paragraph 6; Sharpe, *In the Wake,* 76.

24. Sharpe, *In the Wake,* 77.

25. Erica Edwards, "*What Was African American Literature?* A Symposium," *Los Angeles Review of Books,* June 13, 2011, https://lareviewofbooks.org/article/what-was-african-american-literature-a-symposium/#!.

26. Terrion L. Williamson, *Scandalize My Name: Black Feminist Practice and the Making of Black Social Life* (New York: Fordham University Press), 9.

27. Williamson, *Scandalize My Name,* 15.

28. Sexton, "Social Life of Social Death," 29; Sharpe, *In the Wake,* 50.

29. Ta-Nehisi Coates, *Between the World and Me* (New York: Spiegel and Grau, 2015), 149.

30. My use of the term "post-post-soul" here is a nod to Jeffrey T. Nealon on post-postmodernism, a concept that, he suggests, "marks an intensification and mutation within postmodernism (which in its turn was of course a historical mutation and intensification of certain tendencies within modernism)" (ix). See Nealon, *Post-Postmodernism; or, The Cultural Logic of Just-in-Time Capitalism* (Stanford: Stanford University Press, 2012).

31. Michael Thomas, *Man Gone Down* (New York: Grove, 2007), 5. Hereafter cited parenthetically in the text.

32. For a representative case study on the housing market collapse and disparate recovery for black homeowners, see Michael Fletcher, "A Shattered Foundation: African Americans Who Bought Homes in Prince George's Have Watched Their Wealth Vanish," *Washington Post,* January 24, 2015, https://www.washingtonpost.com/sf/investigative/2015/01/24/the-american-dream-shatters-in-prince-georges-county/?utm_term=.0afc74b773dc; for more on black unemployment, see the Economic Policy Institute's 2015 report, "The Crisis of Black Unemployment: Still Higher Than Pre-Recession Levels," *The American Prospect,* April 2, 2015, https://prospect.org/article/crisis-black-unemployment-still-higher-pre-recession-levels.

33. Kevin K. Gaines, *Uplifting the Race: Black Leadership, Politics, and Culture in the Twentieth Century* (Chapel Hill: University of North Carolina Press, 1996), 14.

34. For more on this phenomenon, see the work of John Logan ("Separate and Unequal: The Neighborhood Gap for Blacks, Hispanics and Asians in Metropolitan America," *US2010 Project,* https://s4.ad.brown.edu/Projects/Diversity/Data/Report/report0727.pdf) or Patrick Sharkey ("Neighborhoods and the Black-White Mobility Gap," *Economic Mobility Project,* https://www.pewtrusts.org/~/media/legacy/uploadedfiles/wwwpewtrustsorg/reports/economic_mobility/pewsharkeyv12pdf.pdf).

35. For a very different reading of the race and class implications of this scene, see the concluding chapter of Ken Warren, *What Was African American Literature?* (Cambridge: Harvard University Press, 2012), esp. 129–39.

36. Darieck Scott, *Extravagant Abjection: Blackness, Power, and Sexuality*

in the African American Literary Imagination (New York: New York University Press, 2010), 257.

37. Scott, *Extravagant Abjection,* 9.

38. See, again, Warren, *What Was African American Literature,* esp. 139.

39. Colson Whitehead, *John Henry Days* (2001; New York: Anchor Books, 2002), 54. Hereafter cited by page number in the text.

40. Perhaps not coincidentally, this scene recalls Toni Morrison's character Consolata in *Paradise* (1997), who alienates her lover when she bites his lip and draws blood.

41. This phrasing from Whitehead seems to make passing reference to the 1964 film *Nothing But a Man,* which starred Abbey Lincoln and Ivan Dixon and told the story of a black railroad worker, Duff Anderson, chafing against his personal and social circumstances in a racist small town near Birmingham, Alabama—another instance of Whitehead drawing direct links between the racial fates of fictional black men across historical periods.

42. For more on this sort of spectatorship as well as the radical potentiality of representations of black suffering, see Courtney R. Baker's *Humane Insight: Looking at Images of African American Suffering and Death* (Urbana: University of Illinois Press, 2016).

43. See Sexton, "Unbearable Blackness," 168.

44. Tavia Nyong'o, *The Amalgamation Waltz: Race, Performance, and the Ruses of Memory* (Minneapolis: University of Minnesota Press, 2009), 34. Nyong'o's historical analysis of Attucks is considerably more nuanced than my summary of Attucks's story would indicate, attending as it does to Attucks's native ancestry and reading him as "a hybrid object between red and black moving fugitively across a landscape" (41), yet Whitehead's novel seems clearly to depend upon the more conventional understanding of Attucks as a black casualty of Revolution.

45. See Brittney Cooper on the notion that "time belongs to white people." Cooper, "The Racial Politics of Time," TEDWomen 2016 Talk, filmed October 2016, San Francisco.

46. For more on literary representation of these sorts of protective performances of decorum, see my book, *Private Lives, Proper Relations: Regulating Black Intimacy* (Minneapolis: University of Minnesota Press, 2007).

47. Bumpurs, a black woman in her sixties with a history of mental illness, was shot in her apartment by NYPD officers on October 29, 1984. Her story returned to news outlets recently after an eerily similar NYPD shooting of a black woman in the Bronx, Deborah Danner. See Alan Feuer, "Fatal Police

Shooting in Bronx Echoes One from 32 Years Ago," *New York Times,* October 19, 2016.

48. Bradley, "Living," paragraph 3.

49. Coates, *Between the World and Me,* 70.

50. Martin Luther King Jr., "I've Been to the Mountaintop" speech, delivered April 3, 1968, Mason Temple (Church of God in Christ Headquarters), Memphis, Tennessee, transcription, http://www.americanrhetoric.com/speeches/mlkivebeentothemountaintop.htm.

51. Cf. Lee Edelman, *No Future: Queer Theory and the Death Drive* (Durham: Duke University Press, 2004).

52. Coates, *Between the World and Me,* 70.

53. Williamson, *Scandalize My Name,* 16.

54. Sexton, "Social Life of Social Death," 28; Williamson, *Scandalize My Name,* 15.

55. The closest the text comes to conceding this link is a moment on page 138, when a young J. is watching a filmstrip in school, a cartoon story about John Henry. An older J. thinks back to this scene, particularly the image of a huge infant John Henry, "born big, forty pounds and gifted with speech straight out the womb," who "ate . . . food in great inhalations." In an aside, the narrator notes, "J. wondering from the summit of the Talcott Motor Lodge, *who is that little boy down there in the classroom who shares his name,* and where did they get that food. He was born a slave. His parents were slaves. Where did they get all that food?" (138, emphasis added). Of course, the little boy "down there in the classroom" might simply refer to a young J. and not to the John of the cartoon—this remaining ambiguity leaves the question of J.'s name unresolved.

56. Sexton, "Social," 29.

Conclusion

1. See Daniel Politi, "Starbucks CEO Apologizes for Arrest of Two Black Men Waiting in Philadelphia Store," *Slate,* April 15, 2018, https://slate.com/news-and-politics/2018/04/starbucks-ceo-apologizes-for-arrest-of-two-black-men-waiting-in-philadelphia-store.html.

2. See the "Visit Philadelphia" website, which describes Rittenhouse Square as such: "One of five original squares planned by city founder William Penn in the late 17th century, Rittenhouse Square is the heart of Center City's most expensive and exclusive neighborhood. With a bevy of high-rise

residences filled with top-end luxury apartments, and some of the best fine dining experiences in the city, residents can marvel at their options, while also enjoying the luxury retail shopping in the area, all of which help surrounds [*sic*] the handsome tree-filled park." www.visitphilly.com/things-to-do/attractions/rittenhouse-square-park/.

3. To this litany of similar stories we might add that of a group of black women, members of an exclusive golf club, who had the police called on them in 2018 for allegedly playing the course "too slowly," a determination that seemed entirely dependent upon the opinion of the group of white men following them in play (the same group that called law enforcement). See Christina Caron, "5 Black Women Were Told to Golf Faster. Then the Club Called the Police," *New York Times,* April 25, 2018, www.nytimes.com/2018/04/25/us/black-women-golfers-york.html.

4. Claudia Rankine, interview by Rich Fahle, "Claudia Rankine on *Citizen: An American Lyric*—2015 L.A. Times Festival of Books," Detroit Public TV, May 18, 2015, www.youtube.com/watch?v=upCFbREUvtk.

5. Claudia Rankine, *Citizen: An American Lyric* (Minneapolis: Graywolf Press, 2014), 28. Hereafter cited parenthetically in the text.

6. While a full analysis of Lawrence's relationship with Tasha is beyond the scope of our discussion here, it is worth noting that on the show Tasha is repeatedly marked, through patterns of speech and styling, as working-class rather than, like Issa and Molly, bourgeois. The end of Lawrence and Tasha's relationship is itself a highly classed moment, as an uncomfortable Lawrence surveys the down-home (read, "ratchet") goings-on at Tasha's family barbecue and decides, seemingly on the spot, to abandon it, and her, in favor of a party with his largely white coworkers.

7. "I don't want the stench of the current administration on this show. . . . I don't want people to look back and be like: 'Oh, this was a Trump show.' I want them to look back and say *Insecure* was an Obama show. Because it is: Obama enabled this show." Jane Mulkerrins, "Issa Rae: 'So Much of the Media Presents Blackness as Fierce and Flawless. I'm Not,'" *The Guardian,* August 5, 2017, www.theguardian.com/tv-and-radio/2017/aug/05/issa-rae-media-presents-blackness-fierce-flawless-insecure.

8. "Hella LA," *Insecure,* season two, episode four, written by Laura Kittrell, Christopher Oscar Peña, Issa Rae, Natasha Rothwell, and Larry Wilmore, directed by Prentice Penny, HBO, August 13, 2017.

9. See Kurt Chirbas, Erik Ortiz, and Corky Siemaszko, "Baltimore County Police Fatally Shoot Korryn Gaines, 23, Wound 5-Year-Old, Son,"

NBC News.com, August 2, 2016, www.nbcnews.com/news/us-news/baltimore-county-police-fatally-shoot-korryn-gaines-boy-5-hurt-n621461; "Experts Point to Brain Injury in N Carolina Police Shooting," *Chicago Tribune,* October 4, 2016, www.chicagotribune.com/news/nationworld/ct-keith-lamont-scott-brain-injury-20161004-story.html; Max Blau, Jason Morris, and Catherine E. Shoichet, "Tulsa Police Shooting Investigated by Justice Department," *CNN.com,* May 18, 2017, www.cnn.com/2016/09/20/us/oklahoma-tulsa-police-shooting/index.html; Jamiel Lynch and Darran Simon, "Former Texas Officer Indicted for Murder in Death of Jordan Edwards," *CNN.com,* July 17, 2017, www.cnn.com/2017/07/17/us/texas-cop-indicted-jordan-edwards-death/index.html.

10. Based on facial features, one of the women appears to be of Asian descent but has long, dyed-blonde hair and fair skin; this, along with her avid participation in fetishizing black men's bodies, makes it reasonable to read her as white passing or white complicit.

11. "After the Winter," *Queen Sugar,* season two, written by Monica Macer, Davita Scarlett, Ava DuVernay, directed by Kat Candler, OWN, June 20, 2017.

12. "Freedom's Plow," *Queen Sugar,* season two, written by Anthony Sparks, Davita Scarlett, Ava DuVernay, directed by Amanda Marsalis, OWN, August 2, 2017.

13. See Gerry Everding, "Police Kill Unarmed Blacks More Often, Especially When They Are Women, Study Finds," *The Source,* Washington University in St. Louis, February 6, 2018, https://source.wustl.edu/2018/02/police-kill-unarmed-blacks-often-especially-women-study-finds/; see also Odis Johnson Jr., Keon Gilbert, and Habiba Ibrahim, "Race, Gender, and the Contexts of Unarmed Fatal Interactions with Police," Institute for Public Health at Washington University in St. Louis, February 2018, https://cpb-us-w2.wpmucdn.com/sites.wustl.edu/dist/b/1205/files/2018/02/Race-Gender-and-Unarmed-1y9md6e.pdf.

14. Frank B. Wilderson III, *Red, White and Black: Cinema and the Structure of U.S. Antagonisms* (Durham: Duke University Press, 2010), 5.

15. Notably, the video humanizes the officer as well, highlighting the way he operates as unwilling cog and weapon in a larger machine of white supremacy.

16. Simone Browne, *Dark Matters: On the Surveillance of Blackness* (Durham: Duke University Press, 2015), 21.

17. Reginald McKnight, *He Sleeps* (New York: Picador, 2001), 155.

Index

Candice M. Jenkins is associate professor of English and African American studies at the University of Illinois, Urbana–Champaign. She is author of *Private Lives, Proper Relations: Regulating Black Intimacy* (Minnesota, 2007).